Visions of Europe

Visions of Europe

Summing up the Political Choices

Godfrey Barker • Samuel H. Beer • Paul Belien
Leslie Blake • Richard Body • Frederick Bonnart
Manfred Brunner • Bill Cash • Eric Elstob
Howard Flight • Ralph Harris • Stephen Hill
Martin Howe • Jean Klein • John Laughland
Rodney Leach • Donald Maitland • Toru Nakakita
Henrik Nielsen • Wilhelm Noelling • Franco Racca
Brian Reading • Philippe Séguin • Norman Tebbit
Margaret Thatcher • Alan Walters

edited by
Stephen Hill

Duckworth

First published in 1993 by
Gerald Duckworth & Co. Ltd.
The Old Piano Factory
48 Hoxton Square, London, N1 6PB
Tel: 071 729 5986
Fax: 071 729 0015

A catalogue record for this book is
available from the British Library.

ISBN 0 7156 2496 2

Typeset by Ray Davies
Printed and bound in Great Britain by
Biddles Ltd, Guildford & King's Lynn

Contents

Contributors

Godfrey Barker is on the staff of the *Daily Telegraph* and writes for the *Sunday Telegraph, Spectator* and other publications on political and other matters.

Samuel H. Beer is Eaton Professor of the Science of Government *Emeritus* at Harvard. He was a Rhodes Scholar at Balliol in the 1930s and a speech writer for Roosevelt. His latest publication, *To Make a Nation: the Rediscovery of American Federalism* has recently been published by Harvard University Press.

Paul Belien is a journalist at the Belgian financial-economic weekly *Trends* in Brussels. He also works for the Centre for the New Europe, a Hayekian pan-European think-tank.

Leslie Blake is a barrister and writer and lecturer on constitutional matters. His most recent book is *Sovereignty: Power beyond Politics*.

Sir Richard Body is Conservative MP for Holland with Boston. He has written more extensively on the EC than any other MP. His many publications include *Our Food, Our Land: Why Contemporary Farming Practices Must Change*, published in 1991 by Rider, and *Europe of Many Circles: Constructing a Wider Europe*, published in 1990 by New Europe Publications Limited.

Col. Frederick Bonnart was born in Vienna, became a British subject, studied at the LSE in London and saw active military service in the Second World War. In 1978 he became editor of *Nato's Sixteen Nations* and has contributed articles to leading newspapers and journals on Nato ever since.

Dr. Manfred Brunner practises law in Munich. In 1988 he became President of the Thomas Dehler Institute. From 1989-92 he was Chief of Cabinet, under Martin Bangemann, of the ECE. He is suing the German Government for breach of the constitution as a result of the government's adoption of the Treaty of Maastricht. The case continues.

Bill Cash, Conservative MP for Stafford, is the leading Euro-Rebel against Maastricht in the UK Parliament; author in February 1991 of the paper on the *The European Community: Reality and Making it Work* for the Conservative Manifesto Committee; and Chairman 1989-91 of the Conservative Backbench Committee on European Affairs. He is author of *Against a Federal Europe* and *Europe: The Crunch*, published by Duckworth. He is Chairman of the European Foundation, founded in 1993.

Eric Elstob is joint managing director of The Foreign and Colonial Trust plc, the largest trust of its type in Britain and Europe.

Howard Flight is a co-founder and joint managing director of Guinness Flight Global Asset Management Limited. He has an MA in Economics from Cambridge and an MBA, majoring in international finance, from the University of Michigan. He is the author of *All You Need To Know About Exchange Rates*, published by Sidgwick & Jackson in 1988.

Lord Harris of High Cross is the founder-president of the Institute of Economic Affairs, a London-based educational charity engaged in economics research, propagating free market views and analysis. He has written several books, including *End of Government*, and is a regular contributor to magazines, journals and research papers.

Stephen Hill is managing director of LICA Development Capital Limited and writes on euro-economics. His publications include *Lions Led by Donkeys: How to Make the Real Economy Work* and *Concordia: The Roots of European Thought*, published by Duckworth in 1992.

Martin Howe is a barrister specialising in intellectual property law and European Community law. He is the author of *Europe and the Constitution after Maastricht*, published by the Society of Conservative Lawyers in 1992 (re-published by Nelson & Pollard, Oxford, in 1993), and author of numerous other published papers and articles on the Maastricht Treaty and European Community law.

Dr. Jean Klein was born in Bohemia and has taught the philosophy of Non-Duality across Europe and the United States for over thirty years. His many publications have been translated into most west European languages and include *The Ease of Being, Be Who You Are, Who am I?* and *Open to the Unknown,* published by Element Books and Third Millennium Publications.

John Laughland lectures in political philosophy at the Institut d'Etudes Politiques de Paris. He is a regular contributor to *The Wall Street Journal, Spectator, Evening Standard* and other publications, for whom he writes on French, German and EC politics. He is a trustee of the Mihai Eminescu Trust in Romania and of the British Helsinki Group.

Rodney Leach, formerly a director of N.M. Rothschild & Sons, is currently a director of Jardine Matheson, Trafalgar House, Kwik Save and other companies and a Trustee of the Post Office Pension Fund.

Sir Donald Maitland, GCMG, OBE was formerly United Kingdom Representative to the United Nations and to the European Community.

Dr. Toru Nakakita is an Associate Professor with the Faculty of Economics of Tokyo University and Senior Economist at the Japan Institute of International Affairs, Tokyo. His many publications include *The Globalisation of Japanese Firms and Its Influence on Japan's Trade with Developing Countries* and *Boeki Furikurhon* (Trade Friction), Yuhikaku, 1983, and his recent contribution to *The Japanese Experience of Economic Reforms,* 1993.

Henrik Overgaard Nielsen is the international director of *The June Movement* in Denmark, which organisation led the anti-Maastricht campaign in 1992-93.

Wilhelm Noelling was the head of the Hamburg Central Bank and a member of the Central Bank Policy Council of the Bundesbank from 1982-92. His latest book, *Monetary Policy in Europe,* has recently been published by Macmillan.

Ing. Franco Racca, executive director of LICA Development Capital Limited, worked for many years in the Strategic Studies Department of FIAT s.p.a. in Turin.

Brian Reading is a director of Lombard Street Research, but the views expressed here are his personal views. (He acknowledges his indebtedness to Martin Wolf of the *Financial Times* for some of the ideas in his contribution.)

Philippe Séguin is President of the French National Assembly. Previously he was Minister of Social Affairs and Employment, 1986-88, having entered politics as a Deputy in Vosges in 1978. He has published several books including *Discours sur la France* and *Ce que J'ai Dit* in 1992, and he co-authored *De l'Europe en général et de la France en particulier*, also in 1992.

Lord Tebbit CH, PC was Secretary of State for Industry, 1983-85, and Chairman of the Conservative and Unionist Party, 1985-87. He is currently a director of British Telecom plc and several other public companies.

Lady Thatcher, OM, PC, FRS was Prime Minister and First Lord of the Treasury, 1979-1990.

Sir Alan Walters, a senior fellow at the American Enterprise Institute, holds professorships at Johns Hopkins University, the University of Birmingham and the London School of Economics. His books include *The Economics of Road User Charges, Money in Boom and Slump, Britain's Economic Renaissance: Margaret Thatcher's Reforms, 1979-1984* and most recently *Sterling in Danger: The Economic Consequences of Pegged Exchange Rates*. He was chief economic adviser to Mrs (now Lady) Thatcher and adviser, *inter alia*, to the World Bank.

Abbreviations

AWACS	Airborne Warning and Command System
CAP	Common Agricultural Policy of the EC
CSCE	Conference on Security and Co-operation in Europe
EBRD	European Bank for Reconstruction and Development, based in London
EC	European Community, which replaces the EEC under the Treaty of Maastricht
ECB	European Central Bank
EEC	European Economic Community, founded by the Treaty of Rome
ECE	Economic Commission for Europe
ECJ	European Court of Justice
ECU	European Currency Unit, *aka* 'ever closer union'
EFTA	European Free Trade Association
EMI	European Monetary Institute
EMS	European Monetary System, of linked exchange rates
EMU	European Monetary Union
EPP	European People's Party
ERM	Exchange Rate Mechanism
ESCB	European System of Central Banks
GATT	General Agreement on Tariffs and Trade, signed in 1946
GGFD	General Government Financial Deficit
GMU	German Monetary Union
GNP	Gross National Product
G7	Group of Seven Leading Economic Powers
IGC	Inter-Governmental Conference
IMF	International Monetary Fund, based in Washington
MEP	Member of the European Parliament
NAFTA	North American Free Trade Association
NECs	Newly Exporting Countries
NICs	Newly Industrialised Countries
OECD	Organisation for Economic Co-operation and Development, based in Paris
OEEC	Organisation for European Economic Co-operation

QMV	Qualified Majority Voting
SEA	Single European Act signed in 1986
SMEs	Small and Medium-Sized Enterprises
VAT/TVA	Value Added Tax/*Tax Valeur Ajouté*
WEU	Western European Union, for common defence

Acknowledgements

As editor, I am indebted to the contributors to this symposium for their ready response to the call to arms and for the speed with which their clarity of thought has been committed to paper.

Many thanks go to Air Chief Marshal Sir John Barraclough, James Bourlet, Bill Cash, Klaus Engelen and John Laughland for introducing me to a number of contributors.

I am grateful to Jonathan Begg for editorial help and to my patient secretary, Joyce Sutherland, who so skilfully typed difficult manuscripts of varying shapes and sizes.

S.R.H.

To my mother, Joan Hill,
who died on 14 July 1993

Introduction to the 13th Nation

Stephen Hill

Already Maastricht has gone hideously wrong.

An extra nation has crept unbidden into the European Community, complete with courtiers, diplomats, a civil service and a spiralling deficit.

It is called Bureaucracy.

Fuelled by the data-handling revolution, its centralised power is set to grow exponentially to unheard-of levels.

Its only allies are Europe's natural losers: those 'black hole' regions that cynically exploit the common decency and goodwill in which the community was conceived.

Feeding on itself, it can do nothing but raise taxes, strangle initiative and inhibit the means of creating employment.

While it smugly contemplates its own creation, it fails to adapt to the post-Iron Curtain Europe, even though the ugly spectre of raw genocide is now on its doorstep.

If Maastricht means anything, it means an inward-looking, undemocratic, authoritarian Bureaucracy that will fatally weaken Europe.

The 13th Nation is the new enemy. The people and leaders of Europe ignore this at their peril.

In 1945 Europe – the cradle of western civilisation – lay in ruins for the second time this century. Unlike its wars of previous centuries, Europe's conflicts in the twentieth century caused global warfare on an unimagined scale. The worldwide fatalities of the First and Second World Wars were over 5 million and 50 million respectively, and Europe's soul was filled with darkness. More important, the destructive power of modern weapons, such as the atomic bomb deployed against Japan in August 1945, now threatened global destruction for mankind in any future conflict.

Nowhere was the need for a future world order that would ensure peace and prosperity more keenly felt than in Japan and Germany. The post-war arrangements in respect of both Japan and the Federal Republic of Germany prohibited the legality and the means for future military aggression abroad. General MacArthur restricted Japan's defence budget to 1% of GNP, but her economic success means that her 'Self Defence Corps' budget is now at £24 billion *per annum,* yet the recent deployment of forty Japanese UN peace-keeping troops on the Cambodian border sparked off demonstrations in Tokyo and anguished debate in the Diet.

Germany's new constitution forbad foreign deployment. Despite recognising Croatia, Germany played no military role in the ensuing war in Yugoslavia – nor in the Gulf War. When a handful of German airforce navigators were required to operate UN Boeing-AWACS aircraft over former Yugoslavian air space, a major public debate was triggered which nearly caused a political and constitutional crisis as the matter went to the Federal Court. Nevertheless, the English-speaking and other wartime Allies now require both Japan and Germany's assistance in maintaining the peace of the world in their respective spheres.

When the worst of the rubble of the Second World War had been cleared away and the wounds had begun to heal, it was seen that international trade and co-operation between the European states was not only economically necessary but vital as the basis for a prosperous peace. The architects of this plan for trade co-operation and ever closer political union, Jean Monnet and Robert Schuman, expounded their blueprint for a pan-European economic and political union at Messina in 1955. Their real aim was the containment of Germany. Their vision quickly found expression in the Treaty of Rome, signed by France, West Germany, Italy and the Benelux Federation two years later. It was the Paris-Bonn axis, however, that was the vital connection in formulating the European order to come. Sir Winston Churchill was the visionary who first saw the need for such an axis. As early as 19 September 1946 he had said at Zurich University: 'I am now going to say something that will astonish you. The first step in the re-creation of the European Family must be a partnership between France and Germany ... France and Germany must take the lead together.' Churchill too had his eye on the containment of German power.

The 1960s saw a dramatic recovery from the devastation of war as the *Wirtschaftswunder,* or German economic miracle, revitalised the Continent's wealth-creating capacity. This demonstrable success served to strengthen the Paris-Bonn strategic axis, as France's economy became ever more entwined with, and dependent upon, West Germany's. It was inevitable that French agriculture and manufacturing should look east to Germany's superior industrial power-base and increasingly wealthy consumer markets.

Britain had to take a pragmatic view of its future too – especially in view of its declining manufacturing base – as it was clear that the EEC marketplace on its doorstep, with nearly 200 million consumers, would play a part in compensating for its far-flung Commonwealth (and former empire), but Britain was never going to curtail its centuries-old tradition, natural to an island race, of constantly seeking out global markets. Nevertheless, Monnet and Schuman's vision of a united and prosperous Europe seemed all but complete when Britain acceded to the Treaty of Rome in 1973, but only after the House of Commons had voted for accession in 1972 by just eight votes.

Harold Wilson, as Prime Minister, had called a national referendum in Britain in 1975 to ratify her membership of the EEC, which Edward Heath had negotiated in 1973. The vote in favour was a decisive two-to-one majority. The people of Britain, irritated by General De Gaulle's continuous rejection of British membership since 1963, warmly embraced the long-awaited invitation to join the Common Market. The British are a nation of inveterate free-traders at heart, who firmly believe in open markets for goods, labour and capital – an approach that has served them well for centuries. Heath had assured the nation that membership of the EEC would put an end to war in Europe and that the sovereignty of Britain would not be put at risk by accession.

Heath, however, was either selectively blind or naively optimistic, for the first part of the preamble of the Treaty of Rome (Article 102,A) recited the intention 'to ensure the convergence of economic and monetary policies which is necessary for the *further development* of the Community'. Now Maastricht adds defence, foreign policy and security to the federalist wish-list.

There was, nevertheless, a distinct sense of relief in Britain at the outcome of the 1975 referendum. The European vision at least as regards a common market had communicated itself to the only independent island nation of western Europe. For the generations that had seen at least one war in Europe, or possibly two, or had grown up under the shadow of the Great Depression or the Cold War, the path to a peaceful future beckoned more strongly than for many centuries. A free market with 250 million consumers seemed to offer a prospect of unprecedented prosperity. Europe would stand united and be as strong as the United States in championing democracy and freedom. Together, the EEC and USA would form a bulwark against communism to the east.

There was a tangible atmosphere of Euro-euphoria in the air in 1973. The fears of an invasion of western Europe were allayed and there was increasing confidence in the ability of NATO to deter

Russian aggression, despite the nuclear threat posed by the USSR's massive build-up of Inter-Continental Ballistic Missiles. At long last western Europe would emerge from centuries of crisis, bitterness and bloodshed to play a constructive role as a world super-power.

The first shock to the dream of *Europa* came with the oil crisis in 1974, which caused the first serious recession in Europe since the war and unleashed inflation. It also caused the Bundesbank's first real monetary crisis. The second shock came with the next oil crisis in 1979, but by then Europe had learnt to manage better its demand for energy and the 1980s saw unparalleled growth. Then in 1986 the members of the EEC, who now numbered twelve, signed the Single European Act. This was intended to usher in the barrier-free common market with a progressive removal of all constraints on trade from midnight on New Year's Eve 1992.

It also limited, however, each nation's veto in favour of Qualified Majority Voting in relation to trade, thereby opening the door for more centralised decision – and policy-making, particularly in the federalisation of agriculture and trade, a process already in operation for over two decades. The members also agreed to search for other forms of convergence and other means of unification to strengthen the common market, such as the extension of the EMS, which had at its core the *franc fort* policy, whereby the French Franc would maintain a close parity with the Deutschemark through interest-rate management. This policy had been closely pursued by the socialist French government since 1985.

The signing of the Single European Act drove the Paris-Bonn axis to accelerate closer economic, monetary and political union. The EEC juggernaut dropped an 'E' about this time, somewhere on an *autobahn* or *autoroute* between the two capitals, and the concept of the EC as a political, rather than simply an economic, union was further enhanced. President Mitterand and Chancellor Kohl, despite denials, assembled the necessary machinery to turn Europe into a Super-State. Their socialist objectives, and that of M. Jacques Delors – not to mention John Major by default – have now utterly undermined the original vision of Adenauer and De Gaulle. At their first meeting, De Gaulle recorded their agreement that there could be no question of submerging the identity of 'our two nations in a stateless institution'. The EEC, however, has now become the EC, the common market is evolving into a new European state, with a superior juridical system, a single currency, a common defence and foreign policy, a minimum social security safety-net and standard employment conditions – all for the benefit of a new citizen, the European.

The new European will have rights of citizenship, freedom of speech and freedom to travel, work and stand in parliamentary elections anywhere in Europe, just as an American has in the US. It may be a bold vision, but is it economically viable and politically realistic? Is this what the peoples of the twelve combining nations actually want? Is it a structure that could include or would exclude the rest of Europe? Is it a structure that will actually create discord rather than harmony.

Fate, however, had already hurled another unsuspected and untimely thunderbolt at the heart of *Europa* in October 1989, which destroyed the Berlin Wall. Communism had collapsed, and with it went the high-tension spring that had focused western European unity and had provided an impenetrable barrier to the endless problems to the east. At first the news was accepted with rejoicing around the world, especially throughout the enlarged German Fatherland. There was one cool voice of reason that foresaw dangers ahead: Margaret Thatcher warned of the absence of democratic and market-oriented institutions on the other side of the former Iron Curtain.

When the euphoria had died down, it became clear that Germany's position itself had dramatically changed too. Since WW2 it had been a federal grouping on the eastern edge of the EC and had not sought to play any overtly significant political role on the world stage. Now it was a nation again with all the implied responsibilities, of which none were more pressing than the condition of the newly liberated nations of eastern Europe and the collapsed former USSR. When the Berlin Wall came down, Germany looked east again and necessarily regarded the west as of secondary importance in terms of economic reconstruction and security. This new perspective was demonstrated by Herr Gensher's instant and unilateral recognition of Croatia and Slovenia in 1991.

Chancellor Kohl cannot be blamed for seizing the opportunity for reunification, but he could perhaps be blamed for a hat-trick of politically forced errors that followed hard upon it. First, he offered partial parity of the near-worthless Ostmark with the mighty Deutschemark. Secondly, he promised pay parity for East German workers by 1995. Thirdly, having unwittingly destroyed any competitive potential that East Germany's economy may have enjoyed before these two measures, he sent the *Treuhand*, the agency for creating a free market economy, into East Germany to privatise anything worth privatising.

The *Treuhand*, however, simply flattened the existing means of production and distribution like an efficient bulldozer. No real plan for the political integration of Germany has ever been made, and so the east still has no effective say in Bonn. The 15,700,000 inhabitants of former East Germany are now bewildered and bankrupt and Germany's budget has gone into an annual deficit of 200 billion Deutschemarks. These figures should be treated with some caution, as they may yet rise further for many years to come.

The terms set for reunification induced the resignation of President Poehl of the Bundesbank and led to a surge in German monetary expansion towards 10% in 1992 and in inflation to over 5%. Poehl's successor, Helmut Schlesinger, had no option under the Bundesbank's charter but to raise interest rates to curb these domestic pressures. France, which had doggedly pursued the mighty Deutschemark under its *franc fort* policy, now found itself saddled with real interest rates of 10%, putting its economy in a massive deflationary squeeze. Britain had only joined the ERM in October 1990 – at an impossibly high rate of 2.95 Deutschemarks to the pound – but could not possibly survive such a tough monetary regime. If John Major did not despair of this error at the time, he must surely have put his head in his hands soon afterwards. Britain's economy had entered recession in 1990, but the German boom continued for two more years as a result of demand from East Germany, as the reunification bonanza Deutschemarks were spent on highly prized consumer durables. When Britain needed recovery in 1992 and 1993, the German economy was itself turning down.

On 16 September 1992 the Exchange Rate Mechanism (ERM) blew up. The pound sterling dropped by 20% (initially), the lira by 10% and the Spanish peseta by 5%. Sweden was also tracking the Deutschemark, and overnight rates for the Kroner (outside the ERM) and Irish punt (inside the ERM) reached several hundred per cent. This was clearly unsustainable and both currencies had to devalue too. France soldiered on phlegmatically with its *franc fort* policy with true Gallic fortitude, but her citizens were deeply despondent. On 2 August 1993 the Deutschemark-franc exchange rate could not withstand the market pressure and the markets effectively killed off the ERM, at least for the time being, but not before the Bank of France had thrown its entire currency reserves away in an attempt to save the franc's parity with the Deutschemark.

Whereas the foreign exchange markets were tearing up the central plank of monetary union of the Treaty of Maastricht, the Swiss electorate had already voted it out in a referendum as they turned their back on the EC. This was not surprising, given Switzerland's long tradition of neutrality and non-involvement in matters 'European'. What was interesting in this referendum was that the French quarter of the population voted strongly for the treaty, while the German three-quarters voted strongly against. When the voters of Denmark did the same thing in May 1992, however, it was a different matter. The clear message to the leaders and Eurocrats was that the people were not with them.

The people of Europe in 1993 are suffering a global recession and Germany has her special problems with reunification. Unemployment, taxes, bankruptcies and inflation are rising in Germany and France and so are national debts across the Continent – except in Luxembourg, which is the smallest EC member state. Not only does the preoccupation of Europe's politicians with the Treaty of Maastricht bear no apparent relationship to the immediate issues, but it has fast become clear that the criteria for monetary union set out in the treaty have ceased to be achievable even in the medium-term, even if it was a desirable aim in the first place.

Then the daily spectre on the EC's doorstep of the horrors of 'ethnic cleansing' in Bosnia-Herzegovina makes a mockery of the treaty's intent to form a common foreign policy and defence, as the only EC foreign policy seems to be to have no foreign policy, other than a show of humanitarian aid sponsored by the UN.

Meanwhile the so-called common market remains riddled with subsidies, biased procurement policies and corruption, and in late 1992 there was even the threat from France of a trade war with America. It is also beginning to dawn on industrialists and politicians that Europe's social security programmes are turning the EC into a high-cost environment that cannot compete effectively on world markets, while the treaty reaffirms the Social Chapter which will only add to payroll on-costs and make the position worse.

Finally, there is a growing perception among the people of Europe that the aim to take control of each nation's currency – a device inspired by Europe's political leaders to dissolve their own authority and disenfranchise their voters in favour of unelected Eurocrats by removing monetary policy to unelected central bankers – is mainly a means to enforce the *fonctionnaire's* vision of a sterile and bureaucratic political union. The European Commission and the other supporting architects of Maastricht do not see that monetary union without a democratically-elected central government will turn into an efficient economic killer-machine of jobs and growth, which are the two main economic requirements demanded most by the peoples of Europe in the global recession. Unemployment in the EC is over

11%, which translates into 17.4 million unemployed, and it is still rising. The politicians offer no solutions. Maastricht is silent on this foremost problem, but prefers instead to lay down national borrowing levels that are being breached in every direction as the fundamental issue of unemployment is not addressed.

What has gone wrong? The majority of the people do not trust the real intent of a centralised organisation headed by unelected Commissioners acquiring such power and so rapidly. The people suspect that a lot of old bones are going to get broken in the process – and for what? The people want democracy not bureaucracy. The people want a vision of Europe that will capture their imagination and inspire them.

The Henley Centre of Britain conducted a survey of 7,000 people in Britain, Germany, France, Italy, The Netherlands and Spain and found that fewer people believe prosperity depends on a United Europe. In Germany, the proportion fell from about half in 1991 to less than a third in 1993. In Britain, the drop was from 42% to 30%: in France from 61% to 47%; and in Italy from 60% to 52%. Support for a single European currency had dropped sharply in Britain – from 41% to 31%. Whereas 59% of West Germans wanted a unified currency in 1991, the figure declined to 35% in 1993. In Britain, barely one in ten feels 'as British as European'. Among Italians the proportion who feel 'as European as Italian' has come down from 50% to 39%. In Germany the equivalent figures were 48% in 1991 and 39% in 1993. Not surprisingly, 69% of those questioned wanted stricter immigration controls, with the figures rising to 77% in East Germany and 73% in Britain.

The first half of 1993 was not a happy time for European politics and politicians. Chancellor Kohl's CDU Party in Germany became increasingly unpopular as recession, inflation, immigration and re-unification taxes began to bite harder and harder; increasingly, the German bankers, electorate and media let it be known that they did not favour EMU and that they would rather keep their Deutsche-marks. The French socialists, who had doggedly followed the *franc fort* policy of maintaining close parity with the mighty Deutschemark for the previous eight years, were roundly thrashed in the polls in March, when the right wing won a landslide victory with 80% of the vote.

In Britain the voters sent a stunning message to the residents of Downing Street, when the Conservative Party's majority of 12,000 at Newbury was overturned by the Liberal-Democrats who won a 22,000 majority in a by-election; more to the point, the Conservatives were routed in the Local Council elections and were then left with control of only one council, that of Buckingham. The electorate were saying 'It's the economy, stupid,' but did they realise how much of the economic mess was being driven by the requirements of the European agenda?

Then the Conservatives lost the fifteenth-safest seat in another by-election defeat in July at Christchurch, where the Liberal-Democrats won with the largest post-war swing of over 35%. One of the several issues where John Major's government parted company with the electorate was its determination to ratify the Treaty of Maastricht over the heads of the people, without allowing them a referendum on perhaps the greatest constitutional change since the publication of the Bill of Rights in 1689. He claimed that his celebrated general election victory of 9 April 1992 endorsed the Conservative Party's manifesto 'commitment' to Maastricht – a commitment that was not expressly stated as such. The treaty was only published in Britain on 12 April, however, and the other two main parties' manifestos also supported Maastricht. So how could anyone in Britain vote against it?

In March 1992 the Danes narrowly rejected the Treaty of Maastricht, but reversed their decision in a May 1993 referendum, but only after having secured significant opt-outs on monetary union, common defence and European citizenship at Edinburgh in December 1992. The French referendum in September 1992 had voted for Maastricht by a margin of less than 1%; if the referendum were held again in 1993, following the decisive removal of President Mitterrand's socialists, there is little doubt that the vote would go the other way.

Then in May 1993 several European socialist politicians were found to be heavily involved in corruption. On 1 May former Prime Minister Beregevoy of France committed suicide after allegations that he had benefited from substantial interest-free loans – or gifts to be more accurate. Next Bjorn Engholm, the leader of Germany's Social Democrats, resigned in shame over his involvement in a five-year-old dirty-tricks scandal that involved the death of a political opponent. At the time more than twenty other Federal investigations into political corruption were running in Germany. In Spain the Socialist Prime Minister, Felipe Gonzalez, was also accused of bribery and was forced to call an early election, which he narrowly won. Meanwhile in Italy the socialist alliance seemed to be, or actually was, involved in wholesale corruption and on a scale which forced constitutional changes. And for good measure an Italian Eurocrat in Brussels did the honourable thing and jumped from a window when he was accused of having his hand in the EC agricultural subsidies till.

The Italian corruption that really matters to Europe begins in Sicily – with drugs. Whereas the Dutch Government's legitimisation of so-called soft drugs has made Amsterdam the narcotics trade centre for northern Europe, the real hard stuff and hard dealing emanates from Palermo. Europe's single market now offers the drug dealers an opportunity as big and attractive as America. The threat is so great that in April 1993 the French Government announced its intention to maintain its border controls – in defiance of the (unratified) Schengen Agreement of 1990, which intended to remove the borders between France, Germany and the Benelux countries as a precursor to a fast-speed Europe. Wherever drugs are pushed crime and corruption follow hard upon them and on a scale that increases with the market opportunity, yet the EC has failed to take effective action in what the electorate perceive to be an obvious target for concerted *federal* action.

The tax-paying voters of Europe are now deeply cynical about the concentration of too much power in their own countries, and now in Brussels too. In short, the political leaders of Europe are widely perceived to be economically complacent, intellectually dishonest, self-serving, intolerant of debate and contemptuous of the will of the people. There is a moral vacuum in the heart of Europe and greed and arrogance in the heart of European politics, of crisis proportions. Now the Treaty of Maastricht threatens a bureaucratic nightmare across the Continent. No wonder the positive visions of Europe seem to have died a death in the recession.

The people want a vision of Europe that will be realistic and workable, among the different nations, and prove enduring. They want freedom, democracy, security, peace and prosperity in all its forms.

The people of Europe, however, are demoralised by the lack of political and cultural leadership. We must awaken their interest and generate enthusiasm for the need to define a realistic shape for Europe's future, which is acceptable for the people. If the people of Europe do not, or are not allowed to, speak, the leaders and the Eurocrats will continue to devise and impose centralising measures and further deny democracy. The fight for Europe's soul is just beginning in earnest, but already the thirteenth nation is casting a dark and cynical shadow across the Continent.

15 August 1993   Andover

From Post-War Ruins to a United Europe

Reflections on the words of Sir Winston Churchill

What were the views of the supreme architect of victory as he surveyed a post-war Europe? In September 1946 Churchill was adamant that 'we must build *a kind of* United States of Europe ... or whatever name or form it may take'. Mindful of the failure of the League of Nations after the First World War, which had failed to achieve US endorsement and then failed in its objectives, he developed his theme in an address to an United Europe meeting at the Albert Hall on 14 May 1947: 'Are the States of Europe to continue for ever to squander the first fruits of their toil upon the erection of new barriers, military fortifications and tariff walls and passport networks against one another?'

Churchill called for Europeans 'to exchange blessings instead of curses', as he revealed the concept of a common market in trade. Churchill was ever the realist who could see the difficulties of formulating and implementing the grand vision: 'In my experience of large enterprises, I have found it is often a mistake to try to settle everything at once. Far off, on the skyline, we can see the peaks of the Delectable Mountains, but we cannot tell what lies between us and them. We know where we want to go, but we cannot foresee all the stages of the journey, nor can we plan our marches as in a military operation. We are not acting in the field of force, but in the domain of opinion. We cannot give orders. We can only persuade. We must go forward step by step ... '

He then stated his preference for 'the federation of the European States and for the creation of a Federal Constitution for Europe', which he hoped would eventually be achieved. He expressed his appreciation of Britain's 'friendly relations' with the associations working for the 'economic integration of Europe'. He pulled back, however, from attempting 'to define or prescribe the structure of constitutions' and was 'content in the first instance to present the idea of United Europe as a moral, cultural and spiritual conception to which all can rally without being disturbed by divergences of structure. It is for the responsible statesmen, who have the conduct of affairs in their hands and the power of executive action, to shape and fashion the structure.'

Consider again Churchill's exact words. His view was that a *United Europe* would be 'a moral, cultural and spiritual conception'. These lofty but vague terms conjure up a vision of a common European idealism rather than a political and economic union. There is not a hint here of monetary union, for example, in which unelected central bankers determine monetary policy across a vast continent. There is not even a hint of the 'Brussels' factor of centralised directives affecting every aspect of citizen's lives.

Interestingly, Adenauer echoed Churchill's vision of unity in his memoirs and in similar terms: 'It was clear to me that a United Europe could only arise if a community of the European peoples could be reconstructed, a community in which each people made its own irreplaceable contribution to the European economy and culture, to western thought, imagination and creativity.' (*Imagination* in this context has more to do with Platonic Ideas than any abstract thinking.) Churchill's *United Europe* was an antithesis to the Europe of 1945 – 'a rubble heap, a charnel-house, a breeding ground of pestilence and hate' – it was a rallying point beyond 'divergences of structure'.

This last phrase merits closer examination too. The use of the plural 'divergences' would indicate that the 'divergences of structure' were at the level of the constituent nations or states – there could hardly be 'divergences of structure' at Churchill's more metaphysical rallying point. This interpretation is borne out by Churchill's continuing thesis on the integration of Germany into the new post-war Europe. In fact he saw no need 'to attempt to forecast the future constitution of Germany'. In his view, without prejudice to the future question of German federation, the old individual States and Principalities of former Germany 'might be invited to take their place in the Council of Europe'. There can be no doubt that Churchill's vision of *United Europe* was a confederation of sovereign states, which would have made even a Federal Germany a transparent structure in the first instance.

'United Europe' in this context, however, most definitely did not include Britain, as Churchill made clear in a speech at Zurich University on 19 September 1946. Churchill was at pains to draw a distinction between Britain and the Continent of Europe: 'We British have our Commonwealth of Nations. These do not weaken, on the contrary they strengthen, the world organisation. They are in fact its main support. And why should there not be a European group which could give a sense of enlarged patriotism and common citizenship to the distracted peoples of this turbulent and mighty continent ... ' For Churchill, Britain and the Continent of Europe would unite at the level of a world organisation – implying the fledgling UN – rather than in the heart of Europe itself.

It was for the continental Europeans to resolve their differences and evolve their unity. Churchill could not 'imagine a regenerated Europe without a strong France ... All my public life I have worked for a strong France and I never lost faith in her destiny, even in the darkest hours.' Churchill viewed the Treaty of Alliance signed in early 1947 as only giving formal expression to 'the community of sentiment that already exists as an indisputable and indestructible fact'. At the time that Churchill was speaking, the need for reconciliation between France and Germany was the paramount issue.

When Churchill considered the Italians' desire for a secure future, he looked to the time 'when free men could travel freely under the sanction of a common citizenship', as they had done in the days of the Roman Empire. The new citizens 'will be as proud to say "I am a European" as once they were to say "*Civis Romanus sum*".' Yet, almost immediately, Churchill doubts the vision as he realises that they will also say 'I am Dutch' and 'I am Belgian' with at least equal force. Perhaps the ease with which an inhabitant of the British Isles says 'I am English' with the same zeal as he or she says 'I am British' could be transferred to a European context. Even this he seemed to doubt, as he concluded somewhat wistfully: 'How simple it would all be, and how crowned with glory, if that should ever arise.'

On another continent, however, Churchill looked to the day when 'eventually there may come – I feel eventually there will come – the principle of common citizenship'. He was speaking this time at Fulton, Missouri on 5 March 1946, but the 'common citizenship' he was talking about on that occasion was between the citizens of the United States and the British Commonwealth, as an extension of the 'special relationship'. In the same speech, Churchill called for the English-speaking peoples to 'work with conscious purpose for a grand pacification of Europe, within the structure of the United Nations and in accordance with its Charter'.

Churchill wondered aloud which countries would be included and which ones left out of United Europe, but he avoided invidious selection and retreated into the general statement that the task was to remove frontiers rather than erect them. All countries of Europe would be welcomed to Churchill's Federal Europe which accorded their peoples the 'fundamental personal rights and liberties on which our democratic European civilisation has been created'.

It was in considering the attitude of Soviet Russia towards *United Europe* that he gave his broadest hint of the shape of his metaphysical rallying point: 'The whole purpose of a united democratic Europe is to give decisive guarantees against aggression', both from foreign invasion and from 'what is even worse, the knock upon the door of the political police to take the loved one far from the protection of law and justice'. With such threats in mind Churchill proposed 'the idea of a Charter of Human Rights, guarded by freedom and sustained by law'. Churchill concluded: 'It is impossible to separate economics and defence from the general political structure. Mutual aid in the economic field and joint military defence must inevitably be accompanied step by step with a parallel policy of closer political unity. It is said with truth that this involves some sacrifice or merger of national sovereignty.' In fact Churchill's views on how to structure United Europe were decidedly ambivalent at times, but his vision of this unity was essentially evolutionary, 'as the gradual assumption by all the nations concerned of that larger sovereignty which can alone protect their diverse and distinctive customs and characteristics and their national traditions'. Churchill's hope was that if the leaders of Europe would 'firmly grasp the larger hopes of humanity, then it may be that we shall move into a happier sunlit age'.

It seems that Churchill had to create the ideal of a United Europe and lend it his endorsement, while skilfully asserting to the rest of Europe that it neither included nor excluded Britain. Churchill described himself as an 'earnest advocate of a United Europe'. He told the Conservative Party Conference at Brighton on 4 October 1947 that he was convinced that 'it is possible to reconcile our position as the centre of the British Empire with full development of close *economic* relations with all the friendly countries of Europe'.

Churchill would not have abandoned Imperial Preference in favour of a European common market; in his somewhat optimistic view the two trading structures could be made compatible. Even in a note to the Cabinet on 29 November 1951, Churchill said he was not opposed to Britain playing her part in the military defence and economic development of a United Europe, but that he did not 'support integral membership of either the United Kingdom or Commonwealth ... We help, we dedicate, we play a part, but we are not merged and do not forfeit our insular or Commonwealth-wide character.' Churchill's priority was first the Commonwealth, then the English-speaking world and third a United Europe.

Even before WW1 Churchill had been a passionate advocate of free trade. When he stood as the Liberal Candidate for Oldham in the 1909 General Election, he made a series of brilliant speeches on economic fundamentals, including trade issues. In his view protective tariffs had 'warped and restricted the growth of the industries of the nations' and had 'been unfairly injurious to the poorer classes', particularly in Germany and America – with their high food prices. He traced a host of ills from corruption in public life to unemployment, low wages and high prices for imported materials as caused by protectionist policies and measures. Churchill favoured open capital markets as well and robustly argued for free inward and external investment as spurs to future production and trade: 'From my experience it seems a profound natural law which governs all our actions that you get nothing for nothing and precious little for twopence-halfpenny!'

As though foreseeing the destructive impact of the Fordney-McCumber and Smoot-Hawley protectionist tariffs imposed by America in the 1920s and 1930s, Churchill warned his 1909 audience that protectionism 'would injure our relations with foreign countries, and it would disturb the course of trade, and it would aggravate that instability among different states and countries from which already we suffer and for which already we pay so heavy a toll in national defence'. Within five years WW1 had broken out; it could only have served to confirm Churchill's view that harmony between nations is best fostered by free trade.

In 1953 the European Defence Community failed. Churchill said: 'We are with Europe but not of it. We are linked but not comprised. We are associated but not absorbed. And should European statesmen address us and say, "Shall we speak for thee?" we should reply, "Nay Sir, for we dwell among our own people".' On 11 May Churchill in the House of Commons explicitly rejected the idea of British entanglement in a 'European federal system'. It was his last official comment on the issue.

Churchill never ceased to cast his gaze westwards and in a recorded speech accepting the Freedom House Award in New York on 9 October 1955 he made plain where he felt Britain's strategic axis really lay: 'I believe in the essential and fundamental unity of the English-speaking peoples – not at the expense of other countries, nor by the creation of elaborate machinery – but as the natural realisation of a great truth. The safety of the world depends on it.'

S.R.H.

17 May 1993   London

The quotations in this chapter are taken mainly from *Post-War Speeches*, Vols. I-III, published by Cassell & Company Limited, including *The Sinews of Peace*; *Europe Unite*; *In the Balance*; *Stemming the Tide* and *The Unwritten Alliance*. The quotations on free trade are taken from *The People's Rights*, published by Jonathan Cape.

Europe's Present Political Architecture

Lady Thatcher

The European Community we have today was created in very different circumstances to deal with very different problems. It was built upon very different assumptions about where the world was heading. And it embodied political ideas and economic theories that in the light of recent history we have to question. In particular, I shall try to answer three questions.

First, how can we best deal with the imbalance in Europe created by the re-unification and revival of Germany?

Second, how can we reform European institutions so that they provide for the diversity of post-Communist Europe and be truly democratic?

Third, how can we ensure that the new Europe contributes to – rather than undermines – the world's economic prosperity and political stability?

Our answers to these questions can no longer be bound by the conventional collectivist wisdom of the 1940s and 50s. That is yesterday's future. We must draw on the ideas of liberty, democracy, free markets and nationhood that have swept the world in the last decade.

The Beginning of the Community

It was Winston Churchill who, with characteristic magnanimity in 1946, with his Zurich speech, argued that Germany should be rehabilitated through what he called 'European Union' as 'an association between France and Germany' which would 'assume direction'. This could not be done overnight, and it took American leadership. In 1947, after travelling through Europe in that terrible winter, when everything froze over, George Marshall, the then Secretary of State, promoted the idea of American help. Marshall Aid was administered by institutions set up *ad hoc* – it had to be, if only because most European states did not have adequate machinery, the Greek delegate being found one day simply making up figures for his country's need – and I expect there were others besides.

The initial impetus was for European recovery. It owed much to simple American good-heartedness. It owed something to commercial calculation: the prosperity of Europe, in free trade conditions, would also be the prosperity of America. But the main thing was the threat from Stalin. Eastern Europe had shown how demoralized peoples could not resist cunningly executed Communist takeovers, and Marshall Aid was intended to set western Europe back on its feet. It was a prodigious success, but we have found, again and again, that institutions devised for one set of problems become obstacles to solving the next set – even that they became problems in their own right. The Common Agricultural Policy is an example. As originally devised, it had a modest aim that was not unreasonable.

Yet we all now know that the CAP is an expensive headache and one quite likely to derail the Uruguay Round. Because of agricultural protection we stop food imports from the poorer countries. They themselves are nowadays vehement supports of market principles: it is from the Cairns Group of developing countries that you hear demands for free trade. Yet in the industrialized part of the world, the tax-payer and the consumer stump up $270 billion in subsidies and higher costs; and the World Bank has calculated that, if the tariff and other barriers were cut by half, then the poorer countries would gain at once, in exports, £50 billion. In case you might think that these sentiments are somehow anti-European, I should say that they come from an editorial in the economic section of the *Frankfurter Allgemeine Zeitung* of 4 May 1992.

Here we have a prime example of yesterday's solutions becoming tomorrow's problems. You could extend this through the European institutions as a whole. They were meant to solve post-war problems, and did so in many ways extremely well. Western Europe did unite against the Soviet threat, and, with Anglo-American precepts, became free and very prosperous. That prosperity, denied to the peoples of eastern Europe and Russia, in the end caused demoralization among their rulers and revolt from below. We are now in a quite different set of circumstances, with the Cold War over.

Looking at European institutions today, I am reminded of a remark made about political parties in the French Third Republic. Some of them had names which reflected radical republican origins from the 1870s, but years later they had become conservative. These radical names, ran the remark, were like the light reaching Earth from stars that were long extinct. Equally with the end of the Cold War we have to look again at the shape of Europe and its institutions.

The German Question

Let me turn first to the new situation created by the re-unification of Germany. And let me say that if I were a German today, I would be proud – proud but also worried. I would be proud of the magnificent achievement of rebuilding my country, entrenching democracy and assuming the undoubtedly preponderant position in Europe. But I would also be worried about the European Community and its direction. The German taxpayer pays dearly for his place in Europe. Britain and Germany have a strong joint interest in ensuring that the other Community countries pay their fair share of the cost – and control the Community's spending more enthusiastically – without leaving us to carry so much of the burden.

Germany is well-equipped to encourage such financial prudence. Indeed I would trust the Bundesbank more than any other European Central Bank to keep down inflation – because the Germans have none-too-distant memories of the total chaos and political extremism which hyper-inflation brings. The Germans are therefore right to be increasingly worried about the terms they agreed for economic and monetary union. Were I a German, I would prefer the Bundesbank to provide our modern equivalent of the gold standard rather than any committee of European central bankers.

But there is an understandable reluctance on the part of Bonn to defend its views and interests so straightforwardly. For years the Germans have been led to believe by their neighbours that their respectability depends on their subordinating their national interest to the joint decisions of the Community. It is better that pretence be stopped. A reunited Germany can't and won't subordinate its national interests in economic or in foreign policy to those of the Community indefinitely. Germany's new pre-eminence is a fact. We will all be better off if we recognise that modern democratic Germany has come of age.

Nevertheless Germany's power is a problem – as much for the Germans as for the rest of Europe. Germany is too large to be just another player in the European game, but not large enough to establish unquestioned supremacy over its neighbours. And the history of Europe since 1870 has largely been concerned with finding the right structure to contain Germany.

It has been Germany's immediate neighbours, the French, who have seen this most clearly. Both Briand in 1929 and Schuman after WW2 proposed structures of economic union to achieve this. Briand's proposal was made just at the moment when the rise of the Nazis made such a visionary scheme impossible and it failed. But Schuman's vision of a European Community was realised because of an almost unique constellation of favourable circumstances. The Soviet threat made European co-operation imperative. Germany was itself divided. Other western nations sought German participation in the defence of western Europe. West Germany needed the respectability that NATO and the Community could give. And American presence in, and leadership of, Europe reduced the fears of Germany's neighbours.

With the collapse of the Soviet Union and reunification of Germany, however, the entire position has changed. A new Europe of some 30 states has come into being, the problem of German power has again surfaced and statesmen have been scrambling to produce a solution to it. At first France hoped that the post-war Franco-German partnership, with France as the senior partner, would continue. Chancellor Kohl's separate and successful negotiations with Mr Gorbachev quickly showed this to be an illusion.

The next response of France and other European countries was to seek to tie down the German Gulliver within the joint decision-making of the European Community. Again, however, this quickly proved to be an illusion. Germany's preponderance within the Community is such that no major decision can really be taken against German wishes. In these circumstances, the Community augments German power rather than containing it.

Let me illustrate this point with two examples where I agree with the German position. The first, as I have mentioned, was the German decision to recognise Croatia and Slovenia which compelled the rest of Europe to follow suit. The second is the refusal of the Bundesbank to pursue imprudent financial policies at the urging of some of the countries of the G7. However much I may sympathise with these policies, the blunt fact is that Germany has followed its own interests rather than the advice of its neighbours who have then been compelled to adjust their own stance.

The Balance of Power

What follows from this is that German power will be best accommodated in a looser Europe in which individual nation states retain their freedom of action. If Germany or any other power then pursues a policy to which other countries object, it will automatically invite a coalition against itself. And the resulting solution will reflect the relative weight of the adversaries. A common foreign policy, however, is liable to express the interests of the largest single actor. And a serious dispute between EC member states locked into a common foreign policy would precipitate a crisis affecting everything covered by the Community.

The general paradox here is that attempts at co-operation that are too ambitious are likely to create conflict. We will have more harmonious relationships between the states of Europe if they continue to have room to make their own decisions and to follow their own interests – as happened in the Gulf War. But it would be idle to deny that such a balance of power – for that is what I have been describing – has sometimes broken down and led to war. And Europe on its own, however organised, will still find the question of German power insoluble. Europe has really enjoyed stability only since America became a European power.

The third response therefore is to keep an American presence in Europe. American power is so substantial that it dwarfs the power of any other single European country. It reassured the rest of Europe in the face of Soviet power until yesterday; and it provides similar comfort against the rise of Germany today – as the Germans themselves appreciate. Why aren't we worried about the abuse of American power? It is difficult to be anxious about a power so little inclined to throw its weight around that our principal worry is that American troops will go home.

And there's the rub. There is pressure from isolationist opinion in the USA to withdraw from Europe. It is both provoked and encouraged by similar thinking in the Community which is protectionist in economics and 'little European' in strategy. In trade, in the GATT negotiations, in NATO's restructuring, we need to pursue policies that will persuade America to remain a European power.

Europe Free and Democratic

If America is required to keep Europe secure, what is required to keep Europe free and democratic?

When the founders of the European Community drew up the Treaty of Rome, they incorporated features from two quite different economic traditions. From Liberalism they took free trade, free markets and competition. From Socialism (in guises as various as Social Catholicism and Corporatism) they took regulation and intervention. And for thirty years – up to the signing of the Single European Act – these two traditions were in a state of perpetual but unacknowledged tension.

Now – with the Commission exploiting the Single European Act to accumulate powers of greater direction and regulation – Europe is reaching the point at which it must choose between these two approaches. Is it to be a tightly regulated, centralised bureaucratic Federal State, imposing uniform standards throughout the Continent? Or is it to be a loose-knit decentralised free-market Europe of sovereign states, based upon competition between different national systems of tax and regulation within a free trade area?

The federalists at least seem to be clear. The Maastricht Treaty met the Commissioner's requirement for a 'single institutional framework' for the Community. Yet, before the ink was even dry on the Treaty, it was reported that the President of the European Commission was seeking more money and more powers for the Commission which would become the Executive of the Community – in other words a European Government. There would seem to be no doubt about the direction in which the European federalists are now anxious to proceed – towards a Federal Europe.

Nor is there any mystery about the urgency with which they press the Federalist cause. Even though they may wish to defer the 'enlargement' of the Community with the accession of eastern Europe, they realise it is impossible. A half-Europe imposed by Soviet tyranny was one thing; a half-Europe imposed by Brussels would be a moral catastrophe depriving the Community of its European legitimacy.

The Commission knows it will have to admit many new members in the next few decades. But it hopes to construct a centralised Super-State in advance – and *irrevocably* – so that the new members will have to apply for entry on federalist terms. And it's just not on.

Imagine a European Community of 30 nations, ranging in their economic productivity from Germany to the Ukraine, and in their political stability from Britain to Poland, all governed from Brussels; all enforcing the same conditions at work; all having the same worker rights as the German Unions; all subject to the same interest rates, monetary, fiscal and economic policies; all agreeing on a common Foreign and defence policy; and all accepting the authority of an Executive and a remote foreign Parliament over '80% of economic and social legislation'.

Such a body is an even more utopian enterprise than the Tower of Babel. For at least the builders of Babel all spoke the same language when they *began*. They were, you might say, *communautaire*.

The thinking behind the Commission's proposals is essentially the thinking of 'yesterday's tomorrow'. It was how the best minds of Europe saw the future in the ruins after WW2. But they made a central intellectual mistake. They assumed that the model for future government was that of a centralised bureaucracy that would collect information upwards, making decisions at the top, and then issue orders downwards. And what seemed the wisdom of the ages in 1945 was in fact a primitive fallacy. Hierarchical bureaucracy may be a suitable method of organising a small business that is exposed to fierce external competition – but it is a recipe for stagnation and inefficiency in almost every other context.

Yet it is precisely this model of a remote, centralised, bureaucratic organisation that the European Commission and its federalist supporters seek to impose on a Community which they acknowledge may soon contain many more countries of widely differing levels of political and economic development, and speaking more than fifteen languages. *'C'est magnifique, mais ce n'est pas la politique.'*

The larger Europe grows, the more diverse must be the forms of co-operation it requires. Instead of a centralised bureaucracy, the model should be a market – not only a market of individuals and companies, but also a market in which the players are governments. Thus governments would compete with each other for foreign investments, top management and high earners through lower taxes and less regulation. Such a market would impose a fiscal discipline on governments because they would not want to drive away expertise and business. It would also help to establish which fiscal and regulatory policies produced the best overall economic results. No wonder socialists don't like it.

To make such a market work, of course, national governments must retain most of their existing powers in social and economic affairs. Since these governments are closer and accountable to their voters – it is doubly desirable that we should keep power at the national level.

The Role of the Commission

In 1996, when the arrangements agreed at Maastricht are due to be reviewed, and probably a good deal earlier, the Community should move in exactly the opposite direction to that proposed by the European federalists.

A Community of sovereign states committed to voluntary co-operation, a lightly regulated free market and international free trade does not need a Commission in its present form. The government of the Community – to the extent that this term is appropriate – is the Council of Ministers, consisting of representatives of democratically elected national governments. The work of the Commission should cease to be legislative in any sense. It should be an administrative body, like any professional civil service, and it should not initiate policy, but rather carry it out. In doing this it should be subject to the scrutiny of the European Parliament acting on the model of Commons Select Committees. In that way, whatever collective policies or regulations are required would emerge from deliberation between democratic governments, accountable to their national parliaments, rather than being imposed by a bureaucracy with its own agenda.

Co-operation in Europe

But need this always be done in the same 'single institutional framework'? New problems arise all the time. Will these always require the same institutions? I doubt it. We need a greater flexibility than the structures of the European Community have allowed until very recently.

A single institutional framework, of its nature, tends to place too much power with the central authorities. It is a good thing that a Common Foreign Policy will continue to be carried on under a separate treaty and will neither be subject to the European Court nor permit the Commission to fire off initiatives at will. If 'Europe' moves into new areas, it must do so under separate treaties which clearly define the powers which have been surrendered.

And why need every new European initiative require the participation of all members of the Community? It will sometimes be the case – especially after enlargement that only some Community members will want to move forward to another stage of integration.

Here I pay tribute to John Major's achievement in persuading the other eleven Community Heads of Government that they could move ahead to a Social Chapter, but not within the treaty and without Britain's participation. It sets a vital precedent. For an enlarged Community can only function if we build in flexibility of that kind.

We should aim at a multi-track Europe in which *ad hoc* groups of different states – such as the Schengen Group – forge varying levels of co-operation and integration on a case-by-case basis. Such a structure would lack graph paper neatness, but it would accommodate the diversity of post-Communist Europe.

The European Parliament

Supporters of federalism argue, no doubt sincerely, that we can accommodate this diversity by giving more powers to the European Parliament. But democracy requires more than that.

To have a genuine European democracy, you would need a Europe-wide public opinion based on a single language; Europe-wide political parties with a common programme understood similarly in all member-states; a Europe-wide political debate in which political and economic concepts and words had the same agreed meaning everywhere. We would be in the same position as the unwieldy Habsburg Empire's Parliament.

The Habsburg Parliament

That parliament was a notorious failure. There were dozens of political parties, and nearly a dozen peoples were represented – Germans, Italians, Czechs, Poles and so on. For the government to get anything through – for instance, in 1889 a modest increase in the number of conscripts – took ages, as all the various interests had to be propitiated. When one or other was not satisfied, its spokesman resorted to obstruction – lengthy speeches in Russian, banging of desk-lids, throwing of ink-wells and on one occasion the blowing of a cavalry trumpet by the Professor of Jurisprudence at the German University of Prague. Measures could not be passed and budgets could only be produced by decree. The longest-lasting prime minister, Count Taaffe, remarked that his highest ambition in politics was the achievement of supportable dissatisfaction on all sides – not a bad description of what the European Community risks becoming.

And because of the irresponsibility of parliaments, the Habsburg Monarchy could really only be ruled by bureaucrats. It took twenty-five signatures for a tax payment to be validated; one in four people in employment worked for the state in some form or another, even in 1914; and so many resources went to all of this that not much was left for defence: even the military bands had to be cut back, Radetzky March and all. Of course it was a tremendous period in cultural terms both in Vienna and in Budapest. We in England have done mightily well by emigration, often forced, to our shores of so many talented people from central Europe. But the fact is that they had to leave their native lands because political life became impossible.

This example could be multiplied again and again. Belgium and Holland, which have so much in common, split apart in 1831. Sweden and Norway, which have even more in common, split apart in 1905. It does seem simply to be a straight-forward rule in modern times that countries which contain two languages, even if they are similar, must in the end divide, unless the one language absorbs the other.

It would be agreeable to think that we could all go back to the work of the Middle Ages, when the educated classes spoke Latin, and the rulers communicated in grunts. But we cannot. Unless we are dealing with international co-operation and alliances, freely entered-into, we create artificial structures which become the problem that they were meant to address. The League of Nations, when the Second World War broke out, resolved to ignore the fact and to discuss, instead, the standardisation of level-crossings.

A Federal Europe

I am sometimes tempted to think that the new Europe which the Commission and Euro-federalists are creating is equally ill-equipped to satisfy the needs of its members and the wishes of their peoples. It is, indeed, a Europe which combines all the most striking failures of our age.

The day of the artificially constructed megastates has gone: so the Euro-federalists are now desperately scurrying to build one.

The Swedish welfare state has failed – even in Sweden: so the Euro-statists press ahead with their Social Chapter.

Large scale immigration has in France and Germany already encouraged the growth of extremist parties: so the European Commission is pressing us to remove frontier controls.

If the European Community proceeds in the direction which the majority of Member State Governments and the Commission seem to want, they will create a structure which brings insecurity, unemployment, national resentment and ethnic conflict.

Insecurity – because Europe's protectionism will strain and possibly sever that link with the United States on which the security of the Continent ultimately depends.

Unemployment – because the pursuit of policies of regulation will increase costs, and price European workers out of jobs. National resentment – because a single currency and a single centralised economic policy, which will come with it, will leave the electorate of a country angry and powerless to change its conditions. Ethnic conflict – because not only will the wealthy European countries be faced with waves of immigration from the south and from the east, but also *within* Europe itself, the effect of a single currency and regulation of wages and social costs will have one of two consequences. Either there will have to be a massive transfer of money from one country to another, which will not in practice be affordable. Or there will be massive migration from the less successful to the more successful countries.

Yet if the future we are being offered contains so very many risks and so few real benefits, why it may be asked is it proving all but irresistible? The answer is simple. It is that in almost every European country there has been a refusal to debate the issues which really matter. And little can matter more than whether the ancient, historic nations of Europe are to have their political institutions and their very identities transformed by stealth into something neither wished nor understood by their electorates. Yet so much is it the touchstone of respectability to accept this ever closer union, now interpreted as a federal destiny, that to question it is to invite affected disbelief or even ridicule. This silent understanding – this Euro-snobbism – between politicians, bureaucracies, academics, journalists and businessmen is destructive of honest debate.

So John Major deserves high praise for ensuring at Maastricht that we would not have either a single currency or the absurd provisions of the Social Chapter forced upon us: our industry, workforce and national prosperity will benefit as a result. Indeed, as long as we in Britain now firmly control our spending and reduce our deficit, we will be poised to surge ahead in Europe. For our taxes are low; our inflation is down: our debt is manageable: our reduced regulations are favourable to business.

We take comfort from the fact that both our Prime Minister and our Foreign Secretary have spoken out sharply against the forces of bureaucracy and federalism.

The Choice

Our choice is clear. Either we exercise democratic control of Europe through co-operation between national governments and parliaments which have legitimacy, experience and closeness to the people.

Or, we transfer decisions to a remote multi-lingual parliament, accountable to no real European public opinion and thus increasingly subordinate to a powerful bureaucracy. No amount of misleading language about pooling sovereignty can change that.

Europe and the Wider World

In world affairs for most of this century Europe has offered problems,
not solutions. The founders of the European Community were consciously trying to change that. Democracy and prosperity in Europe
were to be an example to other people in other continents. Sometimes
this view took an over-ambitious turn with talk of Europe as a third
force brokering between two super-powers of east and west. This
approach was always based upon a disastrous illusion – that western
Europe could at some future date dispense with the military defence
offered by the United States.

Now that the forces of Communism have retreated and the threat
of Soviet tanks and missiles levelled at the heart of Europe has gone,
there is a risk that the old tendency towards de-coupling Europe from
the United States may again emerge. This is something against
which Europeans themselves must guard – and of which the United
States must be aware.

This risk could become reality in several ways.

Trade

First, there is the question of trade. It is a terrible indictment of the
complacency which characterises the modern post-Cold War world
that we have allowed the present GATT round to be stalled for so
long. Free trade is the greatest force for prosperity and peaceful
co-operation.

It does no good to the western alliance when Europe and the United
States come to regard each other as hostile interests. In practice,
whatever the theory may be, economic disputes do sour political
relations. Agricultural subsidies and tariffs lie at the heart of the
dispute, which will not go away unless we in Europe decide that the
Common Agricultural Policy has to be fundamentally changed. That
will go far to determine what kind of Europe we are building.

I would like to see the European Community – embracing the
former Communist countries to its east – agree to develop an Atlantic
free trade area with the United States. That would be a means of
pressing for more open multi-lateral trade throughout the world.
Europe must seek to move the world away from competing regional
trade blocs – not promote them. In such a trading arrangement,
Britain would have a vital role bridging that Atlantic divide – just as
Germany should provide Europe with a bridge to the east and to the
countries of the former Soviet Union.

Eastern Europe

Secondly, we must modify and modernise our defence. The dangers on Europe's eastern border have receded. But let us not forget that on the credibility of NATO's military strength all our wider objectives depend – reassurance for the post-Communist countries, stability in Europe and trans-Atlantic political co-operation.

Communism may have been vanquished, but all too often the Communists themselves have not. The chameleon qualities of the comrades have never been more clearly demonstrated than in their emergence as democratic socialists and varieties of nationalist in the countries of central and eastern Europe. From the powerful positions they retain in the bureaucracy, security apparatus and the armed forces, from their places in not-really privatised enterprises, they are able to obstruct, undermine and plunder.

The systems of proportional representation which so many of these countries have adopted have allowed these tactics to succeed all the more, leading to weak governments and a bewildering multiplicity of parties. All this risks bringing democracy into discredit. If eastern European countries which retain *some* links with a pre-Communist past, and have *some* sort of middle class on which to draw, falter on the path to reform, how will the leaders of the countries of the former Soviet Union dare to proceed further upon it?

We can help by allowing them free access to our markets. I am delighted that Association agreements have been signed between the European Community and several of these countries. I would like speedy action to include the others in similar arrangements. But ten years is too long to wait before the restrictions on trade are removed. And I would like to see these countries offered full membership of the European Community rapidly.

Above all we must offer these countries greater security. Russian troops are still stationed on Polish territory. Moreover, it is understandable that the central and eastern European countries are alarmed at what conflict in the old USSR and the old Yugoslavia may portend. Although I recognise that the Northern Atlantic Co-operation Council has been formed with a view to this, I still feel that the European ex-Communist countries are entitled to that greater degree of reassurance which a separate closer relationship with NATO would bring.

Security

Most of the threats to Europe's and the west's interests, however, no longer come from this Continent. I believe – and I have been urging this on NATO members since 1990 – that the Americans and Europeans ought to be able to deploy our forces under NATO outside the area for which the present North Atlantic Treaty allows. It is impossible to know where the next danger may come from, but two considerations should make us alive to real risks to our security.

First, the break up of the Soviet Union has led to large numbers of advanced weapons becoming available to would-be purchasers at knock-down prices: it would be foolish to imagine that these will not, some of them, fall into the worst possible hands.

Second, Europe cannot ignore its dependence for oil on the Middle East. Saddam Hussein is still in power. Fundamentalism is as strong as ever. Old scores are still unsettled. We must beware. And we must widen our ability to defend our interests and be prepared to act when necessary.

The Community's Wider Role

Finally, the European Community must come to recognise its place in what is called the new world order.

The ending of the Cold War has meant that the international institutions created in the post-war years – the UN and IMF, the World Bank, the GATT – can work much more effectively. This means that the role for the Community is inevitably circumscribed. Within Europe, a wider role for NATO and the CSCE should also be reflected in more modest ambitions for the Community's diplomacy. In Yugoslavia, the Community has shown itself incapable of dealing effectively with security questions. Outside Europe, GATT with its mandate to reduce trade barriers should be the body that establishes the rules of the game in trade. The Community must learn to live within those rules.

All in all, the Community must be prepared to fit in with the new internationalism, not supplant it. Let us make sure that we build a splendid and lasting Europe, rather than one as shabby and ephemeral as the Berlaymont building's EC headquarters in Brussels.

15 May 1992   S'Gravenhaage

Where Have All the Statesmen Gone?

Lord Tebbit

All too rarely do national leaders learn from the errors – or the successes – of the past. Happily for our generation still alive today, the leaders of the post-WW2 era did so. As a result Europe has experienced almost half-a-century without war between the nation states – not to mention a period of unparalleled prosperity in western Europe.

The contrast between the twentieth century's two post-war eras is quite remarkable. Only twenty years after the end of the 1914-18 war we were again at war. Yet the threats to peace at the close of WW2 were almost exactly the same as those in the inter-war years.

In 1919 dangers came from German militarism and imperialism, the devastation of European economies, the rise of protectionism and the threat of economic slump and failure and, although it was then only in its infancy, the threat of Soviet imperialism. The response of the victorious allies was a traditional peace conference and treaty – at Versailles – and the formation of the League of Nations and a descent into craven disarmament and appeasement by the democratic nations.

After 1945 renewed German militarism might well have again torn Europe apart. The threat of economic collapse and the need to rebuild shattered economies was no less urgent. Protectionism remained as strong. The shadow of Soviet imperialism had become a terrible reality with half of Europe falling under a new tyranny, bloodier and more cruel than that of Nazi Germany.

Fortunately the statesmen of the post-WW2 era took a different path. Churchill, Attlee, Bevin, Truman, Marshall, Monnet, Schuman, Adenaeur and Thatcher laid the foundations on which we have built western Europe's best half-century for a very long time indeed.

The North Atlantic Alliance alone has saved western Europe from Soviet aggression. And with NATO forces stationed in West Germany and those of the Warsaw Pact in East Germany there could be no prospect that Germany could set out again on a path of aggression. American military power operating within NATO prevented military conflict for over forty years, decisively won the Cold War and, without battle being joined, liberated the vassal states of the former Soviet Empire. The General Agreement on Tariffs and Trade (GATT) has held back the threat of protectionism and trade wars. The United Nations, though frequently paralysed by east-west rivalry and the Cold War, has been and remains a forum for the discussion and limitation of international disputes.

But it would be hard to overestimate the importance of the selfless generosity of the United States' gift to Europe of Marshall Aid which led to the creation of the OEEC – the Organisation for European Economic Co-operation.

From those beginnings there sprang the ECSC (European Coal and Steel Community) and its nuclear partner, Euratom, and then from the experience of those and the vision of its founding fathers grew the Common Market, the EEC and the European Community.

Marshall Aid was the economic foundation upon which both the European Community and the economic success of western continental Europe were built by the six, and subsequently enlarged by the twelve, partner nations.

Now as we approach the fiftieth anniversary of the Anglo-American liberation of western Europe from the Nazi tyranny, and with the twenty-first century not far ahead, there are threats and dangers which might bring this half-century of success to an end, but they are different from those of 1919 and 1945.

Soviet imperialism may remain a dream somewhere within the former USSR, and the mere existence of a vast and deadly arsenal of weapons only just under political control cannot be ignored, but for the time being economic and political collapse have put paid to such ambitions. As for the Germans, no one would contemplate that the panzers will again roll across Europe. At the moment even the columns of Mercedes, BMWs and VWs seem to have been turned back in the battle for economic leadership.

Certainly protectionism is still alive and well, internally within the European Community, and at the heart of its foreign trade policy, as well as in the wider world. Internally, the Single European Act designed by Britain to break the protectionism of our European Community partners has instead been used against us. Externally the policies of the Community undermine the GATT in trade battles in which Britain is held hostage by the Treaty of Rome, unable to fight for the liberal free trade desperately needed by advanced industrialised and less-developed nations alike.

Happily, Europe, despite its largely self-induced recession, remains by the standards of the inter-war years immensely prosperous and it might seem that all is well, leaving us Europeans complacently to claim the prospect of another half-century of peaceful advancement.

Sadly we seem to lack in this decade leaders who can see that there are dangers ahead. Today's leaders seem to have had eyes at Maastricht only for the problems of the past.

Where then are the dangers to western Europe today? We need to look no further than former Yugoslavia, the newly democratic republics of Central Europe, and the Baltic states and even the former Soviet Union itself.

Former Yugoslavia is an extreme case. Its history has been conquest and rule by Rome, Vienna, Berlin, Moscow and is a particularly cruel one. Nonetheless, it is a vivid warning of what happens if people of distinct ethnic religious and linguistic origins feel threatened by their mutual minority status within a single state.

Further north along the eastern boundary of the European Community, the former vassal states of the Soviet Empire, Hungary, Romania, Poland, Slovakia, Czech lands and the Baltics, struggle to make democracy and capitalism work. If their economies fail, it is unlikely that their democracies will succeed. Many of them have substantial minority populations, not least Germans and Russians. In times of economic failure and possible authoritarian rule such minorities could become either agents or victims of destabilisation advancing westwards.

Maastricht does not address these potential dangers. It exacerbates them.

First, as the width and depth of the responsibilities of the Community and its institutions are to be increased, so it is proposed that membership will be widened by the admission of Austria and the Nordic nations.

A widening torrent of draft directives and policies would flow into the decision-making process of the Council – soon to be not twelve but fifteen or more. The difficulties of thorough discussion, of compromises to satisfy all member states by democratic means, are increased by the square of even the cube of the number of member states. The pressures to move towards a political union and a single government will increase as the Community's responsibilities grow.

Not only will that militate *against* the admission of the Europeans of central and eastern Europe, but it will build growing resentment amongst the peoples of the present European Community memberstates.

Even worse, the proposed single currency will, simultaneously, have similar damaging effects. Even if the economists' criteria of convergence between the economies of member-states is achieved, there is no prospect that there will be sufficient natural convergence between the living standards of the poor Mediterranean peoples and the rich northerners. A single currency requires not only a single government – leaving all of us as potentially disaffected minorities – but a single economic policy. That policy cannot possibly be right for Germany, France, Britain, Greece, Portugal and Finland. Nor can the same Social Chapter costs be borne by such divergent economies.

That is the reason for the creation of the Cohesion Fund – a vast mechanism for taxing the successful to compensate those whose chances of achieving success will have been destroyed by the single currency and the single economic policy. It is a mechanism bound to cause resentment amongst donors and recipients – resentment sharpened by the clear ethnic, religious and linguistic divisions.

And before long the migrants and refugees from the central and east European states would be joined by another tide, mostly but not exclusively, from the Mediterranean.

Maastricht – already seen as a potential failure – will become an incendiary device to recreate blazing conflicts that have been doused by the co-operation and prosperity of the last half of the twentieth century.

There is an alternative. The Maastricht agenda should have been, and the 1996 Inter-Governmental Conference agenda must be, about the reduction of Community responsibility and power to a level which can be managed amongst a family of fifteen or twenty-five states.

The single currency and its inevitable accompaniments of the single economic policy and single government must be totally rejected for the foreseeable future, as simply an impractical proposition.

The Common Agricultural Policy must be redirected towards the production of cheaper food and the elimination of the surpluses which have been dumped to such grievous effect upon the markets and economies of our trading partners.

These changes would allow the nations of the former Soviet Empire, first, access to our markets for the goods which they are able to produce and, as soon as possible, progressive integration into the European family of nation states of the new and revitalised European Community.

None of that would be easy, but not for the first time Europe faces a choice between a difficult and dangerous path to peace and prosperity and a difficult and dangerous path to disaster.

Maastricht is on the road to economic decline, ethnic rivalries, extreme nationalism and the destruction of what has been built upon the vision and boldness of that extraordinary generation of post-war American and European statesmen. There is another road – a better road – but where are the Trumans, Marshalls, Churchills, Attlees, Adenaeurs, Monnets and Schumans of our time?

1 August 1993   London

A Nation at Risk

Godfrey Barker

'I have always noticed that no one pays any attention to warnings or admonitory signs; the only signs that are believed in or paid attention to are fair or flattering ones.'

Goethe, *Elective Affinities*

The Treaty on European Union, signed at Maastricht in 1992, brings the most important constitutional change to Britain since 1832 (the Reform Bill) and before that 1689 (the Bill of Rights and the Glorious Revolution). This is because the Treaty requires surrender to the European Community of liberties which English Parliaments struggled over centuries to win from monarchs – rights which now become subject to new, arbitrary powers created in this Treaty.

At the heart of the liberties which Maastricht confiscates is the freedom of every British citizen not to be taxed without limit and without his consent – a freedom now so largely forgotten as to be taken for granted but which dates back to the Great Charter in 1215, which was asserted by the barons, knights and burgesses who refused to finance in full the wars of Edward I and Edward III and which has since been lost to free Englishmen only under the absolutism of Charles I and Oliver Cromwell. This, more than the freedoms of speech, association, religion and the press, has been the central issue in the fight for liberty across centuries between the English and their rulers.

The Treaty signed at Maastricht on 7 February 1992 takes much of this ancient and precious freedom away.

It hands large powers to Commissioners and bankers in Europe, all unelected and undismissable by ordinary citizens, to tax, fine, levy and borrow at their instigation within few defined limits. The nature of these powers and the erosions of sovereignty that they entail are defined below.

In its 65,000 words – read in detail, we now learn, by all too few of those who rule us – freedoms which every schoolboy studies in 1215, 1352, 1376, 1628, 1640-42, 1660, 1689 and 1832 as the chief theme of 'progress' in English history are made over as a trust, so to speak, for the advancing of the vague, glorious and uncosted visions of 'European Union' and a single European currency.

They cannot be taken back at will; this is not a Treaty rescinded merely by tearing it up: the new powers to tax, fine and levy which are created at Maastricht are enforceable in Europe at law, and no doubt will be. Opt-outs are limited and subject to periodic review. No formula for withdrawal from their sweeping provisions is laid out in these multiple additions to and amendments of the Treaty of Rome.

It is no minor matter, but the very largest issue of our constitution, to hand over hard-won freedoms on so vast a scale to Commissioners, officials and bureaucrats in the European Community who are unelected and unaccountable. To do so – to put faith, in effect, in the arbitrary power of banks, monetary institutions and executives who cannot be called to account – is to reverse, to a significant degree, the story of the development of liberty over 778 years.

Such assertions, to ardent believers in European unity, seem extravagant and unfounded. Yet they can be proved.

The central terrors of the Maastricht Treaty lie in Articles 99 and 100, 103, 104c, 105, 105a, 106 – 108a and 109a-m. These, broadly speaking, take control of national economic policies, banks and capital; they also decide and harmonise taxation. Numerous unlimited powers are also taken in the Statute which sets up the European System of Central Banks (ECSB).

It must be said straightaway – for every believing European will make this prompt objection – that the Prime Minister excepted the UK from many of the most alarming new proposals (see the list in the Protocol relating to the United Kingdom, Cmnd.1934,p.115, paragraphs 5 and 8).

Britain's exemptions apply, however, for only so long as the UK declines to enter Stage 3 of the European Monetary System, the single currency. As John Major tells it, this is safeguard enough for cherished British independence; the right for Britain to opt out of the final achievement of the ECU and out of much future progress towards it entirely justifies our signing the larger text of the Treaty. As an instant political decision on a tense night in Maastricht, Britain's opt-outs no doubt looked like 'game, set and match' for the Prime Minister and for the country too. This is not how it is in the light of day. Our exclusions from Stage 3 and from many of the awesome arbitrary powers which it brings with it are, we know from much repetition, safe for this Parliament and for so long as John Major is with us, but events this summer in the final ratification of Maastricht made clear that neither John Major nor the 1992 House

of Commons enjoy certain immortality. A simple change of leader or
of Government may bring a rapid end to British exemptions. Douglas
Hurd, Kenneth Clarke, John Smith as future Prime Ministers all look
likely to find more enthusiasm for Stage 3 and for fuller European
integration than does John Major, and their arrival in power at some
moment of Conservative self-destruction in 1993-6 does not look an
impossibility.

This Prime Minister had but one course of action available to him
had he wished to ensure that Britain would be safe in perpetuity from
the arbitrary powers created at Maastricht: not to opt out from the
Treaty's worst provisions, but to refuse to sign it altogether and thus
(by the unanimity rule) destroy it.

No one can assume, for now, that the British opt-outs will last for
ever – or that they somehow guarantee our freedom from control by
the unelected bodies for eternity. The likelihood is that they will be
very short-lived indeed. For this reason, this chapter looks at the
complete wording of the Treaty which we have chosen to ratify. Only
a Labour Party change of policy stands between us and its general
application.

A close reading of the Maastricht text – of which so few ministers
who approve it, we now learn, are to be held guilty – makes nonsense
of the bland claim of the Europeans in the 1992-1993 Parliamentary
debates that this Treaty is of minor constitutional import, or of small
significance if set alongside the Single European Act of 1986.

It is, rather, of radical constitutional import and abrogates some
of the most ancient British freedoms and assertions of sovereignty,
The list that follows is, in abbreviated form, a selection of *the principal erosions of parliamentary sovereignty at Westminster* and the
main creations of absolute power within the Treaty:

1. *The Council of Ministers will harmonise indirect taxation, sales,
taxes and excise duties, acting on proposals by the Commission and
'Consulting' the European Parliament and Economic and Social Committee* (Article 99, The Treaty on European Union 1992,
HMSO/Cmnd. 1934, p.16). This is the formal surrender to the ministers of 11 other EC countries of our powers to determine the taxes
which raise 70% of British Government revenue.

2. *The Council shall issue directives, on proposals from the Commission and after 'consulting' the European Parliament, to approximate
laws and regulations of all Member States as relate to the functioning
of the single market* (Article 100, *ibid.*, p.16). The power to proceed by

'directive' from the Commission on this sweeping mandate is the most absolute power handed to a sovereign body by English citizens since Parliament allowed Charles I to collect tunnage and poundage and ship money in the 1630s.

3. *The Council of Ministers will draft by qualified majority voting 'the broad guidelines of the economic policy of the Member States'* (Article 103, par 2 and 4, *ibid.*, p.18). This is the surrender to eleven other countries of sovereign power over our own economic policy. Can a more comprehensive loss of freedom be imagined than lies in these words?

4. *Member States shall avoid excessive government deficits; when they fail the Council may order remedies to be effected upon a specified timetable. These may include denial of loans from the European investment bank, the lodging of capital deposits with the EC by the defaulting states and 'fines of an appropriate size'* (Article 104c *passim, ibid.*, p.20). This clause is presently subject to UK opt-out (p.115). It creates an absolute power for the 11 Finance Ministers to punish member states by forced loans ('non-interest-bearing deposits') and unlimited fines – 'unlimited' being the second meaning of the vague 'appropriate'. The cost of such punishments and indeed of deficit reduction in general, inevitably falls on the taxpayer. It is thus that the Treaty of Maastricht creates the central offence of 'taxation without consent' which has been a right of free Britons since Edward I.

No definition of an 'excessive deficit' is offered in the Treaty. Only a majority vote by the Council shall decide 'if an excessive deficit exists'. (Article 104c.6, p.20).

5. *The European Central Bank will have powers 'to supervise credit institutions and other financial institutions'* (Article 105, *ibid.*, p.21). This sweeping invasion of the right of the private sector in finance to do business within whom it wishes – be it to lend, to make takeovers, to place its funds at will – amounts, in the language of Article 105, to rather more than the power to regulate. The casual phrasing allows a Napoleonic right of interference, but is subject at present to a British opt-out.

6. *The European Central Bank shall be entitled to impose fines or periodic penalty payments on governments which fail to: a. Keep minimum reserves with the ECB: b. operate monetary controls on*

approved guidelines: c. keep the capital of the ECB at approved levels: d. surrender reserves to levels to be determined by majority vote on the first day of Stage 3 of EMS. Fines may also be imposed on governments which defy any other decisions or regulations of the ECB (Article 106.6, 108a, *ibid.*, p.22; Statute of the ESCB, Articles 19.2.20, 28.1, 30.4 and 34.3). This power to impose unlimited fines – to be passed on, obviously enough, to the taxpayer – is currently the subject of a British opt-out. It presents to a majority of the 11 EC ministers a degree of absolute power to punish British citizens by fines not known to monarchs since King John.

7. *The Bank of England shall take no instruction from the British Government in carrying out its duties to the ESCB and in meeting its obligations under the Treaty. Nor shall it seek it* (Article 107, p.22). This deprives an elected Chancellor of the Exchequer of all right of control over the country's national bank. This clause is currently subject to a British opt-out.

8. *A Monetary Committee on which Britain will have less than one-twelfth of the members, will advise the Council of Economic Ministers and the EC Commission on the continued free movement of capital and on compliance of Members with the obligations set out in points 3, 4, 5 and 6 above* (Article 109c.2, *ibid.*, p.24). This is the death of democratic accountability. On this Council of 28 members, Britain will have two seats – the unelected EC Commission and the unelected ECB each, also, enjoying two. For 800 years it has been the right of Parliaments and judges to determine the compliance of English citizens with law made by their consent; a major part of this right now passes, with the Treaty of Maastricht, to a body which no freeborn Britain can call to account.

9. *In extreme balance of payments crisis for a member nation, the EC Commission shall determine the protective measures that state may take; only a qualified majority vote on the Council of Ministers shall lift them* (Article 109h, 1, 2, 3, 109i, 3, *ibid.*, pp.27-28). This amounts to absolute power over our national economic policy in time of crisis. The measures ordered by the unelected EC Commission may include import and exchange controls and higher taxation (to state merely the obvious); we may free ourselves of these only at the vote of 11 other countries.

10. *The Treaty creates 'obligations' on Members to achieve price*

stability and low deficits and to hold their currencies within the margins declared by the ERM for two years without devaluation. Interest rates shall be kept low. In the 1994-97 transition period, decisions by the European Monetary Institute – the shadow European Central Bank – in these areas shall be binding on member states; after 1997 the European Central Bank will enforce monetary regulations with levies of penalty interest and sanctions (Article 109j,1, *ibid.,* p.28: Protocol on the Convergence Criteria, p.112; Statute of the European Monetary Institute, Article 15.4, p.109; Statute of the ESCB, Article 19, p.95). This last provision is currently subject to a British opt-out.

Offences under Article 109j,1, have been committed already – especially with the mass devaluation of the seven currencies against the Deutschemark of August 1993 (an offence disguised by the ridiculous legal fiction of 'a continuing ERM with widened bands of fluctuation'). It will be interesting to see if the Council and Commission decide that some offences by some offenders can be ignored while offences by others will be dealt with more severely. The virtues to which Article 109j subscribes may be beyond dispute; what is not is the mode of their enforcement, over which we are deprived of all democratic control.

11. *The Bank of England must pay up its subscription to the capital of the European Central Bank to support its operational costs, whether we move to Stage 3 or not* (Protocol on the UK, Article 9c, *ibid.,* p.115). This is a new concept in taxation; the payment of a subscription to a club to which we do not, at present, belong.

Much more could be added about the surrender of sovereignty in the areas of foreign and home office policy (Titles V and VI, *ibid.,* pp. 80-86), where Britain loses sole control of policy over asylum and immigration and sole control in the direction of our armed forces, which latter is to be subject henceforth to 'Joint Action' (Article J3.4, p.81).

None of this has anything to do with received tradition in British political practice – the tradition which is supposed to nourish the thoughts and actions of a modern Conservative Party before all other sources of inspiration, even those of a party like the current one which has wholly forgotten its Burke and ignored its Oakeshott.

But this is no surprise. The Treaty of Maastricht is merely the latest of so many Continental triumphs of reason, by which the wisest European minds south and east of Calais periodically tear up the constitutions which they inherit and devise new ones. It must be said, in defence of this practice, that the average life expectancy of a French or German constitution since the mid-nineteenth century has proved to be at least 40 years, and that it may not be the fault of these two nations that the Maastricht Treaty promises to enter the records as a constitution for Europe which died before it took a breath. The blame for the repeated failure of constitutions on the Continent lies in the belief, founded in the deductive confidences of Descartes, that political problems can be resolved by reason alone. That means – to translate 'reason' into the phraseology which ignites the deadened minds in Brussels of 1993 – the illusion that political problems can be resolved by ideology, vision, determination, the Utopianism of 'I have a dream' and detailed planning, disdaining all regard for the past. It has proved a formula for disaster in the past and, with Maastricht, will prove so again.

In Britain, few monarchs and Prime Ministers in 900 years have set out to flout tradition and to rule by their own reason and dogmas; those that have – John, Edward II, Mary, Charles I and James II among kings, Peel and Gladstone most notably among Prime Ministers – have come to a sorry end. The survival, or rather the growth, of the English Constitution over 778 years owes most to our deep respect for traditions and for received liberties, guaranteed by the King in Parliament; it owes little or less to our distrust of political 'blueprints', prescriptive law codes and statutes imposed by Emperors in Rome, Madrid or Vienna on empires thousands of miles wide.

Europe, in contrast, has been racked for centuries by war, turmoil and revolution. If a single thread of explanation can be teased out of so many conflicts, it has been the contempt for local practice in politics and religion of absolute rulers from Spain to Prussia, and a disdain for the tradition of liberty. Democracy is again under threat from the unelected arrogants who throng the committee rooms of Brussels – rulers no less absolute, in their petty way, than the Frederick Williams who have provoked the multitudes in the past and who bring us, in the Maastricht Treaty, one of the most sublimely conceited documents which lawmakers have ever sought to impose upon the suffering peoples of Europe.

Ah! – rejoin the advocates of Maastricht: it was to put a final end to war and conflict in Europe that the spiritual fathers of the Treaty of Rome, Jean Monnet to the fore, dreamed of European Union in the years after 1945. It is their deep awareness of Europe's troubled past which breathes through every clause of that Treaty and of this. It is the historic need to shatter the traditions of nationalism which have inflamed so many conflicts that explains why we, the leaders of

Germany, France, Italy, Holland, Belgium, all of us war-ravaged, find such enthusiasm for Maastricht.

Have we not been here before? The Congressional system born under Napoleon was the nineteenth-century solution to Europe broken by war. It lasted eight years. It envisaged security, wrote Harold Nicholson with strange prescience of how EC policy, and particularly the French attempt to bind up Germany into Europe, would later evolve, 'with reference to the war just terminated rather than with reference to the next war'. This was not, though, the chief reason underlying its ultimate failure: rather it was that national interests inevitably reasserted themselves once the cement of alliance, resistance by the four Great Powers to a common enemy, France, had dissolved. European states have often found common interests in war, rarely in peace. By 1821 England had reverted to what Nicholson calls 'a natural isolationism', reinvolving itself on the Continent after this only to preserve a balance between the competing powers, the balance which Castlereagh called 'a just equilibrium'.

'Too frightened to fight each other, too stupid to agree', so Talleyrand scorned the nations who met at Vienna in 1814-15: but it is only rationalists supremely arrogant and ignorant of history who believe that the traditions, ambitions and liberties of ancient peoples can be obliterated so easily. Napoleon, who told Metternich at Dresden in 1813 that 'a man such as I am cares little for the lives of a million men', put his name to the price which must probably be paid for an enduring European Union: but even England had its own dreaming rationalist in that age in Castlereagh, whose hope was for a Security Council for Europe to do business and keep the peace on an agreed and permanent basis.

This was a vision of a Concert of Europe which oddly prefigures Maastricht and which then as now found few friends at home. It would bring us, objected Canning, the successor to Castlereagh at the Foreign Office, 'deeply in all the politics of the Continent, whereas our true policy has always been not to interfere except in great emergency, and then with commanding force'.

The Concert of Europe was destined to rapid collapse. It was kept alive at Aix la Chapelle, Karlsbad, Troppau, Laibach and Verona from 1819 to 1822 by the same statesmen as had met at Vienna in 1814, but not even this club of intimates, manipulated by the scheming and second-rate Metternich, could fasten agreements on to the changing ambitions and interests of nations now at peace. Britain, the strongest power in Europe, repeatedly refused to intervene in the internal affairs of other countries and by 1822 Canning was in power and ready to announce: 'For "Europe" I shall be desirous now and then to read "England".'

'A natural isolationism' is not far wrong as a generalisation for English, later British, diplomacy towards Europe in the five centuries since we retreated in exhaustion from the Hundred Years' War. Much continental diplomacy in contrast has been devoted to ensnaring us back. 'If England can be won to our side there would be no counter-weight in Europe to prevent your Majesty and the Emperor doing what they like', wrote the Spanish Prime Minister Olivares to Philip III in 1631, explaining that the subjects of Charles I were 'the masters of the world's trade and dictate its terms as they wish'.

Few English Governments have however linked themselves in long-term alliances which they have not come to regret. Our longest and most successful one, the understanding with Portugal dating from 1386, is not by accident the one which we have been least obliged to activate.

By 1850 wiser minds in the Foreign Office than those which exist today were clear as to the interests of England in Europe. Canning put it as admirably as any in the remark quoted above; Palmerston wrote in 1841 that 'it is not usual for England to enter into engage-ments with reference to cases which have not actually arisen', adding that Parliament probably did not approve of 'binding England prospectively'. It was 'not the policy of this country', Lord John Russell told Queen Victoria, 'to make engagements except on a view of the circumstances of the moment'.

What then, in light of historic practice, should be our role when the foreseeable threat in Continental Europe is once again the emergence of an overmighty power? The French solution to Germany is the fevered and impossible dream of Maastricht. The British reply to the emergence of overweening powers in Europe has been to reaffirm the transatlantic alliance, to draw strength from free trade and to search out support from our traditional trading partners round the world, some imperial, some not. Our policy has also been to maintain balance on the Continent by alliances and *ententes*. These are no infallible guarantees of security but in an uncertain world hold out more promise of peace and harmony in Europe than the autocratic prescrip-tions of Maastricht.

This Treaty, in short, trades in many forms of foolishness. The highest, however, is the surrender it demands of free British citizens of liberties which are to be traced far back beyond the concessions of Edward I to the Earls of Norfolk and Hereford in 1297, beyond what

Simon de Montfort extracted from Henry III in 1265 and beyond the rights asserted by armed barons at Runnymede on John in 1215 to a customary law of Anglo-Danish origin – or made, as Whig historians liked to argue in the nineteenth century, in the primeval German forests. The freedom of Englishmen from taxation without consent was a point for boasting against the French by the mid-fifteenth century, when the Chief Justice of England, Sir John Fortescue, stated with pride in 1461 that 'the King of England cannot alter nor change the lawes of the Realme at his pleasure. For why, he governeth his people by power, not only royall, but politique' ('flowing from the people').

Even in 1625 a Tory like Sir Robert Phelps could compare English freedoms favourably with those of our neighbours: 'we are the last monarchy in Christendom that retains our original rights and consti- tution'. 'Rights' were the ground of protest to Charles I in the 1628 Petition, which did not declare what should be common liberty in England but what already was: 'by ... the good laws and statutes of this realm your subjects have inherited this freedom: that they should not be compelled to contribute to any tax aid, tallage, or other like charge not set by common consent in Parliament'.

Inherited or not, this freedom is now confiscated, not wholly but significantly, by the 1992 Treaty signed at Maastricht.

Yet this is a liberty crucial to democracy in these islands, the stuff of revolutionary demand. It was a cause of civil war in England from 1258 to 1265, from 1642 to 1660 and from 1688 to 1690; it was and has been a great theme of 'progress' in English history and is linked to those pivotal dates and 'turning points' in our past which every schoolboy still learns. It has been a privilege of Englishmen centuries before the French, Germans or Spanish ever knew it.

'No taxation without representation' is now a principle casually sacrificed by a Government and Parliament which is, in the deepest sense, ignorant of what has made for greatness in English and British history.

Maastricht, a disaster in the making, is a punishment for an age which knows no history – an age which is steeped in ignorance of the ancient traditions of English liberty, as deep as its nescience of a thousand years of diplomatic history. It is an unrivalled rationalist folly, an idiocy set to consume the wealth of nations, destined to be repudiated by the European peoples with the same ferocity lately unleashed upon the ERM.

10 August 1993   Tampa, Florida

Functional Realities of Trade, Sovereignty and Democracy

Dr. Manfred Brunner

The Maastricht Treaty must be buried and a new path to European unity developed, step by step. The leaders of the twelve member states of the EC must step aside from their personal political tensions and be prepared to understand Europe's position in all its complexity. Whereas they are seeking a Federal Europe of autonomous regions, the aim should be to create an economic union of affiliated autonomous states.

The first step should be the completion of a single market, by dealing right away with the remaining barriers to free trade: namely, open borders, complete internal security, a common right of asylum and uniform regulations covering trade. The principle of *mutual recognition* should be the governing factor for outstanding issues of economic equalisation, rather than the principle of *total harmonisation* as envisaged by Maastricht.

Second, they should attend to the integration of the EFTA countries, which will strengthen the EC, by resuscitating negotiations with individual EFTA states, utilising the experiences gained from attempted federalisation in order to emphasise decentralisation. They must give up the existing framework of legal sanctions and achieve expansion of the EC by negotiation.

Next, the member states should offer membership to those countries to the east now freed from communism, including the Ukraine and White Russia. They should be offered membership at the same level of integration as Spain, Portugal and Greece, with the intention of quickly coming to full membership. The EC must open its borders to the products of all these countries – without reservation.

Furthermore, the EC should move to democratise all its decisions. The European Commission should reduce the number of its representatives and should only issue guidelines on policy; then each policy must be agreed to by members' respective parliaments on a case-by-case basis. This form of democratisation is wholly preferable to enlarging the competence of the European Parliament – as envisaged by Maastricht – because no federal representation of any nation would be possible without the endorsement of its people. In the past, confused decisions of the European Parliament showed how undesirable its centralised procedures were.

The European Commission must be reformed and referred back to its function, namely to act as a co-operative organ of leadership. The Commission must be reduced from 17 to 5 members only. The presidency must be changed annually. Those states which provide commissioners should not be allowed to provide a General Director at the same time. The right of self-determination of the people of Europe shall be established. The EC shall act, for example, on the basis of a common foreign policy which will rest on the principle of self-determination of affiliated nations. This basic principle, however, must be subject to a system of military commitment to deployment within Europe. Any state which refuses to participate fully in such a military system shall lose its membership of the EC. Military responsibilities which transcend measures only applicable to Europe must be solved within the framework of NATO. Any loosening of the bonds of the common defence policy of Europe with America must not be tolerated; the position of France within NATO but outside its military structure is simply untenable.

The legal action which I have initiated in the Constitutional Court of Germany also transgresses the borders of Germany in its significance. What caused me to take this action was the concern over how much sovereignty the European Commission should be allowed to receive from the sovereign member states. My plea to the Court deals with the extent to which democracy must be guaranteed in the context of the European coalition. In Germany itself I am concerned with Article 20 of the Basic Law which, along with Article 79 III, guarantees the sovereignty of the German people, which must by definition be a guarantee for all recorded time. In other words I am concerned here with a constitutional combination of national statehood and democracy.

On the other hand Article 24 of the Basic Law determines partial transfers of sovereignty by way of inter-state alliances which result from a common purpose. In the (so-called *Solange II*) determination of 22 October 1986, the Constitutional Court of Germany determined as follows: the empowering right granted by Article 24 GG must not be understood to be a general power with no constitutional limitation. This regulation is not meant to surrender the individual identity of the Republic of Germany through a violation of its constitutional structure.

Dr. Manfred Brunner

The constitutional structure of Germany is based on Article 20 of the Basic Law. The German constitution only allows for actions by the state which correspond to the powers of the state itself as granted to it in the constitutional structure and to political actions arising from the application of the *democratic principle*. In other words, every consideration rests on the principle of German National Sovereignty.

The *democratic principle* is of fundamental significance for the status of the Basic Law, which means that those chartered with sovereign powers who are not themselves elected democratically and who cannot therefore be called legitimate may not be appointed by the organs of the German Republic to deal with constitutional matters. The rules here must be applied with much more stringency whenever a supranational structure begins to appear with all the trappings of statehood. The rule pertaining to the assessment of such a supranational structure must be determined to be inviolable, which means in other words not just any kind of democracy but only one which is value-connected to the Basic Law, as being essentially liberal and democratic and fully valid according to Article 79 III GG.

The Constitutional Court of Germany has already complained about the existing pre-Maastricht structure of the EC, particularly its failure to establish a catalogue of Basic Law. This absence denies the unconditional priority of the law of the EC above the basic laws incorporated in the Basic Law itself. Under the Maastricht Treaty everything falls within the competence of the European Commission, so that the question arises whether a German citizen of the European union must not be furnished with a European catalogue of Basic Laws, considering that justice must be done to a form of democracy which is based upon a sound constitution.

The principle of *national sovereignty* is another principle which must be observed as a condition precedent to the membership of any political union, let alone one like the EC in which democracy is steadily being restricted. It is beyond dispute that Article 20, II,I demands legitimacy for political action – not just through any people – but through the German people themselves.

A certain psychological tension in the German people in relation to Article 24 Section I is already discernible. Those who gave us the constitution must now decide whether they are prepared – in the light of Article 79 III – to endorse a structure resembling a state [i.e. the EC] which will bind the national government [or may do so with 'Qualitative Majority' voting where Germany, like Britain, only has a 15% minority vote], thereby removing national sovereignty. This problematical difficulty leads the argument directly to the failure to establish a true parliamentary democracy for Europe.

The basic kernel of democracy protected by the German constitution is damaged if and when the voters are unable to express confidence either during elections to the existing national parliament or during elections to the European Parliament. The new rights of the European Parliament are related to the existing single market and are not yet related to the wider issues to which Europe must now address herself. According to the law of the German Supreme Court, it cannot be denied that the *status quo* of the European Parliament touches the frontiers of basic restraints.

The Maastricht Treaty, which enlarges the competence of the European Commission – itself only a new body – cannot therefore receive consent from the German Parliament without a simultaneous institutionalised guarantee of the existing condition of statedom. This guarantee would have to be put in place prior to the transfer of legislative power to the European Parliament; alternatively, the institution of a new process granting individual authorisation by German representatives within the European Council of Ministers could achieve the same result.

At the same time the German Parliament would have to neglect the principle of the division of power which is closely connected with considerations arising from the principle of that division of power when putting the assumed right of German ratification to the test under its constitution. Here it is obvious that the Treaty of Maastricht still increases the tendency towards further accumulation of power at the centre. Until now the thesis could perhaps be justified in that a transfer of power to the European Parliament could be counter-balanced by another form of restraint on the power of the proposed new Super-State.

The implication is the need to put the power of the German Parliament and the European Commission on an equal footing, although the future political union could eventually develop new rights and the desired rules for the division of power would thereby be weakened. This weakening would be determined through instituting fundamental contractual agreements and would not rest on the above-mentioned principles of nationality, which are connected with the enforced equalisation of forces balancing the Commission and the need to take executive decisions. It is significant that the leaders of the twelve EC member states did not pay any particular attention to the principle of the division of power when formulating the Treaty of Maastricht.

Professor Roman Hertzog, the current President of the Supreme Court of Germany, years ago defined the basic principle of the division of power and the principle of an open democracy as a denial of the principle governing a totalitarian democracy, which is an avantgarde concept which compels recognition of the desired common interest.

The desire of the leaders of west European governments is to drag Maastricht out of the mainstream of historical development at the last moment and to move forward against every kind of objection. This is coined as avantgarde thinking. In the same manner the German Chancellor is inclined to close his eyes and behave like a bull in a china shop. This is the same Chancellor who accused Great Britain and Denmark of breaking the Treaty of Rome when they appeared unwilling to build up a Europe based on a violation of the right of nations to self-determination.

The violation of the principle of Article 20, which defines the central state structure embodied in the Basic Law – a violation achieved through the Treaty of Maastricht – could not be 'heard' because of the violation of changes to Article 79 III, because such a change in the constitution would be impossible. For this reason the German Parliament could not appear as a maker of constitutions when deciding this particular question. The fundamental paragraphs dealing with the Basic Law with which we are concerned are those acknowledging that the people are the provider and carrier of constitutional power. The issue of a plebiscite on Maastricht must be in the context of the constitutional question – not in the less significant context of plebiscites generally covering other permissible constitutional changes.

It is amazing that the German Ministers of the Interior and of Justice have so far remained silent in putting this constitutional question to the test. My personal complaint is directed at this constitutional issue and is designed to break through this cartel of silence. Now the Constitutional Court must speak 'in the name of the people'.

28 May 1993   Munchen

La Politique Autrement: Reform it Altogether

Philippe Séguin

It must be recognised that the Treaty of Maastricht played a critically decisive role in the construction of United Europe – but not the role its authors had in mind. Once control of the debate eluded their grasp, the issues totally escaped them. This *magnum opus* of the technocratic mind was intended to enshrine a certain way of making a new Europe, by engineering a piece of legal and monetary machinery that would lead implacably to the emergence of a federal Super-State. This machinery was, however, thrust as a yoke upon the neck of existing economies to force them to converge and, on various legal structures, to drive them on toward uniformity. It was the fruition of the decades-old method of concentrating on the technical side of things, turning a blind eye towards the other major political options and keeping the respective peoples out of the creative process, as if they were neither competent nor of sufficient reason to decide their own political future.

The Maastricht Debate is Over

The Eurocrats thought with Maastricht that the time had come to step up the pace towards *total harmonisation*. This was their big mistake, because instead of the general consent they were expecting and hoping for, they found that they had fired the opening shot in the grandest debate ever inspired by the construction of a United European since the European Defence Community affair forty years ago.

Now with the introduction of Maastricht, the people are deciding to take a hand again in something that mattered to them – the way we are going about building the new Europe. Because that is really what it is all about: not deciding *whether* we want to build a United Europe, but *how* we are going to do it. The conflict is not between pro- and anti-Europeans. It is between those who say that there is only one way possible, the Maastricht route, and those who are convinced that we can and must choose another path.

But basically, this particular debate is already settled. Recent events have shown that the partisans of the single currency and the integrated centralist Europe of the Twelve were wrong. The whole philosophy of Maastricht was encapsulated in this single-currency idea, but this concept has not passed the empirical test. For years now, the European Monetary System has been steered towards the long-term perspective of Monetary Union.

The aim of a single currency has precluded for over a decade any major adjustment of the foreign exchange parities among the Twelve, because it was felt that this was the best way of forcing the various economies and social systems to converge. This illusion went with the wind of the monetary storm of September 1992, which nearly blew away with it a number of hard-won gains. Even as I write, the storm threatens again with the French Franc and Danish Kroner under pressure.*

And it is not just monetary co-operation that has been put into question, but in the long run perhaps the very understanding among the respective European peoples as well. Because the countries which, in spite of the problems, decided to remain hitched to the Deutschemark have suffered from the disastrous repercussions of the cost of German reunification which held real interest rates up, thus aggravating the recession. This slump is so deep that it is creating an extremely dangerous anti-European feeling.

With their grand vision of a single currency and their gamble on forced convergence, the Eurocrats were trying their hand at the magician's trade. And they fumbled another sleight-of-hand too, when they chose to leave out half of Europe by erecting a veritable Gold Curtain down the middle to replace the Iron Curtain, without taking account of the dramatic consequences such a decision would have on the peace and stability of the Continent in its entirety.

Because the great east-west balances have now been replaced by a new order, and because the various peoples are no longer willing to have themselves led around by the nose, it is clear that we must go about making a United Europe in some other way. In the current state of the world, it is urgent to spur this United Europe onward, but on a route other than the one where it has recently gone astray. We have two such spurs in mind: co-operation among governments and a vision that embraces the whole of Europe.

[*Editor's note: the ERM collapsed within two weeks.]

Delegation of Responsibilities without Relinquishing Sovereignty

If we want to build Europe on the basis of national realities – because the nations will always have the last word anyway – then we must deliberately break with this scheme for a federal Super-State that underlies the whole policy of the European Commission and of the Court of Justice of the Communities, which is also the inspiration of the Treaty of Maastricht.

The sovereignty of the several states is the general rule that must be followed. This means not only that the powers of the Commission should be diminished in favour of the European Council, but also that relinquishment of sovereignty must be ruled out. Let us be clear in saying that this means further that we must reaffirm the primacy of national law when it clashes with the European norm, and consent to delegation of competences. This approach is indispensible if co-operation is to be effective.

This point is of crucial importance, because it calls for a radical change in approach. Instead of accruing an ever more pervasive supra-national legal structure, we should now only proceed by consensus, towards a community law which would only proceed by consensus, towards a community law which would be limited to what is strictly necessary. Because of the primacy of national law, this delegated community law would of course be revokable by each of the legislative bodies of the member countries.

Is this something to be afraid of? The answer depends on our idea of democracy. Only by way of this primacy of domestic law can each legislative body rest assured that it will not be slowly and irreversibly dispossessed of its essential legislative power.

Is there any reason to fear that everything would be put into limbo each time there is a change of majority in one or another member country? No – no more than it is to be feared that a parliamentary majority would dissolve the entire legal system of its own country each time there was a political swing in the other direction. If we are willing to accept that the nation's representatives in the various European countries are not by their very nature irresponsible, then there is no reason to worry.

So the problem is to know whether or not we have confidence in representative democracy. We must choose between a supra-national legal edifice of uniformity and integration on the one hand, and the primacy of national law on the other, which allows for the diversity of the various legal systems and still necessitates co-operation. In the former case, whether intentionally or not, Europe would be built against the people's will, or despite it. In the latter, Europe will be cresting the wave of the people's aspirations.

Effective Co-operation

To understand clearly how the Community would operate if the relinquishment of sovereignty were to be ruled out, we have only to stop and take a look at the experience of European Monetary System.

Here is a field where co-operation has worked well for a long time, without the various governments giving up their monetary sovereignty, since any one of them could easily choose to let its currency float at any time. And yet the system held good for thirteen years without any of its members deciding to leave and quit defending their currency. This is because the consensus worked so well that an agreement could be reached each time a re-adjustment was needed. Between 1979 and 1992, there were eleven such readjustments by consensus, such that the parities could be adapted to the circumstances and to the diversity of the national situations.

It was only at the time of German reunification, however, when it was decided to move toward the single currency and freeze the parity structure, instead of agreeing to let the Deutschemark float, that everything was jeopardized. This was because, from then on, monetary co-operation was replaced by automatic devices that would over-ride the will of the different countries.

The lesson to be learned from all this is that, instead of trying to pull out of the monetary crisis by hastening the pace towards the single currency, we would be better off reforming the European Monetary System on a co-operative basis, with broader latitude for fluctuation and for rearranging the parities in a sane manner, to take the drama out of devaluations.

In any case, a choice must now be made between co-operation and integration, with no false pretences or semblances. Once we have settled on this principle, controlling all the legal and institutional mechanics of the Community and its possible derivatives, we must press on with the question of the broadening of the community framework to include the countries of the east and Russia. This is without doubt the major challenge that will be facing the European Community over the final years of this century.

Breathing Life into a Community of all European States

On what may we found this Community of all European states, which we now have to bring to life? It must be founded on peace, economic development and on the preservation of our common heritage.

Peace means a collective European security system along the lines of the United Nations model, in which the terms of the United Nations Charter concerning regional organisations should apply. This collective security system should include only European countries, and be headed by a Security Council with permanent members.

Economic development means monetary co-operation and investment aid to the eastern European countries. It also means a broad Common Market ranging from the Atlantic to Russia, to free the barriers to trade between east and west. Ten years will be needed to set it up, but the foundations must be laid right now; and the perspectives must be traced out clearly, as was done in western Europe in 1957 when the Treaty of Rome was signed.

Preservation of our common heritage means preventing major risks to the environment, and saving our architectural heritage. The threat of nuclear accidents and ecological disaster in the east calls for the assembly of enormous resources to face the latent emergency.

These are the contours that the field of the Community of European States should cover. It could be based on the principle of harmonisation of laws, strictly limited to questions of general interest. Beyond this field, any co-operation would be on a case-by-case basis. That is, it would match the interests, advantages and means of each participant, along the lines of the Airbus and Arianespace ventures.

Specific loyalties could all have their sway, with the Mediterranean side of Europe balancing the North; Danubian Europe balancing the power of Germany; the Atlantic arc finding its constituency. And, in brief, the specific nature of the various situations would be respected; exchanges would be multiplied; efficiency boosted; and equilibrium assured.

Competition would be based on the diversity inherent in this European dimension. Above and beyond that minimum that absolutely must be harmonised, each member would itself remain free to create its own currency and laws, levy direct and indirect taxes and do what it feels best with its own specific advantages.

As concerns the outside world, while leaving room for the specific ties binding England, Spain, France and Portugal to the rest of the world, while remaining on the side of the poor countries, while supporting the domestic development of eastern countries, while refusing to become a fortress turned exclusively inward on itself, the Community of European States would implement a common trade policy that would effectively counter disloyal competition and weigh decisively in international negotiations.

Whereas Europe must remain open to the world, this does not mean that access should just be given away indiscriminately. Competitors whose scruples are so barren that any means is justified, even monetary and social dumping, will not be admitted.

If the Community cannot adapt to the new world situation, it will find itself in the fatal grip of irresistibly advancing unemployment and continuously retreating social benefits.

A European consciousness does exist, and it can serve as a basis for a broad community of peoples. What does not exist is a single, homogeneous European people with some collective will to found a vast multi-national state.

We do have a European consciousness, but we do not have a European national feeling. So much the better. Because if that were the case, Europe would thereby lose this extraordinary diversity, without which it would no longer be itself.

Maastricht embodied a certain kind of technocratic, mercantilist, centralist thinking, and transported it to the height of utter absurdity. Now we must break with this concept. But this does not mean that we should give up the attempt to formulate a new order, or that we have to accept tensions, conflicts, or excessive discrepancies, or that we must encourage each member to withdraw into itself. This would run the risk of new tragedies that would inevitably seal the declining fate of our old Continent.

Quite the contrary, each of us must keep his identity and personality. We must let the many peoples of Europe express their unshakable will toward mutual understanding, easing of tensions and co-operation, an unshakable determination not to let this unique moment slip by. We must work together to realise this unhoped-for opportunity for a United Europe.

19 July 1993   Paris

A Brave New Europe

Bill Cash

'The division of Europe into a number of independent states, connected, however, with each other by the general resemblance of religion, language and manners, is productive of the most beneficial consequences to the liberty of mankind.'

Edward Gibbon, *Decline and Fall of the Roman Empire*, ch. III

Modern leaders in Europe would do well to read Gibbon.

The Two Europes

What is it to be European? We Europeans live geographically in historically sovereign countries on a Continent in which, to a greater or lesser extent, we share or have so far shared a Christian culture, which glorified in its diversity and talented competition from the Renaissance to the nineteenth century.

But there is another Europe. A Europe which has fallen prey to a European internationalism which owes its dark origins to a forbidding and atavistic concept of the *Volk* which, at its worst, has spawned racism and fascism. Twelve of these countries for nearly forty years have drawn together with some success but within an increasingly exclusive legal structure known as the European Community, bound together now by the 'Treaty on European Union'. This other Europe is a Europe grey, dull and uniform, driven now into a Hall of Mirrors by obsolete yet powerful political ambitions grafting on old solutions to new problems, particularly since the re-unification of Germany and the collapse of the old USSR.

History, it is said, repeats itself, but never so much as human nature, pride, greed and ambition. No treaty, no piece of paper, will alter this. This scepticism is what lies at the heart of the arguments of the English Euro-rebels, against the deeper, unnecessary and unrealisable *total harmonisation* which Maastricht represents. Far from being a campaign against Europe, it is a campaign for Europe. A campaign against the faceless bureaucracy and spiritually barren ideology of the Euro-crats in the Community. It is not against the

European Community as a concept, but against its accelerating anti-democratic direction.

This *Brave New Europe*, this undemocratic, authoritarian and social-ist European Community constructed like a massive meccano set, designed to be held tightly together by the supposedly inflexible ERM, with its failed policy in Bosnia, its failure to meet the democratic needs of eastern and central Europe, its failure to match up to the hopes of the Single Market, its failure to reform the Common Agricultural Policy, is light years away from the *New Europe* needed today.

Promise and Performance

It is this fundamental contradiction between promise and perform-ance which is undermining the Community and therefore, more dangerously, Europe as a whole, which is falling into a pit of corrosive contradictions.

Public opinion has now moved against Maastricht. It is seen as a failing experiment which no one properly explained. The opinion polls over the last year in the United Kingdom, in Germany and in France have all shifted decisively against what Maastricht does, or does not, represent. Once ratified, it can only either be unravelled by unani-mous requirement which is to say the least impossible or, when monetary union collapses (as did the Exchange Rate Mechanism), there is widespread chaos with massive political and commercial instability throughout Europe.

The rule of European law itself will collapse with it. This is not a happy prospect. The ultimate irony is that by surrendering democ-racy to unelected bankers, the leaders of Europe have lost their legitimacy in a quest which cannot work. Edouard Balladur, for example, is a captive of the contradiction between the policies of a French Socialist President and a French Conservative electorate and a Europeanism epitomised by the European People's Party in the shape of a former President, Valery Giscard d'Estaing. John Major, with the support of the Labour and Liberal-Democrat Parties and the Christian-Democratic wing of the Conservative Party, but opposed by the federalist tendency, is impaled on the same Morton's Fork.

The Treaty is a massive obstacle to restoring Europe to the relatively peaceful and prosperous condition it has enjoyed, albeit in need of reforms, since 1957. It is neither Christian nor democratic and has precious little in common with, say, traditional Conservatism in the United Kingdom. It owes more to the dangerous 'Conservatism' known to the authoritarian, even racist, tradition elsewhere in Europe.

We heard in the debates in the United Kingdom Parliament from the Foreign Secretary that what is written down is less important than how it works in practice, and Kenneth Clarke, the present Chancellor of the Exchequer, even admitted he had not read the Treaty. The Lord Chancellor, however (our highest judicial title holder), admitted that, 'the Treaty will make changes both within and outside the Community Treaties, some of them substantial. But ... they do not substantially change the constitutional position as it was established in 1972. There is development but not substantial change in these arrangements' (*Hansard* Col. 712, 8 June 1993).

What this otherwise accurate statement omits to point out is that, first, it all depends on how the Maastricht 'development' is woven into the fabric of the Act of 1972 and, secondly, that once the unanimity of all twelve Member States has been secured by ratification, it will need the near impossibility of agreement by each and every one to avoid the federalism which the Prime Minister professed to abhor: 'I will never – come hell or high water – let our distinctive British identity be lost in a federal Europe. Let this Conference not be in any doubt: this Government will not accept a centralised Europe' [the Party Conference in October 1992]. This federalism is what the rest of Europe enthusiastically embraces (including members of the European People's Party allied with the Conservative Party) while six of the Member States are driven by the seduction of subsidies and regional transfer.

Euro-Fantasia

Indeed, Chancellor Kohl, in anticipation of the summit proposed in October 1993 and despite the collapse of the ERM in August, reiterated German demands for a United States of Europe by economic and political union and for the European Monetary Institute and Central Bank to be sited in Frankfurt – where else? – following the ERM debacle. Even more ominously, despite the utter failure of will of the EC over Bosnia and of German insistence on the recognition of Croatia (hailed by his Foreign Minister as 'the greatest victory for German foreign policy since 1945) – Kohl stated that 'War in Europe can only be avoided through European union. Thus the political union of Europe is the most important thing of all'.

The achievement of this fantasy of one country was made immeasurably easier by the legally binding acceptance by all the Member States that no one state (including the UK) could veto the others from going ahead to Stage 3 of economic and monetary union. This single act of appeasement has opened the floodgates to a federal Europe, possibly with the United Kingdom Parliament in the prostrate position of having soon to decide whether or not to stay in the European Community at all. But for this defeat the Community could have turned its attention to the real reforms needed for its renewal instead of facing the prospect of an unworkable monetary system.

Even the European Commission, in an internal paper suppressed in 1992 because of the effect it would probably have on the Maastricht debate, but leaked to the *Financial Times* on 16 August 1993, admits that EMU will bring massive unemployment. With this will come the increased likelihood of strikes and civil disorder, but with less and less political accountability – as the leaders of Europe, including those of the European Economic Area, withdraw from their responsibilities and hand over more decisions to unelected bankers and officials.

The reforms and improvements in accountability in the French National Assembly instigated by its redoubtably anti-federalist and newly elected President, Philippe Séguin, and the reforms demanded in Italy are signs that people are insisting on changes, but will they succeed? As the neutering, under Maastricht, of national parliaments gathers pace, so the paralysis of the real Europe will give way to the prospect of the collapse of the Rule of Law, compounded by waves of immigration from the east, recession and lawlessness.

None of this was necessary. These unpleasant consequences could have been avoided simply by a firm 'No!' when Maastricht was proposed, or by John Major refusing to ratify the Treaty when the ERM, the incubus of political union, fell apart in early August 1993, instead of ratifying it on that very same day.

Positive Alternatives

But can we yet draw back from the *Brave New Europe* which is being constructed – do we have the means or the will to do so in the run-up to 1996? The determination to endorse this unworkable Treaty, even when Denmark first voted 'No' and again when the ERM collapsed, proves that the policy of appeasement, defeatism and the lack of political will is so deep that the federalists and their fellow softliners seem to have most of the cards in their hands – unless they are defeated from within Europe as a whole.

The 'political engineers', with their faith in written constitutions, have worked to a blueprint (based on a legal framework) which has been overtaken by events but not by their adherence to it. Pragmatism is not on their agenda. Indeed, the observation that what is written in the Treaty is somehow less important than how it works in practice reveals a lack of appreciation of the real importance of the legal framework and the power of the European Court of Justice – and of the fact that the European Community is truly European. No longer would it be generally possible to argue under the Maastricht Treaty that we are able to act unilaterally even when our vital interests are at stake. This must be changed.

The ending of the Cold War is not the ending of underlying tensions in Europe, as Yugoslavia clearly shows. The reunification of Germany, the bringing down of the Berlin Wall, the emancipation of Hungary, Poland and Czechoslovakia (now divided) and the dissolution of the old USSR are the salient features of the European landscape. Europe has changed but the thinking of the Euro-engineers has not changed with it. Such is the Maastricht thinking.

Russia, by comparison, was a few years ago the second most powerful nation on earth. It is disintegrating with an accumulated inflation rate of 2,500%. It cannot repay its financial obligations (of which Germany owns one half), nor can it deploy its massive natural resources to generate production of gold or oil because of its political instability.

Their own 'solutions' are counter-productive. One of the original and sensible objectives of the founding fathers was to contain Germany in the aftermath of the Second World War and to achieve reconciliation and harmony between France, Germany and the rest of Europe. The ERM debacles in September 1992 and August 1993 were, understandably (but from the point of view of the doomed but acquiescent advocates of political union in Europe), precipitated by German self-interest. Unfortunately, the imbalance of trading relationships between Germany and the rest of Europe (as high as 85% of all foreign investment in parts of eastern Europe) both collectively and individually works against this objective, even allowing for the annual costs of German reunification of some 180 billion Deutschemarks and the vast transfers promised by Germany to other countries inside and outside the European Community, quite apart from their unreasonable 'underpinning' of the ERM.

It is unrealistic to ignore the power that such an imbalance would give Germany under a majority voting system in the sphere of European government, just as it would be totally unrealistic to ignore the growing aspirations of a strengthened Germany on the European and global stage, encouraged by the new US administration, including pressure for a seat on the UN Security Council and the under- investigated but recent Russo-German Treaty which invites an exchange of German debt for Russian space, aircraft and munitions technology.

Who in practice would run the majority voting systems of the proposed central bank? Germany, already contained within the pre-Maastricht arrangements, is now pressing for more seats in the European Parliament, more political union and more control through its influence in the Christian-Democrat European People's Party.

This also raises the vital issues of accountability and real democracy which in a potentially unstable Europe are needed more than ever. The central bankers are to be independent and unelected and will be unaccountable. They will run monetary and economic policy. National Parliaments will be emasculated. The voters' decisions for their own choice of government and economic priorities in general elections will be subordinated to the faceless pursuit of 'price stability' which even the bankers cannot guarantee, yet which can be achieved (as in the United Kingdom) by self-help. Nor, if they fail to impose their bureaucratic will in a way that results in massive unemployment could the bankers be turned out, whatever turmoil their decisions would have wrought in the meantime.

Maastricht is above all about undemocratic government. Vital national interests must be preserved if popular consent is to be the binding force of the European Community. Without it the system will fail in mutual recrimination or attempts may be made (who knows?) to claim that having 'voluntarily' acquiesced in giving up critical spheres of government, the new rule of law must be 'imposed' or enforced – if necessary by force – but if so, by whom?

Furthermore, the prospect of enlargement to a Community of up to 20 countries – and perhaps more – is now upon us. It is frequently argued by the centralists that to include new Member States (who in any case cannot be denied their right to apply even under the existing Treaty of Rome) would prevent the Community from acting together efficiently. Centralisation would not work on that scale. Much the same could have been argued at any time from the origins of the Community in the 1950s to the present day. However, quite apart from the moral objections to excluding the newly-emergent democracies of eastern Europe, which desperately need to buttress their democracy with free trade, their involvement would also stabilise their fragile relationship with the rest of Europe in mutual self-interest. Their collapse would be a disaster. Yugoslavia is only one dramatic example of what is in prospect if they are denied the opportunity, which they have by right of their courage in throwing off the yoke of communism. Time is not on our side. They must not become the economic satellites of a new Germany, for this would not be in the long-term interests even of Germany.

Free Trade and Freedom of Choice

It is ironic, to say the least, that just as the old USSR has been seeking to democratise itself and to decentralise, the European Community should have been engaged in moving the opposite way. It is no argument that they cannot be compared with the present Community because they were Communist states. The real point is that it is democracy which is the means to freedom to choice and freedom of trade, backed by popular consent. This is what Maastricht singularly fails to recognise.

The debate has lost sight of the real impact which Maastricht will have upon people's daily lives, their jobs and businesses. Which countries (and companies, many of them mega European-champions backed up by national subsidies with help from the European Community) will be the gainers and losers? What would be the impact of ERM if it continues to bind other countries to the Deutschemark? What if they are to be flooded with new immigrants? Will their votes at general elections be worth casting?

The positive arguments of the opponents of Maastricht are very clear. There are important and beneficial aspects of the European Community to bring it up to date with the needs of today and the next century. It is not negative to say 'thus far and no further', if to go further is to destroy the Community and the democracy of Europe with it. To preserve these is the most positive thing a politician in Europe can do. The problem is that almost all the Member States believe that they can push the UK into accepting their terms on all the vital issues – such as a central bank – even at the price of democracy.

The Futility of a European Foreign Policy

To claim the Maastricht Treaty as a victory is extraordinary when compared with what has been conceded, for example, in the field of foreign policy and border controls alone.

No one would ever have thought that foreign policy could be conducted under the jurisdiction of the European Court of Justice. The worst aspects (of Title V) are the loss of our effective and clear unilateral control over our foreign policy and the confusion which is deeply damaging to decisive future action. They do neither one thing nor another, as the overlapping functions of WEU and NATO, the UN and the EC in Yugoslavia have shown. The Common Foreign Policy simply reinforces the sovereignty of Brussels, with our relations with the United States subservient to this and to the European Union.

Title V is wholly out of date. Its wording creates the dangers which the Secretary General of NATO described in April 1993 as a sterile debate between the 'Atlanticists' and the 'Europeanists'. What was needed, but which has been ignored, is the requirement to work with NATO, not for European 'independence'. The Maastricht Treaty is based on the surreal vision of a federal Europe.

We have worked for centuries in alliances and by treaty with other nations. It has worked. Circumstances change, priorities change. This entire Title deprives us, at a stroke, of one of our greatest assets – our pragmatism in changing circumstances – and replaces it with a wholly unnecessary, unexplained system of joint action – perhaps not directly in the hands of the Commission (who are nonetheless fully associated) or enforceable by the Court of Justice, but that was never possible anyway. But what it does do is to put us by Treaty in the position of having to justify why we are taking individual action and sow the seeds of uncertainty and indecision when we can least afford this attitude among the Member States. The Gulf War and Yugoslavia are omens of what is in store.

It is profoundly unwise to bind ourselves to take action on a European scale when all the evidence points to this being counter-productive, incapable of delivery and unnecessary. This applies as much to foreign policy as to the proposals for a Central Bank. It also applies to defence. It is almost impossible to draw a clear line, particularly in times of potential war or emergency, between foreign policy and defence.

Had the provisions of the Treaty on foreign policy and security been in place in the run-up to the Gulf War, would Saddam Hussein have been defeated? It was certainly no thanks to the Member States, one of whom (Belgium) would not even supply a fellow EC member state, namely Britain, with ammunition.

Decentralising the Centralists

Far from being a decentralising Treaty, Maastricht centralises. All the most important areas of government, such as the running of monetary policy and foreign policy, are referred to a higher tier bound together by obligations.

These are in black and white – they cannot be brushed under the carpet and must be renegotiated. The principle of subsidiarity does nothing to alter the main centralising features of the Treaty and, if it is intended to refer back some of the issues to national jurisdiction, then why not set these out in a list of functions? To do so would be clear. Instead they have decided to rely on the smokescreen of subsidiarity which confuses and obscures both the arguments and the issues. If there are powers already granted where the Commission and the Community have become too 'intrusive', these can simply be taken out of express changes to the Treaty. Subsidiarity has nothing to offer if this is done.

If the Single European Act is not working properly, if there is a failure to achieve a level playing field, the remedy is to force the issue through the Courts. If the Commission exceeds its powers, it too must be taken to Court and procedures agreed by Treaty taken to nip such action in the bud. All these systems would decentralise the Community without invoking subsidiarity. The more examples emerge to show what the Commission and others have in mind to 'decentralise', the clearer they reveal the rock of centralisation at the heart of Maastricht.

The *Brave New Europe* could have been avoided, as I sought to warn in February 1991 when I wrote the paper which follows (at the invitation of Douglas Hurd, the Foreign Secretary) for the Conservative Manifesto Committee. I said then that the federalists had their own agenda, that it was not possible by giving in to this to square the circle, and that the federalists would only be prevented by repudiating economic and monetary, and thereby political, union and retaining Britain's own veto. I warned that this would leave us on the outer hub of a two-speed Europe which would undermine the United Kingdom and the European Community itself. I was staggered when even the words 'independent sovereign state' were removed from the final draft. The lines for the battle of Maastricht were drawn – and it is by no means over.

What is being created is a craven, defeatist, self-destructing European Community riddled and corrupted by a fear of freedom – a *Brave New Europe* indeed.

The forces within this Europe – the artificially created Europe engineered at Maastricht – will darken and destabilise Europe as a whole. The real Europeans must continue the battle from within.

12 August 1993   London

Addendum
The European Community – Reality and Making It Work

(1991 Report to the Conservative Party Manifesto Committee,
prepared at the invitation of the Foreign Secretary, Douglas Hurd)

The Theme

The European Community suffers from an air of unreality. This unreality is
a political, indeed a party political, problem compounded by the timing of the
IGCs in relation to our next General Election [April 1992]. Our policy in the
Manifesto must dovetail with Government policy after that Election, which
will be influenced by decisions being taken by all Member States at the IGCs.

There are three kinds of unreality. There is the unreality of the anti-European who believes we should get out now; there is the unreality of those who
cannot or will not face up to the failings of the Community and of political
will or who believe that these will all be resolved once there is a federal
system or a single Government and a single Parliament; and then there is
the unreality of the Euro-establishment, whether in Brussels or in Whitehall,
who are mesmerised by the legal framework of the Treaties and their original
laudable political objectives but who do not see that what was good for the
1950s or for the Franco-German axis does not apply in the same way in the
political landscape of the 1990s. Far too much has changed.

The main thrust of this paper (in relation to the Party's Election Manifesto) is to stress the contribution Britain has made and must continue to
make in the EC and in bringing the Community down to earth whilst
emphasising its benefits. It needs a strong dose of practical, constructive
reality and we need to show we are providing it. This is necessary more than
ever because of the contrast in the public mind between the build-up of
federalism followed by the failure of will over the Gulf War. This is not only
a sensible policy, but has ongoing electoral appeal, particularly in the
aftermath of the Gulf War. The world has changed since the last Manifesto
in 1987, with the changes in the USSR and eastern Europe, the phasing out
of the Cold War, the unification of Germany, the Gulf War, the difficulties in
the GATT and the internal differences and developments in the European
Community itself and its relations with the rest of the world.

The Manifesto cannot promise more than we can deliver and the message
of reality is as essential to British interests as to European. There is no such
thing as 'historical necessity' or 'inevitability' in British policy making or
experience. We need to be flexible and pragmatic, but so too does the EC.

It will be necessary to go through the Manifesto of 1987 and the section
on the European Community in the 1987 Campaign Guide (p.512) and to
bring these up to date. The Manifesto and Government policy must be
convergent, practical and realistic and the British people and Parliament
must be properly informed about what is going on so that proper decisions
can be taken. We need to ask the questions 'why' and 'who are the gainers

and losers as the EC develops or evolves?' e.g. our trade imbalance with the EC, why this is so and whether EC policies will help this to improve.

There are five main areas of policy to consider for the Manifesto:

1. Political Union and Institutional Reform;
2. Economic and Monetary Union;
3. The Single Market, Free Trade, GATT and Agriculture;
4. Wider Europe, USSR, EFTA;
5. Foreign Policy and Defence (including the Gulf War and relations with USA, NATO, WEU).

1. Political Union and Institutional Reform

We want to co-operate but not federate: no single government and parliament. The Gulf War has proved the point that even co-operation became impossible in those circumstances. Co-operation remains a sensible objective but we must be realistic and learn from experience and history, whilst reaffirming our commitment to the EC.

(a) The role of the national parliaments must remain central to our thinking because the European Parliament would be too remote, unaccountable and socialist. A major difficulty is that many of the other Member States have different constitutions and histories (decrees, less questioning, less scrutiny, democracy less well rooted *etc.*). We will not give up our Westminster system of government, nor our control over main areas of tax and expenditure. This affects our policy on EMU (see later).

(b) There is a difference between extending areas of competence under SEA and accepting majority voting for these or similar limited purposes and accepting it in the context of political union. Once consent at this level has been relinquished, we would be in a federal system. The veto remains essential.

(c) With majority voting in the Council of Ministers in new areas of competence (especially SEA), there is less need for the European Commission to have extensive powers.

(d) The Court of Justice has a tendency towards political integrating of use of procedure and interpretation which can only be checked by Treaty amendment. Checks and balances are needed. The Court should not be given the capacity to adjudicate on what are essentially political questions between Member States which cannot be enforced.

(e) 'Subsidiarity' encourages (d) and it is very doubtful that the judges of the Court actually want subsidiarity.

(f) Germany would dominate a Community with political union. It is a fallacy to believe that it would be contained. Majority voting under SEA already contains Germany to some extent. The problem of German domination can only be resolved by attitudes within Germany itself, with or without political union. Without it, at least there can be a balance of interest (or power), particularly in a wider Europe. If there is to be a wider Europe, including EFTA, political union in the federal sense is out of the question. There would be too many countries and this would make majority voting even more unacceptable, but with free trading opportunities.

(g) Political union would also concentrate political power and the legal structure so as to make protectionism more likely and, with it, massive trade wars with USA and Japan. The liberalisation of trade transcends the EC. Free trade has never been more important. (See later on GATT)

(h) Political union raises the questions: Who governs?; By whose consent?; How?; Who would dominate?

Conclusion

We should stress political co-operation and seek political leadership in the EC but not make concessions to political union.

2. Economic and Monetary Union

(a) The evidence from the Delors Report, the draft Central Bank Statutes and the draft Treaty on Economic and Monetary Union is of a determined push towards control, by an independent panel of central bankers, of our economic and monetary policy, with profound and wholly unacceptable implications for our democratic system of government. Containing inflation and securing 'price stability' are necessary and laudable, but so is democracy. *This is the dilemma.* The answer lies more in improved domestic performance within the framework of the Single Market and global opportunities than in institutional answers. These are essentially defeatist. They include majority voting. Even under our own proposals for Treaty amendments, the unanimous decision of the Council would not be referred back to Parliament. Would they include a European financial plan? What is 'Community policy'?

(b) Again 'subsidiarity', on the basis of the proposals so far advanced, would assume that the higher levels of macro-economic power were conceded to the European level, but with no explanation for this in the context of the 1990s. How would it contain Germany? Would it not make the German region more powerful with a cluster of alliances around it within the voting arrangements of the new Bank or Fund? The Germans themselves seem increasingly uncertain about it all unless they are running it.

(c) A single currency would imply a single monetary policy and a Central Bank with loss of accountability evolving away from democracy and the man in the street. Even on its own Euro-terms, a single currency would require economic convergence. This is unrealistic, with inflation in Member States ranging from 3% to 20% and the need for vast regional transfers which the paymasters would not accept or would insist on controlling. Regional policies lead to political manipulation, inefficient industries and regional disparities in productivity.

(d) The binding rules or surveillance rules and the problem of enforcement raise grave issues for democratic decision making over budget deficits, with massive cuts in public expenditure in those Member States running them and the prospects of civil disturbance in the weaker economies. The Gulf War has shown the connection between EMU and defence expenditure. A Euro-defence policy would need to run at about 6% of GDP (as in the USA) but the Euro-average is only 3.1%. Some countries would only be able to contribute – (even if they had the political will, which they do not) – by doubling their defence expenditure and thereby increasing their budget deficits and then being required to reduce them or to reduce their other areas of public expenditure.

(e) Savings in transactions costs on EMU are 0.1% and *negligible*.

(f) EMU as presently conceived by the Commission, and in varying degrees by Germany and France, is a stepping stone to political union and federalism. Its benefits are not demonstrated by the Commission's paper 'One Money One Market' or its earlier papers, yet we are being 'drawn' down a path with unpredictable consequences even on the basis of our own Treaty proposals. Are these tactical or intended?

(g) The German deficit likely in the aftermath of GMU has put further strain on the differences between the Bundesbank, the Finance Ministry and Chancellor Kohl. The interest rate rise of 0.5% was an alternative to raising taxes, which Kohl had repudiated. Germany and France are in disagreement over European economic and monetary policy. France wants economic union, with the Council in control, and her Finance Minister says, 'The German deficit is now a world problem'. Germany is less sure about economic union unless it is once and for all and it serves German interests. Effectively they would run it. France and Britain disagree over the French desire for closer economic union but are both concerned about German domination, its overheating economy and trade imbalance within Europe. *There is uncertainty and much at stake.*

(h) If we have a General Election before the IGC is concluded in the autumn our Manifesto must not commit us to a policy at a time of such uncertainty and at the risk of losing control over our economic and social priorities and of our democracy and accountability. There would be no consent for full EMU Treaty amendments in such circumstances and it would be disingenuous for us then to agree, after the Election, to present Parliament with a Bill to ratify them on the basis of renewed IGC discussions. Nor must we agree to such Treaty amendments now, without the full consent of Parliament in primary legislation, which would or could be triggered at a later time for the same reasons.

Conclusion

A two-tier or two-speed Europe *is a most unattractive idea* – we would be marginalised, lose authority and involvement and would not catch up. We should be clear in the Manifesto that we stick to our current policy of playing Stage 2 long and vague and of repudiating Stage 3 but play for time in the expectation that the differences between the Member States, on EMU, heightened by the disillusionment created by the Gulf War, will cause full EMU to founder, whilst working for flexible, effective and practical co-operation without deep institutional and centralising change. Even ERM and the hard ECU plan, even with Spanish support, could be significantly affected by developments over the next months – we must keep our options open and not be taken in by the spurious argument that now is the time for deep institutional change simply because recent events have shown such disarray.

3. The Single Market – Free Trade – GATT – Agriculture

(a) The Single Market remains an important and worthwhile policy but we must emphasise the need for a level playing field, greater liberalisation of trade, full implementation and enforcement. We must guard against selective and strategic use of 'single market' policies by other Member States invading our markets without equal access to their own. We must ensure that our own training, educational and technical standards meet those of our competitors and that our management meets the challenges it encounters. We need internal audits of comparative performance and assurance by our own companies and trade associations so that they are fully up to date with European legislation and make the most use (with properly trained people) of the scrutiny process in the UK and European Parliaments. We must continue to resist demanding aspects of the Social Charter and prevent cheap labour increasing UK unemployment [i.e. by social dumping].

(b) Free trade is central to our own and global economic performance. It cuts across the EC. Our trade is not confined by any means to the Community. We cannot afford a trade war with the USA. We must avoid protectionism and some ways should be found to improve the negotiating machinery of the EC at GATT, which places far too much control in the hands of the Commission. France and Italy are particularly protectionist and doubtful about GATT. France and Germany have shown up badly on agricultural reform. The failure to reform the CAP, despite a falling farming population and fraud in the CAP, represents a scandal and has been vote based. International financial markets are already global and will increase as telecommunications develop. The UK is well placed in this sphere, at the moment.

(c) There needs to be a stronger GATT dispute reconciliation system to offset the 301 USA Trade Act provisions. There must be increased growth in the developing world, solving their debt problems and providing impetus to their inward investment programmes. The Gulf War will affect oil prices for these countries. The British connection in the Commonwealth offers opportunities in that field, combined with new opportunities in eastern Europe and the Pacific Basin. Uruguay must succeed and the EC has a major part to play in this.

(d) In the sphere of agriculture the OECD has reckoned that £100 billion is transferred by consumers and taxpayers to farmers in OECD countries [OECD 1992 estimate: £140 billion, of which £88 billion is within the EC]. Standard GATT rules must apply to agriculture and to prevent ecological disasters.

4. Wider Europe, USSR and EFTA – Trade and Democracy

Some of the greater hopes for the development of the economies of eastern Europe and particularly in the USSR have been reversed but, despite our determination to support the Baltic States, if necessary by sanctions, we must continue to press for continuing democracy and economic reform in those regions and for improvement in trading relationships with EFTA and Turkey. Investment opportunities in all these areas must be enlarged and not left to Germany which has driven into eastern Europe and signed a separate Treaty with the USSR [in 1990].

5. Defence and Foreign Policy – the EC and the Gulf War

The Gulf War has had a profound effect on the over-extravagant claims made for an EC defence and foreign policy. EC countries have not responded in time or enough to the requirements of the UN resolutions and the need for concerted action in the Gulf. The political will by EC countries was found wanting which, in turn, has had a deep effect on the prospects of political union in EC. The temptation to imagine that the failure of EC countries to work together in the Gulf War means that there is a need for greater combined defence and foreign policy, with moves towards majority voting, must be avoided.

Co-operation in foreign policy will need to be redeveloped but in the fields of security and defence the lessons of the Gulf War cannot be overlooked. The special relationship of the UK with the USA is alive and well and greatly strengthened. Our political and moral authority has been enhanced and the Atlantic Alliance must be fostered through NATO and WEU, not the EC (and certainly no majority voting or mutual defence), and the CSCE will provide a useful forum for widening these efforts. However, in the aftermath of the Gulf War, it may be expected that the USA will not re-establish itself in Europe in the same strength as before, thereby requiring us to develop new means of creating defensive alliances in Europe but with emphasis on co-operation, not unity. Goodwill is not the same as trust. It has become clear that when the need for unity was greatest, it was not forthcoming. The instability in the USSR is dangerous but it remains doubtful whether they will fully trust Germany, especially as it grows stronger. We must therefore give special attention to relationships with eastern European countries and Turkey and develop the opportunities for high technology, satellite, communication and weapons procurement which our relationship with USA offers, even if her physical presence in Europe is reduced. We must ensure that arms control is effective in all regions. The EC has a role to play in this.

Conclusion

Some of the over-enthusiastic claims for the EC need to be put in perspective and its value assessed in more realistic terms. These lessons need to be imported into the IGCs before they are concluded, whether or not a General Election intervenes, and our Manifesto should reflect this.

2 February 1991   London

The Fatal Conceit of Maastricht

Paul Belien

Rome has twice given birth to Maastricht. The Treaty of Maastricht of 1991 owes its existence to the Treaty of Rome of 1957, which marks the birth of the European Community. And the city of Maastricht – *Mosae Trajectum* ('the crossing of the Meuse' in Latin) – was founded by the Romans twenty centuries ago, on the spot where the Roman Road from *Colonia Agrippina* to *Camaracum* crossed the river *Mosa*. *Colonia Agrippina* is the German town of Köln (Cologne) today. *Camaracum* is the French town of Cambrai, on the road from Brussels to Paris. And the Mosa is the Maas (Meuse), the river which forms the border between Belgium and The Netherlands.

That part of the Roman empire was inhabited by the tribe of the *Eburones*. They lived on both sides of the river and, needless to say, they were the same people and on both sides of the *Mosa* they spoke the same language. The Romans called this region *Belgica*, which is the Latin name for The Netherlands (*'Nederlanden'* literally means 'Low Countries').

Since 1830 The Netherlands and Belgium have been totally independent states. The Kingdom of The Netherlands – (sometimes also called Holland, after its most important province) – is the name given to the northern provinces of the ancient Netherlands, while nowadays the southern provinces of the ancient Netherlands are officially called the Kingdom of Belgium. Although the people on one side of the Maas carry Belgian passports whilst those on the other side have Dutch ones, they are still one and the same people and they speak the same language – Limburgian, a dialect of Dutch.

Until 1839 the two Netherlandic states of Belgium and The Netherlands quarrelled over two provinces: the duchy of Luxemburg and the duchy of Limburg. The dispute was solved by cutting both in two. The western part of Luxemburg went to Belgium while the eastern part became an independent state, the Grand Duchy of Luxemburg, with the monarch of Holland (the dynasty of Orange-Nassau) as its head of state. The personal union lasted until 1890, but Luxemburg still has the same flag as The Netherlands.

Limburg was also cut in half. The left bank of the Maas went to Belgium, the right bank to The Netherlands. Limburg's capital Maastricht, although situated mainly on the left bank, went to The Netherlands (as did the title Duke of Limburg, which was bestowed on the Orange king of Holland). The city thus lost the entire western half of its hinterland.

Rome not only founded Maastricht, it also founded the first pan-European empire. Except for the Germans, the Danes and the Irish, all contemporary member states of the European Community were involved, even the British. In the fifth century, the empire collapsed under Germanic pressure. The second pan-European empire was founded in the ninth century. This time the Germans were involved, but not the British. Maastricht was very close to the centre of this second European unification. After the departure of the Romans, the region along the Maas had been settled by the tribe of the Franks. Although this people gave its name to the French, they gave their language to the Dutch, and more particularly to the Limburgians. The Limburg dialect is the closest language there is today to the language of the Franks. The oldest written text in Dutch is from this region.

It was one of these Franks who united Europe and refounded the 'Holy Roman Empire'. He was born in the dynasty of the lords of Herstal, a village 20 kilometres to the south of Maastricht on the left bank of the Maas, in present-day Belgium, and he had his European capital in Aachen, 30 kilometres to the east of Maastricht, in present-day Germany. He probably crossed the Maas a couple of times along the old Roman road to Maastricht. There is a popular nursery rhyme in the region which goes (in Dutch) *'Tussen Keulen en Parijs ligt de weg naar Rome'* or (in English) 'Between Cologne and Paris lies the way to Rome'. And, indeed, in December 800, the hero of the people of the Maas was crowned emperor of Europe in Rome: *Carolus Magnus*, 'Charles the Great' or 'Charlemagne'.

Charlemagne appears to have been a wise and modest man. His son, Louis the Pious, was also a modest man. After Louis' death, however, the empire fell apart, giving birth to the nation-states of both Germany and France. In the 12 centuries that followed, a couple of dictators considered the nation-states of France and Germany too small for them and tried to follow in Charlemagne's footsteps. 'Europe' was a rallying call used by both the Corsican Napoleon Bonaparte and the Austrian Adolf Hitler. Neither succeeded in keeping his European empire together for more than ten years, but neither were modest men. Together with the collapse of their conceited vision of Europe, they brought ruin on the nation-state they started out with. Then Jacques Delors crossed the old Roman road in Maastricht. Being a Socialist, he is not modest either. Maastricht might well become his Waterloo, and together with his conceited vision of Europe, he might also ruin the modest achievements of Europe thus far.

The peoples of the Benelux are among the most fervent defenders of supranational integration. It is not difficult to see why. Limburgians and Luxemburgians on both sides of the border are aware of the artificiality of this division of their land and their people. So are

N

Key
—————— Existing country borders
– – – – – Duchy borders
•••••••• Linguistic borders

the people of Brabant, the old duchy that was also divided up between Belgium and The Netherlands: the northern third of its territory went to The Netherlands, the southern part, with the capital Brussels and the title of Duke of Brabant, went to the king of Belgium. The same also applies to the people of Flanders, who lost the northern fifth of their country to Holland while the rest, together with the title of Count of Flanders, also went to the king of Belgium. Until 1839 the city of Ghent, the capital of Flanders, although it had been bestowed on Belgium, was locally ruled by staunch francophone 'Orangists', who professed loyalty to William of Orange, the king of The Netherlands.

The partition of The Netherlands also lies at the roots of Belgium's identity crisis as a state and the ensuing linguistic conflict which still threatens to tear the country apart. Belgium is only a half-state and, as such, cannot solve its nationality problem. The Belgians are perhaps the only European people who take no pride in their nation-state at all. They would have no qualms about participating in a 'Europe of the regions', directly under Europe, with no intermediate nation-states at all. Belgium is no nation, it is an artificial state, and so would the new Europe be. As the British Historian Hugh Seton-Watson wrote in *Nations and States*: 'The formation of the Dutch nation is a case of the division in two of a community which ... was growing into a single modern nation; but [was pulled and kept] apart, making one into a nation [The Netherlands] and leaving the other [Belgium] in uncertain status'.

Why is Belgium with its two main language groups, Dutch (Flemish) and French, not a viable national entity, while multi-ethnic Switzerland, with four language groups, has such a strong sense of national identity that the nation in a referendum rejected membership of a larger European framework? Because in Switzerland the 65% majority of the German-speaking Swiss is big enough to ensure that the country does not fall apart when the second group, the 20% French-speaking Swiss, vote the other way (as was the case in the referendum on Europe). In Belgium the 59% Dutch-speaking majority experiences constant frustration. It never has its way in issues where the 39% French-speaking minority thinks otherwise. Within a Benelux framework, however, the linguistic situation would be an almost exact copy of the Swiss: 70% Dutch versus 20% French and two minor languages (German and Frisian). Paradoxically the situation of the French minority in such a situation would be better than it is in Belgium. As the Swiss experience shows, a majority which does not feel threatened can afford a greater benevolence towards the minority.

After having forced their peoples to live next to, but totally separate from, one another for over one hundred years, the war experience of the early 1940s brought the exiled Dutch and Belgian governments together. In September 1944 the governments of Belgium, The Netherlands and Luxemburg signed the Treaty of London, which created the Benelux, the first European supranational organisation, designed to establish an economic union between the three countries. Benelux was a modest institution. In its charter it never envisaged a transfer of national sovereignty to a supranational level, although many hoped that this would eventually follow, thus wiping out the borders that divide three peoples who throughout most of their history had always belonged to the same nation anyway.

As Benelux was a modest operation it worked remarkably well. If it had been allowed to continue unhindered its slow but spontaneous growth, it might well have resulted, half a century after its creation, in 1994 in a complete political, economic and monetary union between its three member states. As it is, Belgium and Luxemburg have already been a monetary union since 1921. However, things did not turn out this way. In the early 1950s a territorial copy of the Europe of Charlemagne seemed to come to life. The six countries over which that great son of the Maas region had reigned – the Benelux, France, Italy and the Western half of Germany – decided to set up a number of organisations for economic cooperation. The initiative for the first of these organisations, the *European Coal and Steel Community* of 1952, was taken by a Luxemburgian, Robert Schuman, who had settled in France and became the French prime minister in 1947. Other pan-European economic organisations between these six countries followed. Unlike the Benelux, a substantial transfer of sovereignty from the national governments to the supranational level was envisaged. The process resulted in the signing of the Treaty of Rome on 25 March 1957. The European Economic Community (EEC) was born.

The founding fathers of the EEC envisioned a politically united Europe. Economic liberalisation was seen as a first step towards this goal. But they were modest people. They were careful not to aim too high and to take their time. The treaty of 1957 stipulated that the EEC should constitute one frontier-free market for all goods and services by 1 January 1970.

Unfortunately, the EC aborted Benelux. The latter would undoubtedly also have led to a substantial transfer of national sovereignty to a supranational Benelux institution, if it had been allowed to grow spontaneously. However, as the three Benelux-countries had agreed to transfer national sovereignty within the broader EC project, Benelux became superfluous. From the mid-1950s on, Benelux no longer had any significance. It became a dormant institution – 'this Sleeping Beauty, waiting to be awakened', as the Belgian minister of Foreign Affairs, Mark Eyskens, said in 1990.

The EEC of the Treaty of Rome was set up as an instrument for economic liberalisation. Transferring national sovereignty from the level of the national government to the level of the Community government (the *Commission*) is a good thing if the supranational level prevents the national levels from becoming too interventionist. The net result should be less government interference. However, as EEC bureaucracy expanded, the opposite happened.

As long as the EEC remained a vehicle for economic liberalisation, its member states were reluctant to surrender sovereignty. This attitude was due more to socialism than to nationalism. When the EEC was founded in 1957 the countries of Western Europe had already succumbed to the temptation against which Friedrich von Hayek had warned in his book *The Road to Serfdom* in 1944: they had become *welfare states*, where the national governments are held to be primarily responsible for the protection and promotion of the economic and social welfare of their citizens.

The acceptance of the notion that a citizen has a right to state aid whenever he finds himself in social or economic difficulties, entails that any project limiting the power of the national state is almost doomed from the beginning – unless the institution replacing the national state takes over its welfare functions. This was the case with the EEC's *Common Agricultural Policy* (CAP), set up in 1962. The CAP, which devours almost two-thirds of the annual EC budget, is a gigantic multinational welfare operation for farmers who, without it, would long have gone out of business. It has proved a financial and economic disaster. But in terms of supranational co-operation it is a success.

In 1966 the so-called *Luxemburg Compromise* granted member states the right to veto any Community decision whenever they felt a 'vital interest' threatened. In practice the EEC's welfare-state governments invoked vital interests threatened each time a segment of their population risked experiencing a social or economic disadvantage as a result of economic liberalisation on the European level. On New Year's Day 1970 the frontier-free market for goods and services, promised by the Treaty of Rome, was nowhere in sight, not even between the three Benelux countries who had foolishly given up their pan-Netherlandic integration in favour of pan-Europe.

Although not very successful, the EEC (apart from the CAP) more or less remained an instrument for economic liberalisation until the end of the 1970s. This explains why in 1973 the British entry into the EEC was strongly opposed by the Labour Party and backed by the Conservative Party. Today, however, Labour enthusiastically embraces 'Europe' while some Conservatives are rather critical. Some observers have called this 'the sharpest role reversal in recent British politics', but it is in Brussels that things took a sharp turn, not in London.

As the original six 'Charlemagne' members of 1957 were joined by Denmark, Great Britain and Ireland (1973), Greece (1981), and Portugal and Spain (1986), it became ever more difficult to set up mechanisms for supranational liberalisation of the market. The more welfare states were involved, the greater the probability of welfare-state-inspired vetos. Most of the new members did not join because they adhered to free-market principles, but because it was a way of getting their agriculture and industry subsidised.

The outlook of the European Commission has also changed. The goal of the Commissioners is no longer the economic liberalisation envisaged by the Rome Treaty, but sometimes plain economic interventionism. The Commission has seventeen members, two from each of the five larger member states and one from each of the seven smaller ones. In small countries like Belgium there is a silent agreement among the main political parties to have a rota for the one commissioner the country is allowed to nominate every four years. If a Christian-Democrat politician has been commissioner during the previous term, the next goes to a Socialist, and the next to a Liberal. A big country with two European commissioners usually nominates one from a right-wing party and one from the left. Britain has one Conservative and one Labour commissioner, Germany one Christian Democrat and one Liberal. Because the Commission encompasses the whole political spectrum, it still includes some advocates of free-market principles, but it also contains advocates of a planned economy. Inevitably the economic policy it creates is a mixed bag. The EC has become the champion of a 'mixed economy' – or, as its defenders would say, 'capitalism tempered by socialism' – the typical economic system of the welfare state.

In 1985 Jacques Delors became president of the European Commission. For the presidency of the Commission there is also an unwritten agreement between the member states to apply a rotation system, based on both nationality and ideological affiliation. In 1985 it was the turn of a Frenchman and a Socialist. This was Delors' chance. He is a former French Socialist minister and a charming, intelligent and capable politician. He is not a hard-line Socialist who believes in a planned economy, but a moderate one who believes in a 'mixed' economy of the welfare state. He clearly understood the enormous potential of the EC, not as a vehicle of economic liberalisation, but as a vehicle of the welfare state.

Delors was one of the first to notice that by the early 1980s economies had become increasingly international, which made it impossible for the individual welfare states to retain national control over their economies. Consequently, the welfare state, which depended on the money and wealth generated by the free economy, had to follow the economy to the supranational level. As the internationalisation of economies was proceeding at an ever increasing pace, Delors knew he had to act fast. He immediately started improving the EEC's institutional mechanisms so that supranational integration would proceed smoothly and quickly. Within a year after his accession, the *Single European Act* (December 1985) had been passed.

The Single European Act abolished the unilateral veto of the member states (except for various welfare reasons, such as 'health, safety, environmental protection, consumer protection, or protection of there working environment') and introduced a weighted voting system. The Single Act also reset the date by which the EC should be a frontier-free market for goods and services to December 31, 1992. The latter could be seen as a paradox: a goal of liberalisation, such as the creation of a frontier-free market, to serve an interventionist welfare purpose. But Delors understood that a frontier-free market would lead to the extra economic growth which was needed to generate the necessary money for the survival of the welfare mechanism.

Delors reversed the whole mentality behind the EEC. He added a 'social dimension' to the European project and he turned the EC bureaucracy into an instrument which was to intervene regularly in the national economies in order to actively 'create' a free market. One thing, however, Delors did not understand: a bureaucracy cannot construct a free market; a free market creates itself, spontaneously. A government, whether it be national, European or local, cannot 'create' freedom, it can only let freedom happen. Liberty, as Isaiah Berlin (a Latvian) has warned, should be a negative concept rather than a positive one. It has more to do with what a political authority does not, than with what it does. Positive liberty, as Leszek Kolakowski (a Pole) has remarked, is a Marxist concept. It more often leads to less freedom than to more.

However, west European politicians and bureaucrats do not like this message. The 17 EC commissioners and the thirteen thousand civil servants working for them in the Charlemagne building and other office buildings of the Commission in Brussels were pleased with Delors' message to start 'constructing Europe'. It made them feel important. This was the fatal conceit.

Socialism, as Hayek (an Austrian) wrote, is a form of constructivism, and constructivism is immodest: certain politicians and bureaucrats think that they know better than the people themselves what is good for the people. The problem with Socialism is not that these constructivists do not mean well (they often do) but that they suffer from a lack of knowledge. The constructivist mentality sees society as a system that can be centrally directed. The government centralises all knowledge which is present in society and formulates the collective goals accordingly.*

However, as society grows more and more complicated, it becomes ever more difficult to centralise knowledge in one bureaucratic centre. The system becomes self-defeating through its lack of knowledge about reality. Socialism works in the closed, almost 'tribal' order of the group, where everybody more or less knows what everybody else's goals and needs are, but not in the open and ever more complicated, extended order of the modern world. In the open extended order one can also more or less know what the goals and needs of people are, not by centralising information, but by looking to the market. The market, on condition that it is open and free, is, as Michael Polanyi (a Hungarian) pointed out, a *medium of communication* which conveys information about how people behave in accordance with the knowledge they have about their own situations. The market is a reservoir of knowledge which is constantly being updated and which is vital for the survival of the open extended order. Without it the societal order breaks down and society can only survive if it closes itself, or if it 'tribalises'. Protectionism is the economic result of such tribalisation. It is the consequence of socialism and nationalism.

Tribalisation or 'group egoism' is what the Treaty of Maastricht is all about. Maastricht is the culmination of the Delors mentality which has permeated the EC. Maastricht cannot work because Socialism cannot work. It cannot work as the former Socialist regimes in

[*Editor's note: The same tendency is apparent with the Christian-Democrats.]

Eastern Europe could not work. They also lacked knowledge and were totally out of touch with reality. They ultimately perished. But not without having first destroyed the whole economy and brought poverty to the people. Maastricht might do just that, because the European commissioners and their thousands of civil servants do not have the slightest knowledge about the European realities: the goals, the aspirations and the needs of the peoples of Europe. They cannot have, for nobody can. Only the market, always adapting and adjusting itself to new phenomena and evolutions, can communicate these.

Europe does not need Maastricht, or any other new Treaty, to make it more free and prosperous. In order to become more free, Europe needs more freedom. The Delors Commission began replacing the various local (national) government regulators by a European super-regulator claiming to be intent on 'liberalising' the market. Once more, positive liberty has led to less freedom. Competition between the various national regulators at least had the advantage that the citizens and companies of Europe could move their money and economic activity to the most business friendly and economically sound countries. The European super-regulator robs them of this advantage. But the East European experience in 1989 has proven that the market will ultimately prevail as it *knows* more than the regulator. In the knowledge society of the twenty-first century, the EC will not be able to halt the internationalisation of economies and the spread of information beyond the borders of Europe. If Luxemburg is forced by EC interventionism to give up its favourable climate for international banking, the banks will move to the Cayman Islands, the Netherlands Antilles or other distant places. For the citizen it takes only a push on a button to transfer money, whether to a bank in his home town, in Luxemburg or at the other side of the world.

Delors' Europe will turn out to have been an unattainable vision, but before this is realised it may have caused great damage to Europe – west as well as east. Indeed, the new EC mentality which caused the change of the founding fathers' negative concept of liberty, as expressed in the Treaty of Rome of 1957, into the positive concept, embodied in the Treaty of Maastricht of 1991, is also apparent in the attitude of the Community towards other nations, especially Eastern Europe. So long as the EEC was an instrument for true liberalisation it was an *open* organisation, welcoming new members even when this brought additional problems. When the mentality of group egoism gained hold of the Community, it acted as Socialist systems do everywhere: it closed its borders to the outside world. By the end of the 1980s the EC had become a closed instead of an open society.

European nationals applying for membership were told to wait until the group had consolidated. When the Iron Curtain fell in 1989 the EC did not welcome the liberated East European nations in and did not open its market to their goods. Instead it shut them out because it did not consider them fit to participate in the 'open' market of the EC. They were no welfare states, as they did not generate any wealth (yet) for redistribution by national or supranational welfare mechanisms.

The loyalty of Delors and the new Socialist 'Europhiles' to Europe is false. Their loyalty is only a loyalty to the welfare state. Their 'Europe' does not include ancient European nations like Poland, Hungary, Latvia and others, who have first-hand experience of what Socialism really is, and their European ideal is *conditional*. It depends on the 'social dimension' that is being given to the EC. This 'social dimension' is Delors' highest priority, endorsed by Europe's leaders at Maastricht as one of its prime objectives. The European Commission wants to push forward a *European Charter of Fundamental Social Rights*. It would guarantee, among other things, the right of every worker to be covered by a collective bargaining agreement and the creation of a European Company Statute providing for worker participation on company boards. In 1989 the French president François Mitterrand made it clear that he was not prepared to accept the frontier-free market and lift restrictions on the free movement of capital within the Community if the Community did not get its Social Charter. Mitterrand backed Maastricht: it paves the way for the 'social Europe'.

The mentality of the Maastricht Treaty of 1991 is totally wrong. Europe should be an open society, a liberal economy, driven by modest political projects. Instead it promises to be a closed society with a 'mixed' economy and ever more interventionism by the EC bureaucracy in all areas of life, driven by an impossible political project: a European monetary union by the end of the century.

Such a structure is self-defeating in our expanding world where the need for the optimisation of human knowledge is growing, an optimisation which can only be provided by the spontaneous communication channel of the open, free and extended market. The hard-line socialist regimes of the planned economy in eastern Europe could not survive in the knowledge society our world is becoming, but neither can the moderate socialist welfare regimes of the mixed economy in western Europe, not even when they act on the supranational level of the EC. This construction might implode as suddenly and completely as the regimes in the East. In this collapse the valuable achievements of supranational co-operation in Europe will also be lost. One of these is the monetary union between Belgium and Luxemburg. For the first time since 1921 this union has come under pressure from the monetary instability which threatens the EC as a result of the ambitious monetary plans of Jacques Delors.

1 June 1993   Antwerpen

The Nature of Sovereignty and Citizenship

Leslie Blake

There are two principles in contention in any new constitution for
Europe. On one hand the cornerstone of the English constitution, a
word meaning 'that by which we stand together', was defined by
Henry de Bracton, the thirteenth-century lawyer: 'The king must not
be under man but under God and under the law, because law makes
the king'. On the other hand is the earlier dictum of Roman Law
jurisdictions throughout continental Europe, defined by Justinian:
'What pleases the prince has the force of law' because 'the people
conferred on him its whole sovereignty and authority'.

In today's language, 'What pleases the European *Commission* has
the force of law' is not far from the truth. The Commissioners, headed
at present by M.Delors, have extensive law-making and executive
powers. They are the geyser from which all the directives, regulations
and decisions flow. They formulate the thinking of the Council of
Ministers. Under Maastricht there is of necessity a daunting process
of reconciliation if the European Parliament does not agree.

Sir John Fortescue noted and wrote about the two different constitutional concepts in 1470, in a delightful dialogue with the young Prince
Edward, son of Henry VI, with whom he shared exile on the Continent. His book *In Praise of the Laws of England* is really a training
manual for English pre-Machiavellian kings:

> 'For the king of England is not able to change the laws of his kingdom
> at pleasure, for he rules his people with a government not only regal
> but also political. If he were to preside over them with a power entirely
> regal, he would be able to change the laws of his realm, and also impose
> on them tallages and other burdens without consulting them; this is
> the sort of dominion which the civil laws indicate when they state that
> 'What pleased the prince has the force of law.' But the case is far
> otherwise with the King ruling his people politically, because he is not
> able himself to change the laws without the assent of his subjects nor
> to burden an unwilling people with strange imposts, so that, ruled by

laws that they themselves desire, they freely enjoy their properties,
and are despoiled neither by their own king nor any other.'

'Nor to burden an unwilling people with strange imposts': how can
this be said of the European Community? And 'consulting the people':
how is this possible when a Member of the European Parliament
supposedly represents 500,000 citizens, the majority of whom do not
bother to vote him or her into, or out of, office?

The words 'king under law, for the law makes the king' have echoed
down the centuries of English history. There was Fortescue at a time
of civil war. There was Chief Justice Coke standing up courageously
to James I's assertion that he, too, could declare what the law was,
to suit his own purposes. Coke said that the law was the golden wand
and measure to try the causes of subjects and which protected a king
in safety and peace. James was greatly offended and said that meant
he was under the law, which in his opinion was a treasonable
assertion. Coke then reminded him of Bracton's above-mentioned
words.

Charles II was left in no doubt of the implications in a sermon
preached before him at his restoration. Lord Denning had recently to
state the same principle – 'Be you ever so high, the law is yet higher'
– to an Attorney-General who refused to give his reasons to the court
for a certain course of action. And in the United States President
Nixon, who claimed executive privilege over the Watergate tapes, was
overruled by a Supreme Court which would not exclude even the
supreme executive officer from the reach of the criminal law.

The practical demonstration of the working of these two contradictory principles – 'the king is under law' and 'what pleases the prince
carries the force of law' – is this: in Britain the Queen's servants, down
to police officers, are permitted only to work within the powers
specifically granted to them by law. If they exceed those powers they
are struck down by the courts, whereas under the common law the
ordinary citizen is free to say or do anything which does not harm
another. The common law is a law based on *duties* and not on *rights*.
On the Continent, however, the citizen enjoys only those rights which
are granted to him by the state: conversely the state's servants (for
example, the prefect in France) have wide and relatively undefined
powers to do what they will, which may be questioned, if at all, by
special administrative tribunals outside the jurisdiction of the ordinary courts.

Jeremy Bentham observed that charters of prescriptive rights,
such as the European Convention on Human Rights and Fundamen-

tal Freedoms, are 'nonsense upon stilts'. (Note the plural; it is significant – freedom cannot be divided.) Edmund Burke was equally
scathing:

> 'We know that we have made no discoveries, and we believe that no
> discoveries are to be made, in morality, nor in the idea of liberty, nor
> many of the great principles of government which were understood long
> before we were born ... . In England ... we have not been drawn and
> trussed in order that we may be filled, like stuffed birds, with chaff and
> rags and paltry blurred sheets of paper about the rights of man.'

The general public may not have realised that there are already
'paltry blurred sheets of paper' in the form of a draft constitution
prepared by the Committee on Institutional Affairs of the European
Parliament (dated 3 February 1993). These are an indication of what
may come in the future and were being formulated for the 'European
Union', even before Maastricht has been ratified. Here is no 'king in
parliament', the hallmark of sovereignty in Britain and other constitutional monarchies, the product of Bracton's concept of the 'king
under law'. Rather, it is difficult to find where 'the king' lies, since
there are no less than three king-like presidents, each vying for power
and attention: the president of the Council of Ministers (shared on a
six-month basis by each member state); the unelected president of
the European Commission, elected by the European Parliament for
five years; and the president of the European Parliament.

Effectively, the president of the European Commission will be
sovereign while the presidency of the Council 'will be regulated by an
organic law'; that is, by a law adopted by the European Parliament
by a majority of (all) its members. No such regulation is imposed on
the Commission's president. The same Article empowers him, 'acting
in agreement with the Commission', 'to dissolve the European Parliament'. The Commission itself 'shall have the power to initiate
legislation'; 'shall participate in the legislative power'; and 'shall have
a *general supervisory power* regarding compliance with the provisions
of the Constitution'.

What, then, is this business of 'pooling sovereignty' in the face of
the above? It is plain that there is no intention of vesting sovereignty
in anyone other than the head of a spreading bureaucracy. The real
question is whether there is any need to introduce another level of
government into the daily life of the new European citizen.

There are other worrying features about this constitution-in-wait-
ing. Supposedly, the United Kingdom does not subscribe to the

'Protocol on Social Policy' attached to the Maastricht Treaty. Much has been made in our own Parliament of this derogation. Yet, if the draft constitution does go through as presently planned, the United Kingdom will find itself committed to so-called 'Human Rights' (set out under Article 8 of the Working Document), which include an almost complete code of social policy which the United Kingdom intends to avoid.

The words of the Working Document are bland and meaningless. Its preamble states: 'the Union shall respect the identity of the Member States which form part of the Union on the basis of the principles of solidarity, economic and social progress, subsidiarity and the active participation of local and regional authorities'. With such a bundle of basics, what is there left to respect in national identity?

If Europe wants to come together it must also do so culturally, free of governmental interference, in a way akin to the vision of both Churchill and Adenauer. The Florentine Renaissance, for a prime example, was truly European. It revitalised the life and arts across the Continent and was the source of our rich European cultural inheritance. Unfortunately there is no real evidence of a cultural revival which would feed the metaphysical rallying point that Churchill dreamed of after WW2.

If one looks back at the origins of the Florentine Renaissance itself, one finds its active agent, the philosopher-priest Marsilio Ficino (1433-99) skilfully blending the Christian tradition with Platonic teaching to provide the impetus for the modern age. Associated with him and his Academy were the most conspicuously brilliant men ever to have been assembled in modern Europe. These were the men who embodied the Renaissance: Lorenzo de'Medici, Alberti, Poliziano, Landino, Pico della Mirandola; and the artists Botticelli, Michelangelo, Raphael, Titian, Dürer and many others. Professor Kristeller has said that the whole intellectual life of Florence in his time was under Ficino's influence. At a time when religion and culture are in definite ebb across Europe, something of the same impetus may come from the recent interest in the teachings of the East, as exemplified by the works of Dom Bede Griffiths (recently deceased) who lived in India and sought the common Indo-European ground which undoubtedly exists in Christian and Vedic teachings. Essentially this consists in expressing the non-duality of peoples with their divinity.

Certainly any renewal of common humanity must be based on religious and moral statements, not on badly drafted constitutional papers intent on extending bureaucratic regulations and control over people's lives. Lord Denning said, 'Without religion there can be no morality; without morality there can be no law'. Marsilio Ficino himself wrote to lawyers in *circa* 1457, a few years before Fortescue's pronouncements, in these terms:

> 'Yet, although there appear to be many laws in the state there are not many souls. For, just as many skills and many levels of citizen do not make many states but only one if they move towards the same goal and according to similar principles, so there may be many magistrates' regulations in a city yet there is but one public law. This is the common rule of living justly, which leads to the public happiness. God and nature prepare us for this law, regulations guide us towards it, and God alone finally makes us conform to it. For from the divine law spring both the law of the stars and the law of men.'

This is the real challenge to those who would try to build a Federal Europe on the basis of bureaucracy perpetrated by unelected official-dom: whence comes their authority? Those would-be federalists who drafted the Treaty of Maastricht did not rise to the challenge. They envisaged a president of the European Commission and tried to daub him or her with a touch of sovereign legitimacy, but were not surprisingly defeated by the very absence. So they cast around and borrowed from Catholicism the idea of 'subsidiarity', the concept by which the sovereign authority is delegated to the bishops in their various dioceses. This is a religious concept which is not susceptible of adaption to political affairs in a democratic context. Christ's admonition 'Render unto Caesar ... ' has been completely ignored, even by the Christian Democrats, who are seeking to reintroduce obsolete and dangerous notions of the Holy Roman Empire. The problem remains because the concept fails to address in the context of a Federal Europe, the question 'subsidiarity from whom?'

It was at this point that the Federalists realised that they would have to play a *mass trick* on the citizens of the EC's member states, by demanding that each nation surrender its sovereign powers to the unelected Commissioners, so that the latter could hand back certain powers – as yet undefined – to the same member states as an act of 'subsidiarity'. This absurd non-ceremony could hardly be performed in public, as everyone would then see just how absurd it was. So the political leaders decided that these matters would be settled, not by open national parliaments, but by closed Inter-Governmental Conferences, and then even refused to answer why business was being done in this way.

The citizens of the EC's member states, however, began to realise

– and are realising more and more – the implications of the vast transfer of sovereign national powers to Brussels proposed by the federalists in their conspiracy of silence. (At the time of the first reading of the Maastricht Bill in the British House of Commons, no copy of the treaty was available to the public and many parliamentarians could not procure a copy either.) It is not, nor can it come to, good: when the people of Europe realise that they have been misled by their elected representatives, there will be a strong reaction. The evolution of European unity cannot be achieved by 'living unjustly', and a bureaucratic president can never assume sovereign legitimacy over so many different nations. Unfortunately, the failure to enter into honest and open debate on these fundamental issues is a sure sign of weakness – that 'what pleases the European Commission' does not meet the wishes of the people, whom they were never elected to govern.

1 June 1993   London

Sovereignty versus Federalism

John Laughland

'If we are to succeed in the great struggle of ideas that is under way, we must first of all know what we believe.'
Friedrich von Hayek, *The Constitution of Liberty*

There is a sweet irony in being asked to provide a 'positive alternative' to Maastricht: because the principled objections of the so-called 'Euro-sceptics' have been consistently winning the arguments, the pro-Maastricht case has itself become fundamentally negative. While John Major defends the treaty more for what it omits than for what it contains, Douglas Hurd is reduced to arguing that, although flawed, Maastricht is the only thing on offer. The second Danish referendum campaign, like the French one last year, was based on a fundamentally negative message: either vote for Maastricht or there will be chaos. Indeed, the increasingly vociferous denunciations of the anti-Maastricht camp as merely negative are themselves a sign that the treaty's defenders are on the defensive.

To this extent, the battle is half-won; continued rigorous defence of principles will ensure complete victory. In this sense the pro-Maastricht rhetorical demand for an alternative 'positive plan' is a trap, for the anti-Maastricht cause will not be advanced by replacing one constructivist plan for European union with another, nor even by just wrecking the treaty or its application.

This is because the mistake which the European Community has committed by wandering into the Maastricht miasma is more profound than simply signing a bad text. It is to have strayed from the fundamental principles of democracy and the rule of law. This basic fault has produced three interconnected (and basically negative) claims, to which anti-Maastrichteers should give clear and principled affirmative answers.

Independent Statehood and Political Authority are the Essential Bases for Democracy

The pro-Maastrichteers often make the negative claim that national sovereignty and federalism are either out-dated concepts, or incapable of definition. Sir Leon Brittan has compared sovereignty to medieval astronomy, 'smashed by new facts'; while he and other pro-Maastrichteers are fond of pretending that *federalism* has different meanings in Britain and on the Continent. It is strange to argue in favour of the political unification of the EC while at the same time holding that linguistic and cultural differences make it impossible to agree on even the most basic political concepts; these claims, however, are little more than a cheap way of ducking the issue.

Whatever their exact meaning, *sovereignty* and *federalism* are clearly properties of states. To deny that these terms have any meaning is ultimately to deny that there is such a thing as statehood. Indeed, one European federalist has even written that, 'The idea of the state itself has become an anachronism.' In any federation, however *decentralised* – (Germany being far less decentralised than is usually claimed) – the federal government and federal law are, by definition, recognised as having supreme authority. The question 'Do we want a federal Europe?' can be rephrased as 'Do we want the European Community to become a state?'

Indeed, national sovereignty is the defining characteristic of an independent state. It means constitutional independence. A constitution is the totality of rules for the exercise of political authority in a legal order. Political authority is the fundamental fact about any state: if the government is generally recognised as having the right to govern, then it is legitimate and has authority. A legal order is the rule of law which reposes on, and flows from, this fundamental recognition of political authority. Political authority in a democracy is based on consent, while the authority of the law comes from natural justice. In other words, those who deny the concept of sovereignty are denying the notion of authority (or legitimacy) itself. For them there is only one thing: power.

Without the recognition of a political authority – the sense that a country represents a political unit – there can be no constitution, and thus the rule of law and political participation (democracy) cannot occur. Despite the growth of international law, the political and legal order to which the overwhelming majority of people in a democracy relate is that of the nation-state. The language, the political practices, the terms of the debate and the historical and cultural frame of reference are more or less understood by citizens; national politics more easily reflect people's real concerns; national politicians are relatively accessible to the man in the street, and so on. It is in order to preserve democracy that nation-states are essential.

Political Constructivism Destroys the Rule of Law

A corollary of the confusion between power and authority is the confusion between law and legislation. The bureaucratic-administrative tendency equates the two, and thinks of government as merely the administration of society for the achievement of certain ends. A corollary of this is the view that what is important is how the law is applied, not what the law is. Unless the anti-Maastricht camp restates its principles clearly, the constructivist logic of Maastricht will continue to undermine both democracy and the rule of law

There is a widely held view in many EC countries that what is decided one day can be revoked the next at the legislator's whim. In France, for instance, politicians in Jacques Chirac's entourage happily dismiss Maastricht as nothing but a piece of paper, signed for the purpose of foreign policy expediency, and applicable or bendable at will. Even Simone Veil, the leading pro-European French cabinet minister, has repeatedly declared that what mattered in the French referendum was not the text of the treaty itself but the 'symbolic gesture of voting in favour of Europe'. Finally, Douglas Hurd, who has often demonstrated worrying ignorance of the exact contents of the treaty, brushes off his blunders by saying that 'what matters is how the treaty operates in practice, not what is written down'. It is difficult to imagine franker admissions that they both intend to bend the law, and it is astonishing that politicians with the moral and political stature of Douglas Hurd and Madame Veil can make such remarks with impunity.

Underneath, this attitude is merely our old friend economic *dirigisme* in political disguise. It is only curious that, although widely excoriated in the economic realm, its threat to the integrity of the political realm is not always understood. Just as a market needs the stability of neutral, abstract rules, so society demands that the law be respected as it is. This explains why the most ardent pro-federalists are hysterically opposed to free trade. Both Alain Peyrefitte, the senior French politician and academician and former Interior Minister under De Gaulle, and Joseph Rovan, a professor at the Sorbonne and one of France's foremost 'experts' on Germany, both luridly compared the speculators who forced the ERM to its knees in August 1993 to terrorists; both argued that the United Nations should deal with this 'new world danger' in the same way as they had dealt with Saddam Hussein!

The opposite view is that the business of government is to uphold the law, whose justice has a transcendent source. Judges and legislators *discover* the law, they do not invent it. The challenge for the anti-Maastricht camp is to reassert this classical view of law and justice, for, despite the pretence that Maastricht represents some new kind of constitutional construction, the truth is that there is nothing new in bureaucracy as an alternative to democracy. On the contrary, the struggle between the two concepts of law and government which underlies the debate is as old as political life itself: ancient history begins with the rivalry between free, law-abiding Athens and dirigiste, authoritarian Sparta.

In its modern form, however, bureaucracy as a form of government started to flourish with nineteenth-century imperialism. The administrator who rules by reports, of the kind we know and love in the EEC, was originally a feature of British India. Lord Cromer, the British Consul-General of Egypt, and one of the theorists of imperialist bureaucracy, proclaimed (like the supporters of the EEC) that it was 'a hybrid form of government for which there is no precedent'. Like many undemocratic systems, it is popular with the people who run it. One British judge in India asked, 'If despotism and bureaucracy work so well in India, may not that at some time be used as an argument for introducing something of the same system in England?'

It was also in the nineteenth century that philosophical justifications of bureaucratic rule developed, most notably in the philosophies of Jeremy Bentham in England and Auguste Comte and Saint-Simon in France. With typically hubristic pretensions at scientific certainty, the last of these declared that his theories would 'replace the government of men with the administration of things,' while Bentham devised an absurd 'felicific calculus', with coefficients of the durability and probability of the future happiness to be produced of legislation. But it is as stupid to think that an economy can be planned as it is to think that the effects of legislation on the complex organism of society could be known in advance by the legislator.

The EC's positivist and constructivist tendencies are reflected in its predilection for experts, reports, 'independent bodies', directives and its overall desire to dismantle the political and legal institutions of the Member States. It is frequently asserted that the 'European construction' is a 'constant process', but these are not only just weasel expressions to duck the obvious faults of the treaty. They are incompatible with the very notion of law itself, because it is an essential characteristic of law that an authoritative and final judgement can occur between two mutually exclusive options, a judgement whose source is justice and conformity to the law. Laws are derived from a sense of justice, not from some supposed finality: to fail to apply the law, or to bend the manner of its application according to individual cases, is to undermine the very notion of law itself.

It is no coincidence that federalists should happily use the phrase 'European construction', for they assume that the legislator is omniscient and that it is within their capacity to 'construct' a political constitution. This partly derives from the dominant rationalist political traditions on the Continent, especially in France. British notions of democracy and the rule of law are not deeply rooted in the political culture of most Continental countries, and politics there has long since haemorrhaged into the mere 'administration of things', which Engels hoped communism would produce. It is, therefore, no coincidence that France, Germany, Italy and Spain have all more or less corrupt political systems.

Nonetheless there have always been people in Britain who preferred continental-style government by experts to that of an accountable parliament. Disraeli denounced the 'Jacobinical sect in the City of London' which thought Britain's traditional political institutions archaic – an interesting anticipation of the support given to Maastricht by the *Financial Times* in our own day. Even the apparently liberal John Stuart Mill admired the centralised authoritarian administration of Prussia, which based its reputation for being a *Rechtstaat* (a state of law) on a mistaken identification of the rule of law with mere respect for the formal process of legislation, instead of having a legal and governmental system which was actually based on justice.

However, the reason why Britain has been blessed with exceptionally long political stability is that the Westminster tradition of accountability and open debate, its liveliness and effectiveness, and the history of mass political parties which are organically in touch with public opinion, have all been achieved only by an internal balance of forces, and as a result of historical, cultural and geographical factors, which are far too delicate and subtle to have been planned by any individual. It is only by maintaining the robustness of institutions such as the UK Parliament that Europe can withstand the nefarious effects of rationalistic tinkering.

Politics Must be Clear, Principled and Honest

One cannot but be struck by the explicitly anti-democratic nature of many pro-Maastricht arguments, and the contempt they express for elections and voters. The official position of the European Movement is to refuse a referendum in Britain on the grounds that the result is unpredictable and the future of the nation would thereby be put in jeopardy; the *Financial Times* declared the Westminster Parliament 'an obstacle to Britain's role in Europe'; while the Konrad Adenauer Stiftung, a German government think-tank, argued after the first Danish referendum that it was a mere protest vote and that 'if Europe does not succeed in finding *a new type of voter* then governing will became even more difficult than it is already.' Even Douglas Hurd expressed the same sentiment after that vote.

There is also a dishonest tendency among federalists to use spurious technical arguments to advance their political aims. The worst example of this is the ludicrous claim that saving transaction costs between currencies is a sufficient argument for monetary union, when the savings represented by such a step are negligible. Moreover European monetary union is a monetary reform which, like all others, is as much political as economic: as the German Bundesbank never tires of pointing out, it is a political measure which requires a single European government to be in place.

Finally, much pro-Maastricht discourse is notable for its obscurity and surreal nature, such as John Major's claim that Maastricht is not a centralising or federal treaty, or the juridical nonsense of 'subsidiarity'. Such unclarity is itself worrying, relying as it does on a contempt for truth itself.

This is not what politics should be. As the ancient Greeks understood, true politics is an art, not a science. It is a matter of judgement and courage, not something you can look up in the book. Political decisions should bear the personal hallmark of those who take them, not the anonymous stamp of an official. Being an eminently human activity, politics sometimes demands symbolic acts instead of just new committees; it is a question of public performance, like that of an actor, rather than work done in corridors and behind closed doors. True politics may be stylish, or humorous: bureaucratic rule is only ever boring, which is why in order to divert attention the pro-Maastrichteers desperately try to portray those against Maastricht as 'Boring!'

These apparently theoretical remarks have a real basis in truth and daily life, and failure to understand them explains why the

Maastricht treaty is unravelling. Since its whole logic undermines the notion of authority, the politicians who support it have none, and thus lose elections. (This goes some way to explaining the crisis of authority affecting governments all over Europe.) Qualities like courage, credibility and integrity are the very stuff of politics, as of economics. For instance, the pound's crash in September 1992 was not so much the result of technical factors, such as the weakness of the British economy and high German interest rates, but of a severe *political* vacuum: politicians all over Europe have insisted that there was no alternative to Maastricht, and it was partly the absence of any contingency plan in case of a French 'no' which terrified the markets so spectacularly.

Or again, in the summer of 1992 it was reported that John Major believed that British interest rate policy could make the pound sterling dislodge the Deutschemark from its pre-eminent position as the strongest currency in Europe. But a currency's strength does not derive simply from technical things like monetary policy. The Deutschemark is strong because it is the *German* currency: because of long-accumulated confidence in the anti-inflationary instincts of the German people, and because of the robust institutional reputation of the Bundesbank. By definition, such confidence cannot pertain to a merely technical procedure.

For this and other reasons, it is clear that defence of principles is politically successful as well as a moral imperative. Had Jacques Chirac opposed Maastricht in the French referendum he would now be President of France. Had John Major stood out against monetary union he would have won new friends in France and Germany, whose voices are not being raised (a course of action which would, incidentally, have improved Britain's standing and influence in the Community).

Honesty, then, is the best policy. Conversely, to continue in the same technocratic groove will inevitably lead to more rude shocks and spectacular failures. Last October the President of the Czech Republic, Vaclav Havel, was awarded membership of the French Academy of Moral and Political Sciences. One of the most perspicacious critics of post-totalitarian bureaucracy, he confessed that he had failed to preserve the unity of his country because he had fallen victim to the same reformist rage and frenzy which Edmund Burke had denounced in 1790, and which he identified with the Communist or Rationalist mentality:

'Detached from the human soul, the mind can only lead to violence

when it sets itself up as the principal motor of politics. The world revolts
against any order imposed by the brain, a brain which seems to have
forgotten that it is but a small part of the world's infinitely rich
architecture. The more the world is constrained by rationalist categories, the greater are the violent explosions with which it surprises
us ...

'If politicians learn to wait, in the best sense of the word, thus
showing their respect for the intrinsic order of things and for their
unfathomable depths; if they understand that everything in this world
takes its time, beyond what they expect from the world and from
History: if they also know what the world and History expect from
them, then humanity will not finish as badly as we sometimes fear.'

Conclusion:
Britain's Role – the Balance of Power in Europe

The most pernicious pro-Maastricht 'argument' is the one which says
that, whatever happens, we must be 'in Europe'. This is, at bottom,
a profoundly insular view, which assumes that the Continent is a
bloc, and that the only question for Britain is to be 'in' or 'out'. Because
the Lord Howes of this world meet only like-minded bureaucrats and
ministers, they inevitably think that the whole of 'Europe' thinks the
same way. But, as the pro-Maastrichteers may soon find out, Europe
is far more varied than the place they know from their camping
holidays. There are tensions between countries as well as within
them, and Britain has a traditional role to play with respect to this.

Britain should not be detached from Europe, for this is the
defeatist, opt-out mentality to which John Major subscribes. On
the contrary, we should be prepared to defend our principles, and
to inspire the people of Europe by so doing. Had the British
government behaved with a true European vision, it would have
vetoed both monetary union and the social chapter *for Europe as
a whole*. Both those central planks of Maastricht are already
breaking up under the pressure of economic and political realities:
had we warned Europe of what she is now discovering, and stood
out clearly against them, we would have saved Europe from the
pain and waste of the collapse of those policies, as well as gaining
prestige for having done so.

Britain is an offshore island and no amount of vacuous speech-writ-
ing can change that fact. This means that our geo-political role in
Europe must always be based on broader horizons than those of some
Continentals. This means keeping the EC open to the sea (especially

the Atlantic), open to eastern Europe, and above all ensuring a balance of power on the Continent, by preventing any one country from dominating the others. The last century of European history has revealed this traditional British preoccupation to have been one of the profoundest and most valuable insights into the way the Continent should operate: it is no coincidence that Kaiser Wilhelm II and Hitler both explictly rejected it.

8 August 1993

Paris

Nationhood Means Self-Government

Sir Richard Body

Happy the country with no history; and how much more true is that of a whole continent. Of all the continents, Europe can claim the most history; and no part of the world has been so afflicted by human conflict and the misery of one war after another. The historian who has made a study of the sorry record can look at Europe in 1993, and he can marvel at the view.

Events in Bosnia are the tragic exception, but for the first time ever in our Continent's history there is no conflict dividing her peoples. Some 600 million men and women who have for more than a thousand years found countless issues to quarrel about, now find none. A united Europe? No; but at long last we have the ground fertile enough to grow the seeds of co-operation between the nations.

It seems we have a choice. We can go ahead with the further integration of the Twelve, so that some kind of European union is established, to which other nations may or may not wish to join. No matter how many others decide to accept Brussels as the capital of the new Super-State, it is rather fanciful to suppose that either Russia or the Ukraine, to name only two, will find it an irresistible magnet. Thus, for a certainty, Europe will become divided once more: the golden chance of a new harmony will fade away.

There is, as this symposium shows, a multiplicity of ways to encourage the peoples of Europe to live together with some degree of harmony. What is important is to recognise the fundamental flaw in the supra-national intentions of the European Community. History gives us innumerable examples of federal or supra-national unions being established. Many have come and gone; and just a few survive. These survivors have one common denominator: their member-states are homogeneous; culturally and linguistically they are one with one another. True, Canada survives still, but between Quebec and anglophone provinces the divide grows, and no one can be certain for how much longer the federation will continue with Quebec a member. The one true exception, though, is Switzerland, but only because the three nations are divided into near autonomous cantons, all of the same size, so that none can dominate the other two.

The alternative for Europe then, is to steer away from this supra-national or federal course. We should look again at the Treaty of Rome. Article 189 tells us that the legislation passed by the institutions of the Community overrides any laws of a member-state. There is the rub! Section 2 of the European Communities Act, 1972 enshrines the principle in our own Statute Book; and it cannot be repealed too quickly. All member-states should do the same, and then a practical harmonious alternative will fall into place.

An Inter-Governmental Conference in itself can never do much harm and usually can achieve much good. Much needs to be done in this way if the peoples of Europe – all forty countries that is – are to live in harmony. How else are we to overcome the environmental hazards that cross the frontiers like acid rain or the biological death of the North Sea? Is it not sensible to bring down many of the trade barriers that individual member-states have erected? If we want to enjoy the right to move freely across the frontiers, to what extent can we or should we control immigration? There are a dozen grounds for holding Inter-Governmental Conferences now for cross-frontier problems that exist today.

Now when ministers with their advisers confer, they meet to consider a problem they have in common; they may talk rather too much, perhaps adjourn to eat and drink too much, but eventually they may understand one another rather better and reach an agreement. Almost always the outcome will make it necessary for new laws to be passed and more revenue raised to put the agreement into effect. In so far as any law has to be made or revenue raised, the removal of Article 189 of the Rome Treaty would require the agreement reached by the ministers to be ratified and approved by the national parliaments. In a word, the international approach would replace the supra-national.

Why is this the key to progress in a reformed Community? Lord Palmerston summed it up: 'a nation has no friends, only interests'. Any alliance between two or more nations will only endure while their interests converge. As soon as they differ, the alliance will begin to weaken, and it will founder altogether once a clash of interests cannot be repaired. A community that is purely European will find a place for every one of its nations, but they should only take part in a common policy if satisfied that it is in their own interest. The role of the Commission should be to identify the interests of various groups of nation-states; in some cases it will be possible to include all parts of the Continent; in others the majority, but in many cases a minority. What does it matter that only two or three of Europe's nations manage to attend the Inter-Continental Conference? Far better that the few should co-operate freely and contentedly than that they should meet to horse-trade, bicker and override the *bona fide* interests of minorities. And who better to judge what are the interests of a nation than the elected representatives in the national parliaments? If it is said that they are not the appropriate body to do so, it is difficult to sustain the argument for democracy.

The Gettysburg description of democracy may lack precision, but Abraham Lincoln gave us the essential flavour by adding 'government by the people'. This crucial element is undermined by the Treaties of Rome and Maastricht, for together they permit a programme of far-reaching legislation and taxation to pass from national parliaments to supra-national institutions. So many laws are passed today and so much taxation is imposed, that we are in danger of losing sight of their purpose. It is to take away our freedom.

Nothing is achieved by a new law unless it stops people doing something they want to do or coerces them into not doing what they would wish. Likewise, there is no point in taxation if we give the money willingly, and every penny taken out of our own pockets by taxation is a penny less to spend as we would wish. Anyone who breaks the law, no matter how trivial, or fails to pay the tax, no matter how trivial, faces a penalty; and the ultimate penalty (the penalty for persisting to disobey) is the loss of freedom that comes with a sentence of imprisonment. Laws and taxes are the armoury of government, without which no form of government is possible.

The test of whether or not a nation lives in a democracy depends, surely, on whether those two powers of coercion are in the hands of the people who are themselves to be coerced. The transfer of even the slightest of those powers puts a limit upon the democratic process.

So let the vision be of a democratic Europe. Her peoples should be set free to behave as they wish and spend their money as they will, with those freedoms curbed only by the laws and taxes decided by the people through their elected representatives, to whom they entrust exclusively the powers of coercion; and because they are elected, will make themselves accountable for what they do.

One last point, but it may be the most important. When a nation loses its self-government, can it keep its self-esteem? To take away from people the power to make decisions in their everyday lives is to wound the confidence they have in themselves, so it must be with the whole nation, not least a nation with a proud history of self-government.History tells us that nations only truly prosper when they have this feeling of self-esteem and self-confidence. In such periods of a nation's history come the great achievements in the arts, literature and architecture, in social cohesion and national unity, as well as in the material things as trade and industry, in engineering and scientific advancement. And the converse must be true. Take away the self-esteem, no great works of art are seen, no uplifting music is to be heard, literature and architecture decline, crime and violence is tolerated, and the material things become tawdry.

History, without a doubt, can tell us which way Europe ought to go.

4 August 1993   Palace of Westminster

Justice and the European Super-State

Martin Howe

What is it that makes the European Community fundamentally different from the many other and varied international treaty arrangements under which states co-operate together in the modern world? The answer is *Community law:* a body of legal rules contained in, or made under, the Community Treaties.

Community law penetrates into the internal legal systems of the member states and creates rights and obligations which are directly enforceable by and against businesses and private citizens. It is interpreted and ultimately enforced by the Community's own institutions, paramount amongst which is the European Court of Justice (ECJ) at Luxembourg.

That Court itself clearly defined the nature of Community law in the early and seminal leading case of *Van Gend en loos* (1963):

> 'This Treaty is more than an agreement which merely creates mutual obligations between the contracting states. This view is confirmed by the preamble to the Treaty which refers not only to governments but to peoples. ... the Community constitutes a new legal order in international law for whose benefit the states have limited their sovereign rights, albeit within limited fields, and the subjects of which comprise not only the Member States but also their nationals.'

In further cases, the ECJ has made clear that national courts must directly apply Community law in preference to their own national laws in the event of a conflict, even if this involves overriding the fundamental or constitutional law of their own country. It follows that both governmental and national legislative acts, including (in the United Kingdom) even Acts of Parliament, must be stuck down if they conflict with Community law. As Mr Justice Hoffmann said in the *Stoke-on-Trent* case in 1990:

> 'The Treaty of Rome is the supreme law of this country, taking precedence over Acts of Parliament. Our entry into the Community meant that (subject to our undoubted but probably theoretical right to withdraw from the Community altogether) Parliament surrendered its

sovereign right to legislate contrary to the Treaty on the matters of social and economic policy which it regulated.'

The interpretation of both the content and the scope of Community law is a matter ultimately not for the national courts or authorities, but for the ECJ. The ECJ performs this function either on a 'reference' from a national court (which is an appeal in all but name), or in direct actions brought against member states by the Commission. Maastricht gives the ECJ the power to impose fines on member states who fail to comply with its judgements.

The European Community thus displays the basic features of a federal state. Sovereignty is exercised within certain fields by the central authorities to the exclusion of the local or provincial authorities. Federal laws apply directly within all units of the federal state and override any local laws with which they conflict. The content and scope of federal laws, and the consequent restriction on the scope of autonomy of the lower units, are determined not by the lower units but by the organs of the federal authorities, most importantly by the supreme constitutional court or ECJ.

In this structure, the Community Treaties fulfil the role of the written constitution. Many politicians, among whom can be included the present British government, seem incapable of understanding the essential nature of these Treaties. They seem to think that they are mere political agreements, which can be respected when it suits but disregarded if it becomes convenient to do so.

In ordinary international treaties, vagueness and inadequacies of drafting give room for manoeuvre. States can, by and large, suit themselves as to how they interpret them. But with the Community Treaties, it is quite the reverse. Vagueness and gaps in the Treaties are filled in by hard-edged judgements from the ECJ. Vagueness and gaps are routinely interpreted so as to extend the scope of Community powers and to limit the residual powers of the member states.

The ECJ is entrusted with the role of deciding the extent of Community powers and therefore the extent of its own powers. What is its approach to this task? Interestingly, the Court itself has explained its approach to this role in the clearest possible terms when it compared the proposed European Economic Area Treaty with the Treaty of Rome:

'An international treaty is to be interpreted not only on the basis of its wording, but in the light of its objectives. The Rome Treaty aims to achieve economic integration leading to the establishment of an inter-

nal market and economic and monetary union. Article I of the Single
European Act makes it clear that the objective of all the Community
treaties is to contribute together to making concrete progress towards
European unity. It follows from the foregoing that the provisions of the
Rome Treaty on free movement and competition, far from being an end
in themselves, are only means for attaining those objectives.

'The EEA is to be established on the basis of an international treaty
which, essentially, merely creates rights and obligations as between its
members and provides for no transfer of sovereign rights to the inter-
governmental institutions which it sets up. In contrast, the Rome
Treaty, albeit concluded in the form of an international agreement,
none the less constitutes the constitutional charter of a Community
based on the rule of law. As the Court of Justice has consistently held,
the Community treaties established a new legal order for the benefit
of which the States have limited their sovereign rights, in ever wider
fields, and the subjects of which comprise not only the member-States
but also their nationals. The essential characteristics of the Community legal order which has been thus established are in particular its
primacy over the law of the member-States and the direct effect of a
whole series of provisions which are applicable to their nationals and
to the member-States themselves.'

In the *Van Gend* case in 1963, the ECJ referred to the member states
as having limited their sovereign rights in *limited fields,* but by the
time of the EEA Treaty case in 1991 this had changed to *ever wider
fields.* Because of the differences in the fundamental nature of the
two treaties, the Court concluded that the parts of the EEA treaty
and of the Treaty of Rome on free movement and competition, even
though identically worded, would be interpreted differently. By
reaching this conclusion, the Court was actually making a comment
on its own technique of interpreting the Community treaties, which
is to interpret them in such a way as best 'to make concrete progress
towards European union', and on the presupposition that Community
law will expand into 'ever wider fields'.

This illustrates the essential nature of the Court. It is a mistake
to compare it with a conventional, impartial law court. It sees its
essential purpose as to give judgements which favour the process of
European integration in aid of 'ever closer union'. The composition of
the court leads to this: the majority of its judges have not previously
been judges in their own countries, and many are from political
backgrounds. ECJ membership is treated as a political appointment
in many of the nominating member states.

The ECJ has a habit of giving judgements which seem to have a slender, or even non-existent, basis in the actual words of the Treaties: its conclusions are often 'inherent in the scheme of the treaties', or justified by their 'spirit'. The Court's impatience with the slowness of the process of European integration has led it to by-pass irritating restrictions which appear to be present in the actual wording of the treaties.

Thus Article 119 of the Treaty of Rome requires member states to apply 'the principle' of equal pay for equal work between the sexes. There are many different detailed ways in which such a broadly expressed general principle can be applied in practice, and Article 119 was manifestly a broad guideline directed to member states which was never intended to give rise directly to private rights as between employers and employees.

However, in 1976, the ECJ surprisingly decided that this 'principle' was directly applicable, so that it created private rights enforceable before the courts of member states. Once having said this, the ECJ was then committed in further cases to defining in detail the precise scope of the rights it had conjured into existence, including detailed application of the principle of equal pay to occupational pension entitlements.

In a field requiring carefully considered legislation, particularly covering the way in which the equal pay principle should affect accumulated pension entitlements for past services, the Court's judgements were like the work of a rogue elephant. In order to cope with some of the uncertainties created, a special protocol had to be added to the Maastricht treaty, and the ECJ itself has placed temporal limitations on the effects of its judgements, making explicitly clear that it is actually engaged in judicial legislation rather than interpretation.

In the field of free movement of goods, the ECJ in a series of cases has expanded a treaty provision designed to outlaw quotas and other similar non-tariff barriers on imports from other member states, into a general power to control all trading rules, even if they do not discriminate particularly against imported goods. Thus, even national rules on Sunday trading can stand only if they pass the Community law test of 'proportionality'. The original framers of the Rome Treaty would have been astonished if they had been told that their rules on non-tariff barriers could be stretched that far.

Yet another ECJ invention of great importance is the doctrine that Community directives can be relied on directly before the courts of member states. The framers of the Treaty of Rome plainly intended that regulations should apply directly within member states, but directives would simply oblige the member states to pass their own legislation to achieve the objectives of the directive.

However, the ECJ has progressively decided that directives can be enforced in the courts of member states against the state of 'emanations of the State'. More recently it has decided that citizens can sue member states for damages for non-implementation of a directive, a development which will have the most profound and far-reaching effects. Such a right to sue for damages in nowhere to be found in the text of the Treaty but, in the Court's view, is 'inherent in the scheme of the Treaty'.

What is wrong with such 'creative' judicial interpretation, in aid of the objective of 'making concrete progress towards European union'? The answer is that the ECJ is entrusted with the task of maintaining the proper division of powers between the Community and the member states. If it fails to act neutrally in that task, and instead acts as the fervent advancer of the powers of the Community, it destroys any democratic legitimacy for the Community's exercise of power. The people of the member states, in many cases by referendum, vote for one treaty: but what in fact they get is that treaty 'interpreted' out of recognition by the activities of the ECJ.

For this reason, the ECJ must be regarded as potentially one of the most serious threats to democracy in western Europe today: a small group of men determinedly engaged on an agenda of their own, subject to little external control or accountability.

In a constitutional order, whatever is the body charged with final interpretation, the question must arise: '*Quis custodiet ipsos custodes?*' Although reforms can be suggested which could improve the impartiality of the ECJ, there is ultimately a problem in ensuring with certainty that any body in the position of the ECJ will be self-denying enough to impose effective limitations on its own powers.

The leads to a more fundamental question: is a body such as the ECJ actually necessary at all for the proper and democratic functioning of the European Communities? Is it actually necessary to have a Community legal order which penetrates into the internal legal systems of the member states, or is it quite sufficient to operate a system of treaty obligations at inter-governmental level, not directly affecting the law courts or private citizens? The ECJ itself was pointed to see European Economic Area Treaty as achieving free movement and fair competition through bodies acting at inter-governmental level alone. GATT likewise functions without a GATT court and without a GATT legal order enforceable before the courts of its member states. Humble disputes panels operating at inter-governmental level seem to be adequate for its purposes.

The creation of a Community legal order is in fact not necessary for the creation or functioning of an outward looking, free-trading Community of nation states. Such a legal order *is necessary* for the creation of a European Super-State in which the member states are subordinate units in a federal or even unitary system. That in fact is why the Community legal order was built into the Rome Treaty in the first place, and why its removal would be the best and surest way of diverting the Community onto a path of open development suited to the turn of the twentieth century.

12 August 1993   Temple, London

What's Wrong with European Politics

Henrik Overgaard Nielsen

The Two Danish Referendums

As the Danes have voted twice on the same Maastricht Treaty, they are probably the best informed European electorate on the current issues facing the European Community. Unfortunately, this would appear to amount to rather little, as in spite of our 20-year membership of the EC, many of the facts in the referendum campaign were uncharted territory for a large majority of voters. This level of ignorance is one of the greatest problems about EC co-operation. Virtually all political activity takes place so far away from the ordinary citizens, that they are precluded from obtaining knowledge about the activities of the EC.

I should like to list some of the more important issues of the campaign. This is of course only my personal evaluation of the main themes, but I draw on the experience of having participated in daily public meetings during both referendum campaigns. The Danes are a homogeneous people. Our small country of five million has no significant groups of immigrants and we all speak the same language. We are generally proud of our democracy whose vitality is rooted in and expressed by thriving local groups.

The pro-Maastricht 'Yes' supporters in both the Danish referendums embraced all the 'big battalions', including seven out of eight political parties in the Danish parliament: the *Folketing*, employers' associations, the vast majority of trade unions, nearly all captains of industry, forty-four out of forty-six national newspapers and, of course, the whole panoply of EC political machinery.

On the 'No' side, we had one political party on the far right which has little influence in mainstream politics; four members of parliament who voted against their own parties, out of one hundred and seventy-nine MPs; a small group of campaigning trade unionists, one newspaper which came out in our favour, and one which was consistently balanced, two national grassroots movements; the June Movement (which opposes Maastricht and further European integration), the People's Movement (which recommends that Denmark should leave the EC), and finally several regionally based organisations of varying political persuasions.

The most significant issues of the campaign were whether Denmark should retain its right of self-determination. (Would the *Folketing* continue to take the important decisions on behalf of the Danish people?). And what would happen if Denmark rejected the Maastricht Treaty once more?

The EC has existed since the establishment of the European Coal and Steel Community in 1953, and its underlying vision has always been the federalist one of a United States of Europe. This vision has consistently attracted the support of a small minority of Europeans. Even now, after 18 May, it still only represents approximately 8% of Danish opinion, but it looks as though the federalist bandwagon will roll on, and as a democratically minded person this disturbs me.

How did the Establishment persuade 57% of Danes to vote for a European Union in the second referendum? The main argument employed was the same as used in other EC countries; that if we don't participate we will be left outside in the cold and none of the others will have anything to do with us. The argument has many sides. For example, Chancellor Kohl says that the movement towards European Union will continue with or without Denmark or Britain. The Danish Ministry of Finance similarly commissioned a report that concluded that if Denmark voted 'No', she would be excluded from the EC and this would increase unemployment by 50%, and the politicians and captains of industry stated that foreign investment in Denmark would dry up after a 'No' vote. There are even examples of companies that negotiated building contracts for the purpose of expansion and incorporated in those contracts a clause to the effect that if Denmark voted 'No', the contracts would be null and void. Naturally, the companies made these contracts public by means of press releases.

After the first 1992 Danish referendum, an objective survey was undertaken by the University of Aarhus of the voting patterns and motivations of the Danes. It showed that the main reason for voting 'Yes' in support of the Maastricht Treaty was the belief that Denmark's economic performance would improve as a result. The main reason for a 'No' vote was fear that the Maastricht Treaty would harm Danish democracy and transfer further powers to the EC.

There is no reason to believe that the considerations affecting the behaviour of Danish voters changed significantly by 18 May 1993, apart from an increased fear of the consequences of a 'No' vote instilled by the Establishment. Would the other EC countries have turned against Denmark if we had been obstinate enough to have rejected Maastricht once again? It is hard to say what would have happened if Denmark had voted 'No', but the idea of little Denmark changing the future development of Europe was too much for many.

In conclusion, it can be confidently asserted that the Danes voted 'Yes' for fear of damaging their economy, not because they want a European Union.

How Did We End Up Here?

The same pattern prevails across Europe – but especially in Denmark – namely, the Establishment versus the people. The Eurocrats' desire for power conflicts with the ordinary citizen's wish to control his own destiny. How has this situation come about?

There is a broad tendency for our politicians not to be in harmony with their people's wishes. This seems odd in a democratic country, where, in theory, political success for politicians depends upon giving the voters what they want. Why then do the majority of our politicians apparently wish to commit political suicide? Is it because the pressure from the political establishment is so great that no one dares to defy it? A modern version of the Emperor's new clothes? Is there really no responsible politician who dares to criticise the concept of European Union?

Can it be seriously suggested that the 51% and 43% of the Danish population who dared to defy their leaders by voting 'No' in the two referenda are all right-wing or left-wing nationalist extremists? Or is their desire for power so great that our politicians don't give a damn about the voters because once every sixth year they take over the Presidency of the Council of Ministers and consequently become the leaders of 360 million people?

Alternatively, does the reason for their behaviour lie in the fact that they have a vision of Europe which they have not been able to communicate to the voter? Do they really have a vision which cannot be understood by the voters, their countrymen? It would then, in Denmark anyway, be the first time that our elected politicians could agree on anything that looked remotely like being visionary.

The real explanation for the current gulf between politicians and people flows from the fact that we have given birth to a bureaucratic monster which is now accumulating power because they are not in contact with their own national roots but only with other European colleagues who are in the same situation. They only fraternise with each other and have no idea of what the ordinary European thinks or feels.

As a result, they have come to believe that the interests of ordinary European citizens are best served by increasing the power of EC institutions – as if the cause of 'Europe' – free trade, friendly co-operation, etc. – is identical with the interests of European bureaucrats.

The following comments are a summary of my alternative vision for the Europe of the future. The views expressed here are my own and cannot be regarded as the official view of the June Movement.

I shall discuss two subjects specifically, namely trade and the environment. I believe them both to be of primary importance in any system of European co-operation. Lastly, I shall talk about the most important political subject, namely democracy, where I feel there are great problems in the EC and in Denmark.

Environment

One of the most important concerns (within the EC) that Danes have is the environment. Pollution knows no borders and fighting it is very expensive indeed. It is therefore clear that an effective environmental policy demands international co-operation.

In the absence of such co-operation, attempts to reduce pollution will suffer from the fact that no country will want to impose extra costs on its industries in the form of more stringent environmental regulations if the only result of this is to benefit international competitors who do not require or observe the same 'green' standards.

Co-ordinated measures agreed by majority voting in the EC can be a starting point for such co-operation and can be extended to embrace other countries.

EC and international co-operation to preserve the environment should strive to set minimum standards which must be observed by everyone – whilst leaving individual countries free to impose higher standards of environmental protection. This would have the advantage of allowing different countries to engage in the war against pollution at their own pace whilst preventing unfair competition from countries whose industries are burdened by fewer or less costly environmental regulations.

The Maastricht Treaty's articles relating to the environment are a step in the right direction, but unfortunately will not help the overall problem thrown up by current EC environmental legislation.

The reason for this is that approximately two-thirds of all environmental issues are not covered by the environment articles but by the articles dealing with technical trade problems. This means that the directives are not minimal ones, setting minimum standards, but maximum ones, imposing maximum standards.

Hence, for instance, Denmark's desire to ensure that paint products should be properly labelled – so that consumers know what chemical and other ingredients these products contain – can only be translated into law with EC permission since it is defined as a technical trade problem. In Danish eyes, however, it is an environmental issue affecting working conditions since we do not want Danish painters to get brain damage because they work with organic solvents without knowing it.

If other countries do not want to protect their painters, that is their own decision, but that Denmark is not allowed to demand the sort of labelling we require is not the kind of co-operation we want or need.

Trade

Free trade has been a goal of many philosophers and economists down the ages. The principle of trading without customs barriers and unnecessary technical restrictions designed to protect home industries makes economic and political sense because it maximises prosperity and at the same time encourages peaceful relations between nations bound together by growing ties of economic interdependence.

Free trade and economic co-operation within the European Community must therefore be encouraged to the fullest possible extent, not only within Europe but throughout the world. But does the achievement of this objective really require common health and common cultural policies?

These days, especially, both the Third World and the new and vulnerable democracies of eastern Europe need free trade rather than aid. These countries don't need millions of pounds in charity but simply the opportunity to sell their goods in the industrialised world.

Everybody agrees for the time being that the new democracies in eastern Europe need help, but the EC still has a large positive trade balance with these countries because they cannot sell their commercially viable products freely in EC markets. Their way is barred by the EC's Common Agricultural Policy and other restrictions designed to prevent the EC countries' own products being undercut.

The principle of an enlightened trading policy has to be that every country makes whatever it is best at, meaning no custom barriers or subsidies. This will save taxpayers and consumers considerable sums. The whole of the Common Agricultural Policy has developed into a corrupt farce, and everyone agrees that something has to be done about it, but they just cannot agree on what.

Our trade partners outside the EC have also many restrictions and subsidies they ought to remove, but the EC should take the initiative by getting rid of its own trade restrictions. Through this we would not only get cheaper goods but also a slimmed-down bureaucracy in 'Brussels', freed from the continued need to measure the circumference of cucumbers.

Common EC policies should concentrate only on achieving free trade and environmental preservation. Other areas of co-operation should be purely European Inter-Governmental. We don't need therefore a European parliament with 518 members or a European bureaucracy interfering in our daily lives. We don't need harmonisation which means standardisation, since it is the differences between countries which make trade and travel worthwhile.

Democracy

Currently, European democracy is in a state of crisis. Scandal after scandal involving leading politicians hits the headlines, and it would appear that elected representatives have no contact with the voters any more. At the same time we see left-wing and right-wing extremists turning to violence in order to make an impact on the political process. One cannot sympathise with the methods of these extremists, but I believe the only way to rid ourselves of them is to give back to the people a belief in their ability to influence their governments.

The decision-making process is becoming more and more centralised yet the original concept of democracy was based on a public meeting attended by all those entitled to vote. There the voters' aspirations, opinions and decisions were communicated directly to their representatives, maintaining direct contact between politicians and people. At the moment, however, the voters' decisions are made after fifteen- to thirty-second soundbites, which are the equivalent of a political commercial. From the television stations' point of view, these soundbites are only there to keep the voters glued to their television sets long enough to see the 'real' commercials.

If the people of Europe are to believe in their own capacity to effect their own destiny, decisions have to be made closer to the citizen. When most EC decisions are taken behind closed doors, and – as in Denmark – it is difficult to see any real difference between the viewpoints of our politicians and political parties, the only thing that remains to interest the people are the scandals. We have to move the decisions back to the citizens so that there will be a greater encouragement to participate in political life.

This is the view of many Danes about the future of Europe. If this Danish perspective is relevant to other European countries, it might help to give us all a greater understanding of each other. At least it can be said that our outlook runs directly counter to the centralising and anti-democratic tendency currently dominating the development of the European Community.

1 July 1993   Naestved

What's Wrong with the Politics of European Federalism

Samuel H. Beer

Modern government cannot be carried on without wide and deep support among the people it serves. If the burdens are to be borne and the benefits appreciated, politicians must enjoy the active and understanding consent of the citizens. This necessity constrains the governance of the European Community as well as the governance of its member nations. One must therefore ask how it will be possible to achieve the 'ever closer union' proposed by the Maastricht Treaty despite the slight and indifferent support the Community enjoys among the European people.

The last phrase states the problem: Is there such an entity as 'the European people'?

What it means to be 'a people' is not a matter merely of sentiment, but especially of behaviour. What individuals say to pollsters does show that a majority look favourably on the union, with a minority feeling themselves to be citizens of Europe as well as of their respective nation-states. But when one looks at what the majority do, evidence of any deep commitment is scant.

Given the immense changes in power and policy that are confidently proposed, one would suppose that some great mass movement throughout the Continent had arisen to bring them about. That has usually been the case with other comparable developments of modern government, such as the rise of the welfare state in the twentieth century. That vast expansion of social services and economic regulation was accompanied and in large part impelled by the activity of social democratic political parties and their affiliated organisations. The creation of the United States of Europe would make no lesser call on the ideal and material resources of the Continent. Yet as a possible future it has found no equivalent political agent.

The European cause has led to no realignment of political parties. In the elections to the European Parliament in some countries pan-European issues have become more prominent and in a few instances political groupings, notably the European Liberals, have campaigned on common manifestos. MEP elections, however, are more accurately characterised as twelve different national elections than as a co-ordinated continental affair. For the most part the same parties that dominate national elections also put forward the candidates for Strasbourg and the support for these candidates rises and falls with the standing of these parties in their domestic forums. On average and in most countries the turnout for MEP elections has been much lower than for national elections and in the course of the three elections of 1979, 1984 and 1989 the turnout has declined. Confirming the unimportance of the choice in voters' eyes, few leaders in national politics have shifted their ambitions to the European Parliament.

What it comes to, in the words of a Canadian historian, is that 'the sense of European citizenship is weak and shallow compared to the robust sense of national citizenship' in the member states of the Community. Or as a Swiss scholar has concluded, the Europeans are still in *nation*-states, while being hardly, if at all, compatriots in Europe. In this democratic age, one way a population shows itself to be a people is by generating political activity directed at controlling the powers governing it. The cause of European union has produced no such grass-roots, cross-national effort. In short, there is no 'European people', but as stated in the preamble to the Treaty of Paris of 1951 from which the Community grew, 'several peoples'.

What difference does it make whether Europe is one people or several peoples? Specifically, what difference does it make to such centralisation as is proposed by the Maastricht Treaty? The experience of the Americans in establishing their own United States suggests a quite definite answer.

In our beginnings we too faced the problem of reconciling unity and diversity, and not infrequently the champions of European union have thought that they could follow the American example. The most vivid expression of this hope that I can recall was voiced by one of our graduate students some years ago. A Dutchman, he strongly supported closer union and, around the time the Strasbourg parliament was being formed, he and I occasionally talked about its long-term significance. One day in 1979 after the first meeting, he rushed into my office full of enthusiasm and poured fourth his vision of this event as the decisive moment when the democracy of Europe, like the American Continental Congress in 1774, would meet and establish its United States.

In his passion for a united and democratic Europe he was not misguided in looking to that body for a promising analogy. Speaking through the Congress the Americans first called themselves 'one people' when they declared their independence in 1776. They demonstrated their union, however, far more emphatically by what they did than by what they said.

The delegates who met in Philadelphia in 1774 were not representatives of the established governments of the thirteen colonies. They could not have received that sanction since in nearly all colonies, the governor, a royal appointee, would have blocked the action. The Congress, therefore, was a revolutionary body, chosen in various extraneous institutional ways which made them delegates not of governments, but of voluntary associations of individuals. There were the whigs, a political party constituting a continent-wide movement committed to a common political outlook and connected by a network of communication and action. The whigs did not include everyone. Slaves, Indians and women did not vote and, then, there were also the tories, a substantial minority, who actually preferred to be ruled by a king. A good majority of the politically active population, however, the whigs claimed to speak for 'the people', or as they sometimes said, perhaps recognising their partiality, 'the *good people*' of the several colonies.

This self-created people was the constituent power which created and shaped the new republican state. Acting through the Continental Congress, this people conducted the agitation against the British, authorised the rebel colonies to form themselves into states, declared the independence of these states collectively, and went on to fight the war and make the peace. They were not monolithic in their opinions. Their frequent division into 'conservatives' and 'radicals', however, actually helped them arrive at a balanced and practical consensus on what to do and when to do it. This was one revolution that did not devour its own children. Moreover, when the first constitution they gave themselves, the Articles of Confederation, proved to be weak and oppressive, this people again showed their capacity for united action by giving themselves a new structure of government, the Constitution of 1787-88.

The leaders in the drafting and adoption of the Constitution were centralisers. They reduced the powers of the states and aided those of the general government, especially in military, financial and economic matters, framing these grants of power, moreover, in such a way that their application could be extended as new needs arose. They created new institutions which would enable the power of the American people as a whole to be brought to bear on the action of the general government, not only in its establishment but also in its daily operation. They left no doubt as to the ultimate source of authority in the nation, declaring in a celebrated Preamble that 'We, the People of the United States do ordain ... this constitution.'

At the time, this nationalist conception of the union was bitterly contested by a powerful minority in whose view sovereignty originated and permanently remained in the separate peoples of the several states. The Constitution therefore should and could only be established by agreement or compact among the states as had been done when the Articles of Confederation were adopted. Each state was considered to have an 'individuality' which made it the primary political community for its particular people. Their interests therefore would permit and require only a severely limited delegation of power to the centre. Retaining sovereign power, each state was the final judge of any infraction of the compact by other parties to it and also of what action should be taken in response, including nullification, interposition and ultimately secession. Looking at the Constitution from this point of view, the famed patriot Patrick Henry said that the Preamble should read, 'We, the States', not 'We, the People', a usage which he regarded as 'pernicious, impolite, and dangerous.' This compact theory, needless to say, was the ideological foundation of the attempt of the southern states to secede which precipitated the Civil War in 1861.

According to present-day usage, both the national and the compact theories are 'federal' in the sense conventional in jurisprudence and political science that each theory provides for an allocation of power between levels of government sanctioned by an exceptionally authoritative legal instrument. On this much the two theories agree, although for the compact federalists the basic law, the Constitution, is a mere treaty among equal states, while for the national federalists it is the command of the sovereign power. On this understanding, any federal state, whether based on the less centralised compact or the more centralised national model, is constitutionally decentralised, as compared with a unitary state such as Britain in which a central government controls local governments, and indeed creates them and gives to them and takes away from them their powers.

Before the debate over the Constitution, however, the term federal, then spelled 'foederal', referred to the compact model, the word itself coming from the Latin *foedus*, meaning 'treaty' or 'compact'. Then as now, however, controversy led to confusion in the use of words. For whatever reason, from which the search for political advantage is not to be excluded, the centralising nationalists appropriated that term for their cause, happily taking the name 'Federalists'. Their opponents accordingly were known as 'Anti-Federalists'.

For the friends of a 'federal' Europe today to be identified as the centralisers echoes that earlier American usage. When I dip into the current controversy in Britain as reported in Hansard and the press, regardless of terminology, the main theses of the two opposing positions, 'a federal union' versus a 'loose alliance', continually remind me of the national and the compact outlooks. To invoke the American experience, however, also directs attention to the importance of grass-roots democratic politics to the prospects of closer union.

Discussion of the 'democratic deficit' of the Community is usually limited to the need to enlarge the powers and enhance the activity of the Strasbourg parliament. Critics sometimes also deplore the lack of that greater participation which would give the European voters control over what is done at Brussels. What is missing from these critiques is the recognition that democracy not only gives power over government, but can also mobilise the consent which strengthens government and paves the way to closer union.

The movement toward closer union is commonly treated as if it resulted solely from bureaucratic leadership and the high politics of national statesmanship. My argument has been that further integration also must have a foundation in grass-roots politics. Such participation, however, cannot be brought into existence merely by giving a set of individuals the right to vote for members of a parliament. Those individuals must also be moved by ideas and sentiments that impel them to use this instrument of self-government and to support its outcomes. That means having opinions, expressing them in political organisations, taking part in public debate, voting in elections and accepting the disappointments of defeat as well as seeking the joys of victory. The peoples of the democratic nation-states of Europe continually demonstrate this capacity in their domestic politics. If there is to be a strong federal union, this population as a whole must generate a commitment comparable in sentiment and behaviour to the nationhood of its member states. Only a European people can create a United States of Europe.

14 July 1993   Boston

What's Wrong with British Elitism

Eric Elstob

Having thought about the wide subject matter of this book, I decided that the one topic that no one else would write about, perhaps because they do not realise that it even exists, is the peculiar attitude of the British elites to the rest of the world. It is an attitude of remarkable self-sufficiency, a sense of detachment and also a lack of interest. When Bacon wrote that 'no man is an island' he did not allow for his fellow Englishmen. In the most general sense this attitude might not particularly matter in relation to America or Japan; but the facts of geography should at least compel the British elites to pay attention to Europe. Yet the member of the British establishment today is less cosmopolitan than his eighteenth- or nineteenth-century forebear. He may have travelled more; but what he has seen is airports, hotels, offices, art galleries and beaches. Unlike the young man of the age of enlightenment on his Grand Tour he has not stayed for months in the homes of his peers abroad, sharing their interests and learning their concerns. I know of one senior British businessman who boasts how, in a geisha house in Tokyo, he sent his sashimi back to be fried. What the geisha thought, being from that class of remarkable, well-travelled, well-informed, well-educated women, would be amusing to know.

Europe impinges on Britain in a fundamentally different way to America or the Far East. Britain's trade patterns should make this obvious to anyone; but it is probably more obvious to the businessman from another continent than it is to the British elites, certainly to the elites not directly involved in commerce. There is a subconscious scepticism among the British about foreigners. 'Can any good thing come out of Nazareth?' Or indeed the rest of the planet? It is worth trying to analyse what lies behind this scepticism, as the innate hostility to anything foreign affects profoundly both British society and the British economy.

A prime reason must be the tone of British education. The way history is taught here presents mainland Europe as a kind of football pitch for military away matches – (the British very sensibly do not play home games in that particular sport.) This explains the atmosphere of the Heysel Stadium murders in 1985. Even then the history is selective. For every thousand Englishmen who know about the battle of Agincourt, only one will know Bouvines – where their home side suffered an away-defeat!

The legacy of the twentieth-century wars in Europe, when the British were effectively cut off from the mainland for thirty years by fighting and the Great Depression, is that at least two generations of the British elite had no opportunity to travel normally in Europe, and had their perception shrunk to France and the Low Countries, with Germany and the Slav states as complete outsiders.

It is a truism to refer to the fact that Britain is an island. However, interesting the phrase 'continent-isolated' may be as an example of the philosophical concept of phenomenology, in the real world it is just silly. How many Londoners appreciate that it is now possible for them to reach Prague in a long day's drive? Land frontiers are always permeable; and the motor-car effectively abolishes them unless reinforced by physical barriers like an Iron Curtain. Psychologically the bullet-train from London to Paris will be very important as it will make the journey as simple as going to Edinburgh. Perhaps this is the subconscious reason why the British elite has shown such crass critical path analysis over the rail-link to the Channel Tunnel.

Another powerful barrier is language. Although logically one European language should be no more divisive between people than another; the fact that English has become the Latin of the modern world means that we are spoilt to a degree that we do not realise. (One has to ask in passing what British children do in the time saved when young Frenchmen and Germans are learning English. There is no marked British superiority in other subjects.) When a continental dinner party has to talk English, the result is to leave the Englishman as a tourist not a guest, cutting him off from what really interests and matters to the rest of the table. How often in an evening in Paris or Munich I have noted the surprise of my fellow guests that we are using the local language, only to hear it rationalised as 'Ah; but you had one European parent!' – my mother was Swedish.

The result is that the British elites are largely ignorant of the concerns, policies, ambitions of their equivalents in mainland Europe. In the modern world this is economically very dangerous. Although the trend towards economic consolidation started in Europe, it was the inevitable result of modern transport of large-scale manufacturing and of global marketing. North America has formally acknowledged this with the creation of NAFTA. In the Far East the same consolidation is taking place informally, in deference to the political history of the region during this century. In the twenty-first century the existence of these three economic blocs is as certain as anything can be in human affairs. The relationship of Britain to this tri-polar world will be crucial for her prosperity.

Economic integration will lead inexorably to a greater degree of political and social integration. Anything else would be at the very least profoundly undemocratic. The history of the Exchange Rate Mechanism is instructive. What should have been a rational discussion was drowned by political shouting – to be fair, not only by the British. The successful change in policy forced on the United Kingdom by the currency markets in September 1992 is being presented as a proof of the virtues of non-co-operation which has the effect of reinforcing the impression among the other countries of Europe that the British are solely negative towards anything that hints at closer co-operation with their fellow states. There is nothing wrong with the ERM in itself, except that the Deutschemark is in it. So long as the German economic cycle is out of sync with the rest of Europe as the result of reunification, Germany will naturally need the opposite monetary policy to everybody else.

There is an element of truth in this among many of the British elite. Some of the arguments in favour of insularity are bizarre. There may conceivably be a risk of rabid rabbits crossing to Kent through the Channel Tunnel; but in that case the French are being irresponsibly casual. Once the Tunnel is open it is also almost inevitable that sooner or later a French politician is going to be bitten by Lord Tebbit. Why dirty beaches should be seen as the touchstone of national sovereignty is not immediately obvious.

For any analysis to be useful it must shed some light on the future. What does the British elite really want? This is an extremely difficult question to answer, because this elite is so divided within itself. There are broadly three groups.

To the first, membership of the European Community is quite simply a mistake. It is politically wrong because it allows foreign influences into British life; and it is economically unnecessary, because Britain can be an off-shore industrial state like Hong Kong. Admittedly the GNP per capita of Hong Kong is now greater than that of Britain, but the conclusion begs the question of Hong Kong's relationship with China.

The second group consists of the reluctant realists, who accept some inevitable British integration into Europe, but hope and expect that it can be postponed for their lifetime. This is the old doctrine of unripe time; although I have heard an interesting variant that it is too late to take a step, or the doctrine of overripe time.

Lastly there are the so-called pro-Europeans who see both commercial and possibly political advantages in Membership of the European Community, and accept that in order to mould and optimise the EC it is necessary to do it from within.

In the coming years the age profile of these groups will be a key determining factor in European unity. The younger generation of elites, both in Britain and on the mainland, take take the *acquis communautaire* for granted. They study at foreign business schools, work for multi-national companies, travel casually across their continent. To them the idea of needing a visa to cross the Channel is quite simply inconceivable. Also the generation at home and abroad who in their hearts think of Britain as the heroic saviour of the open society from totalitarianism is dying. Their grandchildren are just as likely to see Britain as sulky and negative – not a commercially useful reputation to have.

There is evidence that the attitude of the British elites is changing. The public image of the European Community is of necessity bad since national politicians put all the blame for necessary but unpopular policies onto Brussels. The existence of a plausible scapegoat must have achieved significant improvements in the lives of European citizens by accelerating desirable but initially unpleasant reforms. However, the EC has now existed long enough for tangible benefits to be identified and these will be apparent to the younger elites.

The cost to Britain of her ambivalence remains. The choices are straightforward. From the point of view of material prosperity a full commitment to the European Community is best. Although it is a perfectly logical choice for Britain to become like Hoxha's Albania, totally cut off from the world around her, it is scarcely a rational one. Fortunately, the British are a rational rather than a logical nation.

When I submitted this piece thus far to the editor, he informed me that Lord Tebbit was a fellow invitee to the symposium! I put my trust in the British sense of humour, Norman.

The editor also reminded me that I had perhaps overlooked an obvious role model of my would-be non-insular Briton. I must confess I felt a twinge of chagrin, even embarrassment, at my glaring omission. It so happened that the editor and I were brought up after WW2 in the same West Country market-town and I need look no further than the exemplary European business career of the late Herbert Hill of Birfield Limited, acquired by GKN in 1966.

Having performed valuable work in the economic recovery of Rhineland-Westphalia in 1945, Hill returned to the Continent in the early 1950s with Birfield, an engineering group based on Hardy-Spicer in Birmingham and Laycock in Sheffield – hence Birfield. Hill persuaded the German and French to co-operate to build a European motor components business, namely the late Walterscheid Mueller of Dusseldorf and Robert Glaenzer of Paris. Hardy-Spicer developed the front-wheel drive and Hill involved Issigonis to design the ubiquitous Mini in 1959, the first transverse-mounted engine design. In the early 1960s Birfield Transmissioni S.p.a. was established as a successful manufacturing implant in Brunico, northern Italy. Next came a tie-up with Dana Corporation of America. Hill was expanding eastwards into Czechoslovakia too; unfortunately Dubcek was ousted, but not before Birfield's chauffeur had driven the Rolls Royce to Moscow for the 1966 World Expo. Today, GKN is the leading world supplier of automotive drive components; Glaenzer-Spicer in France, until recently led by Gerard de La Passe who was recruited by Hill nearly forty years ago, succeeded in licensing the Japanese car industry in the late 1980s to realise the global opportunity.

Then the editor cited the example of Bill Cash, MP, the well-known 'Euro-rebel'. I had not realised that he had worked with certain leaders in France, Germany, Spain and Denmark and has now founded the new *European Foundation*, a pan-European think-tank, to generate debate and policy right across Europe. Would Herbert Hill have approved of Bill Cash's vision of Europe, free of Maastricht, I asked. 'Most definitely', replied the editor. 'Birfield was built up across Europe when Britain was not even in the common market. The British led the way and persuaded the French and Germans to co-operate as a matter of practical and mutual advantage – the principle of mutual recognition. And Birfield weren't the only ones; what about Redland and British Aerospace?'

Britons like the late Herbert Hill and the quick Bill Cash are the rare cosmopolitans of the British elite, who have done their country great service. They need to be heard, and listened to, in the next stage of the European debate which is now beginning.

4 June 1993   City of London

Alors, Delors! Deceiver or Dunce?

Lord Harris of High Cross

In the bewildering clash of parliamentary argument over Maastricht, there are just a few statements that might carry wide, if not universal, accord among the *cognoscenti*. They remained obscured partly because the media find polarisation more newsworthy and partly because the partisans on both sides prefer not to dwell on things they agree about publicly for fear of giving points to their opponents.

Thus even the fiercest antagonists might agree (privately) that there is an elevated, long-term case to be made for the pure vision of European political unification. For their part, protagonists must acknowledge (privately) that the Treaty on European Union is supported enthusiastically by their continental allies as a further stage in 'the process' of building a unitary federal state complete with European citizenship, a single currency, uniform economic policies and a common foreign and defence policy.

If even the strongest British supporters of Maastricht in both Houses of Parliament have studiously refrained from acknowledging this reality, it is because of another fact which again few would question, namely that public opinion is still overwhelmingly on the side of the sceptics. Finally, sceptics themselves would have to admit that such opposition is based on ignorance buttressed by instinct rather than deep knowledge of Maastricht.

Against this background, I would say that of all the battles we fought in twelve days of debates in the House of Lords, the defeat of the referendum – and with it the prospect of an open public debate – was an historic missed opportunity. Paradoxically, that triumph of the Euro-ruling class may prove the undoing of their long-run hopes for European political union. Even before the Bill was through Parliament, the new Belgian Presidency blurted out that Maastricht 'is not the end of the road; it is just the starting point.' Plainly, 'the centre of Europe' to which Douglas Hurd, like his predecessor Geoffrey Howe, and their apparatchiks at the Foreign Office so desperately aspire, will continue to prove a strenuous battlefield. John Major, or his successor, will again find himself struggling against the federalists, corporatists, socialists, protectionists and regulationists, not forgetting M Delors' flat-earthers. It would have been easier for our representatives to fight Britain's corner if they had been sure he had the backing of an informed public.

Having learned so much myself from the Lords' debates, I had no doubt that the strongest case for consulting the people was that the resulting campaign would have likewise educated the electorate on the key issues. It cannot be denied that the European project has so far been the handiwork of deals struck in secret sessions between a precariously narrow political elite in all twelve countries. In Britain the collusion of the three front benches has denied a strong voice to sceptics. In the Lords, among Brussels placemen, pensioners and apologists, there were pairs of former Commissioners batting for both Labour and Liberal Democrats (respectively, Lord Richard/Clinton-Davis and Jenkins/Thomson now joined by Dahrendorf) with Lord Cockfield fielding all round the wicket for the Tories, plus several past and present MEPs whom Lord Stockton declared his surprising ambition to join.

The amendment calling for a 'consultative referendum' was moved at Report stage by Lord Blake, the respected Oxford academic who was elevated in 1971 by none other than Edward Heath and who was once described as 'the nearest thing the Tories have to a written constitution.' His central argument was that the Treaty introduced 'irrevocably and irreversibly' significant constitutional changes.

So far from treating this weighty testimony with the solemnity Tories might be expected to show for constitutional pleadings, Government spokesmen followed Labour, first in denying that Maastricht was an innovation, secondly in downgrading the constitutional role of the second chamber and, thirdly, in declaring the referendum to be alien to our constitution (despite its use four times in the last twenty years). Thus, having been forbidden to perform its everyday revising duty by tidying-up loose drafting – for fear of the Bill going back to the Commons and Bill Cash – the Lords were treated to solemn warnings from Ministers against appearing to challenge the elected House by daring to exercise its well-established role of giving 'the other place' pause for second thoughts. So far from behaving undemocratically, Lord Blake explained that a vote for his amendment provided 'a golden chance to show that the peers are in favour of the people.'

The most cynical argument against the referendum was that Maastricht had been supported by massive majorities in the Commons. Even peers who lacked friends in 'the lower house' must have read about the unprecedented whipping, culminating in physical intimidation, necessary for the Government to scrape through one key division by three votes.

Of course, things are managed with more decorum in the Lords. Yet the crushing defeat of the referendum by 445 votes against 176 was procured only by support from Labour and Liberal Democrats, reinforced by a rare three-line whip commanding Tory back-benchers: 'Your Lordship's attendance, unless inadvisable for reasons of ill-health, is therefore essential.'

The sad truth is that once the Prime Minister had pledged his personal survival on getting the Maastricht Treaty through, his Government was committed to employing all means, fair and foul, to carry the day. Its central strategy was to play on the fear of Britain being consigned by its partners to outer darkness on the 'periphery' or 'margins' of Europe, despite the fact that Treaty changes require unanimity so that the other eleven could not depart from the *status quo* without our agreement.

The Confederation of British Industry obligingly lent its support to orchestrating the Government line. Thus before the grand debate opened, members of the House of Lords received a circular from the President of the CBI which started from 'prime concern' for the Single Market, and went on to express hostility to Brussels for its 'dirigiste philosophy ... Napoleonic edicts ... arrogance', before playing on the fear factor: 'This is no reason to abandon the Single Market *as the so-called Europe-sceptics would wish.*' I emphasise those words because there never was any question of abandoning the Single Market. Indeed, the real threat to our shared goal of creating a truly competitive market comes from the long visible collectivist social and economic philosophy of the Commission and the European Court of Justice (ECJ) which Maastricht powerfully reinforces.

The game was unintentionally given away at the opening of the second reading by Lord Cockfield who, as the Commissioner responsible for the 1992 action programme, knows more than most what he is talking about. He seemed to take fiendish pleasure in teasing Lady Thatcher (sitting almost next to him) that in 1983 she had signed at Stuttgart a 'Solemn Declaration on European Union' which committed all twelve to 'a united Europe ... the European Social Charter ... convergence of economic development ... progress towards Economic and Monetary Union ... an industrial strategy ... transfer of resources to less prosperous regions ... ' and much other generalised mischief. For Lord Cockfield, Maastricht simply dotted the i's and crossed the t's on 'policies to which the Community has long since been committed.'

This doctrine is all the more alarming in the light of the special role and method of the European Court sitting in Luxembourg as the supreme legal authority with power to hand down judgements that over-rule national legislation and domestic courts. In the dreaded Stuttgart Declaration, it has 'an essential role to play in progress towards European Union, by securing compliance with, and *development of,* Community Law.'

Unlike British courts, its judgements take into account the underlying objectives of the Community, including what it explicitly expressed as 'making concrete progress towards European units.' As the standard textbook by Lasok and Bridge has explained: ' ... references to the spirit or the aims of the Treaties enable the Court to fill the gaps in the system ... (It) consciously acted ... as an architect of European integration.' Worse still, of the thirteen judges, it transpires that some were previously politicians and only three had previous judicial experience. How can the British Government hope that such an innovative Court will scrupulously respect Mr Major's boasted 'opt-outs' from either Monetary Union or Social Chapter when both fly in the face, not only of the spirit, but of the letter of earlier undertakings?

Such a hope becomes even more bleak in the light of the political/economic philosophy of the Council. Even without the dogmatic Catholic social thinking of Jacques Delors, the cards would be stacked against the competitive market economy of British classical liberal thinking which finds no echo on the Continent. The dominant tradition of France, Germany, Italy, Spain and other partners has long been corporatist, preferring co-operation and consensus to competition and contention. A small illustration from the political arena was that the 200 hours our MPs spent vigorously debating the details of Maastricht were far more than the total of all the eleven parliaments.

Even worse, the Commission has exclusive power to originate directives and regularly exploits the Single European Act (SEA) to bring social measures before the Council under Qualified Majority Voting (QMV) in order to defeat the British veto. The best-known example of the Commission's deviousness was the attempt to enforce the 48-hour working week directive through Article 118a of SEA which is supposed to be confined to 'Health and safety at work.' (Citizen Delors boasts of working fourteen hours a day!) Instead of simply denouncing such a ruse, leaving the Council meeting, and appointing tougher permanent representatives for next time, the

British minister sought to water it down and then appealed to the ECJ, whose verdict is now grimly awaited with no certainty of a just ruling. The prospect of winning this and other cases has worsened under Maastricht by the Prime Minister agreeing to enlarge the objectives of the treaty by including 'Social Cohesion', which will inevitably bring the Social Chapter into the UK by the back door. Already, on 2 August, the European Court has adjudicated unlimited damages for sex discrimination at work.

An even more revealing example of duplicity is the Commission's Directive on employment conditions for part-time workers which has been brought forward under Article 100a that justified QMV to speed the removal of barriers and complete the Single Market. Although this Article specifically excludes, *inter alia*, 'the rights and interests of employed persons', the Directive aims to impose on part-time workers proportionately similar benefits to full-timers in pensions, holidays, dismissal and seniority allowances.

The devious justification offered for using Article 100a single market powers is five-fold as follows. Firstly, part-time working is increasing; secondly, arrangements vary widely between countries; thirdly, such variation risks distorting competition; fourthly, differences in treatment affect indirect costs; and so fifthly, to the spurious conclusion: 'it is necessary to approximate the relevant national rules in order to eliminate the disparities which give rise to distortions of competition'.

As with so many Commission efforts at *harmonisation*, this argument beautifully exposes the favourite Delorean 'level playing field' as more akin to delirious flat-earth economics. Does not all trade between companies, districts or countries, follow from variation in the costs of capital, labour, land or location, due to natural or acquired comparative advantages? *Mon pauvre Jacques*. He has got it back to front. Is he trying to deceive or is he a dunce? True, free trade tends to approximate costs by the simple process of spreading the products of localised or efficient resources more evenly throughout the market. But that is the *ex-post* outcome, not the *ex-ante* condition of competition.

A contemporary example should bring the analysis to life. When I first studied economics at Cambridge, union leaders regularly denounced imports from Hong Kong as 'social dumping' by capitalists who paid their workers a handful of rice a day. Fifty years later, despite restrictions on exports from the far east, imperfectly free trade has enabled Hong Kongers to trade up until their wages are now above those of some European countries.

The logic of this Brussels distemper of *dementia delorsia* would be to impose a common European bedtime so as to prevent all those industrious foreigners stealing a march by working through the night. My friends have begged me to suppress this little jest in case the humourless German Commissioner Bangemann – remember the Commissar against prawn-flavoured crisps and for uniform condoms? – gets to hear of it. He would presumably start pondering whether 10.30 or 11pm would be the best time to close Europe down – in the interests of health, safety and/or undistorted competition you understand.

The example of the Commission's attempts to impose social policies by majority voting raises severe doubts about how long our opt-out will survive. No less serious is the question-mark over our exemption from the stage three of monetary union. Lord Tebbit asked repeatedly whether HMG was in favour of the principle that a single money, eventually and irreversibly, should replace all national currencies; but answer came there none. The best the Minister could say was that they did not have to make up their mind about such matters until after the appointed day in 1997 or 1999. Alas, there are at least two possibly fatal flaws in so facile a stance.

The multiplying critics, having been proved right by the collapse of the ERM, had warned us about the damage to the whole of Europe. Under the title of 'optimal currency area', technical economic analysis suggests that countries using a single money must be of similar structure, at a similar stage of development and progressing at similar rates of growth. It could succeed for the same reason that a three-legged race can work if the partners tied together are of like size, strength and speed, and so long as they are heading in the same direction. In the absence of such conformity, the monetary policy appropriate for the most prosperous economies will exert contractionary pressures on the laggards, just as *within* Britain since the 1930s declining industries condemned Scotland and the North East to the status of depressed areas calling for large and continuing subsidies.

It is to tackle such uncomfortable realities that the Maastricht Treaty is full of talk about convergence and cohesion funds. But the presumed time-table of 1997 or 1999 bears no relation to the protracted period of adjustment that economic history has shown to be necessary, especially in times of rapid technical progress and unprecedented change in trading, investment and other relationships around the world. Even if an optimum currency area could be identified, it would swiftly be disturbed by events that affect some parts differently from others. The disruption caused by German reunification is only a special case of this general, inescapable proposition.

So monetary union for Europe is one of those flights from reality that is almost certain to bring a fearful reckoning. If anyone asks how leading politicians can take the project so seriously, he should be reminded of the Keynesian-collectivist consensus on incomes policy, state industry, union power, mixed economy, subsidisation and welfare state that held all parties in thrall till Margaret Thatcher broke the spell in 1979.

There is a second possibly fatal flaw lurking behind the confident ministerial assurance about Britain's opt-out from stage three of EMU. The Treaty is perfectly explicit in requiring countries that stay outside to peruse economic convergence as a qualification for joining the ERM and meanwhile to treat their economic and exchange rate policy 'as a matter of common interest'. But already, before Maastricht has come into effect, Delors and others have criticised Britain's floating currency as giving an unfair competitive advantage to our exports by making them cheaper in terms of other national currencies. Again, there is a delicious disregard for elementary economic analysis which teaches that one effect of an increased sale for 'cheap' British exports would in due time be to raise demand for our currency and therefore its price, thereby rendering our exports less cheap.

Even if Brussels glimpsed this commonsense analysis, the Treaty on European Union has as its centrepiece the goal of economic, political and *monetary union*. Since the dunces will not grasp such economic verities – which are indeed scorned by the constructivists – any effort for Britain to remain indefinitely outside the collapsed ERM can be argued by our partners only to put them at a competitive disadvantage, but also to put us in plain defiance of our solemn and repeated undertakings. At the very least we will be exposed to unceasing pressure to join fully in stage two as a necessary preliminary to putting ourselves in a position to decide on the opt-out. If we continued to delay and prevaricate about our intentions, it is almost certain we would be taken to the European Court, either by the Commission or another member state, and it is difficult to see how we could deny not having taken EMU seriously. If the Court found against us, we might regret our boasted part in arming it with the new power to impose unspecified fines on future defaulters, which we had assumed would principally be Italy!

The more I have contemplated Britain's future in Europe after Maastricht, the less can I find aught for our comfort. Leaving aside the undiminished scandal of the CAP, the prized Single Market is already faltering from cloying *harmonisation* and costly social regulation, which the imperialism of the Commission and Court will seek to intensify. The accumulated *acquis communautaire* (le rag-bag) will obstruct enlargement to the east. And Delors' only answer to the prospect of increasing competition from China and the Asian tigers is to propose 'a global social charter'!

It is difficult to disagree with the Tory cynics who have supported Maastricht on the basis that it won't happen, except that they say, 'Don't worry'. I have increasingly concluded that unless we can restore the primacy of the competitive market in Europe, we should instead re-learn the Hong Kong lesson of prosperity through unilateral free trade.

2 August 1993   Barnet

Economic Realities Facing Europe

Brian Reading

Liberalisation versus Regimentation

Maastricht is a blind alley. Most people recognise this. Many politicians don't, but they led Europe into it and will be the last to admit it. They made economic and monetary union an objective in its own right, then chose convergence criteria to achieve it, framed exclusively to ensure that the planned single currency would be as sound as Europe's soundest, rather than as debauched as some members allow their currencies to be. Europe's governments and central bankers looked back to the inflationary 1970s, believing that the problems of the past must also ineluctably be those of the future.

The Community's founding fathers thought in similar terms, but justifiably so. Their vision of Europe's future was formulated with recent and bitter memories of the 1930s economic depression, high unemployment, national economic rivalry culminating yet again in the devastating military conflict of WW2. They sought rising prosperity to eliminate national rivalry and domestic discord. They liberalised rather than regimented.

All post-war European governments shared the same objectives: rapid growth, low unemployment and equitable societies in which the old, sick, poor and jobless shared fairly in national prosperity. Price stability was given no special priority. Inflation was not perceived to be a peacetime problem. Hitherto it was always a wartime phenomenon, or had followed in its aftermath, especially amongst defeated nations (see Chart 1). Rising prosperity was the antidote to poverty, inequity, fascism, communism, nationalism and, above all, war. Liberal trade between nations was the recipe for rapid growth, the welfare state its consort to ensure domestic social harmony. This was the social compact post-war European governments offered their people, and it was widely popular.

So what went wrong? The burdens imposed on those who produce the wealth of nations, by offering tolerable living standards to all those unable to contribute (mostly through no fault of their own) has escalated to levels never originally envisaged. A wedge of taxation

Chart 1: World Inflation since Cromwell

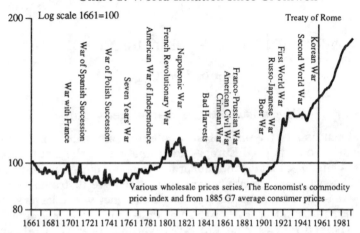

Log scale 1661=100

200

Treaty of Rome

War with France
War of Spanish Succession
War of Polish Succession
Seven Years' War
American War of Independence
French Revolutionary War
Napoleonic War
Bad Harvests
Crimean War
American Civil War
Franco-Prussian War
Boer War
Russo-Japanese War
First World War
Second World War
Korean War

100

Various wholesale prices series, The Economist's commodity
price index and from 1885 G7 average consumer prices

80

1661 1681 1701 1721 1741 1761 1781 1801 1821 1841 1861 1881 1901 1921 1941 1961 1981

has been driven between the value of output and the rewards to those
who produced it. Chart 2 shows how large it has become. In Germany,
for example, the average hourly cost of employing labour is $22, but
the average worker gets to keep from one extra hour's work barely a
third of this, $7.70 net. The unemployed German worker, by compari-
son, gets $7.50 (gross) for not working!

See how much smaller the British and Spanish tax bites are
compared with the French and German, and how marginal take-
home pay compares with unemployment benefits across Europe. The
incentive to employ labour and capital is the prospect that the value
of the output will exceed the cost of producing it. Increased tax costs
raise overall costs and thereby reduce the amount of capital and
labour it is worth employing. But the fewer people productively
employed, the larger the tax wedge needed to support the unemployed. The result is a vicious circle, in which the system ends up
fighting itself.

The cost of the social compact has been increased by high and rising
unemployment and will be further increased by Europe's ageing
population. With rising living standards, Europeans opted for
smaller families. The surfeit of post-war baby-boomers had promised
themselves too affluent an old age, at the expense of their too few
sons and daughters. Free immigration from poorer countries, which
could and would solve this problem, is unacceptable.

Chart 2: The Tax Bite
Industrial hourly wage costs

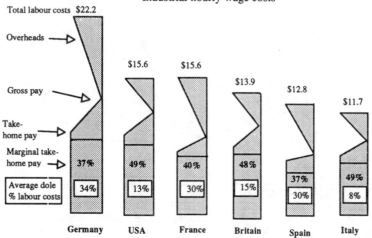

Total labour costs $22.2

Overheads →

Gross pay →

Take-home pay →

Marginal take-home pay →

Average dole % labour costs

	Germany	USA	France	Britain	Spain	Italy
Marginal take-home pay	37%	49%	40%	48%	37%	49%
Average dole	34%	13%	30%	15%	30%	8%

$22.2 $15.6 $15.6 $13.9 $12.8 $11.7

Unemployment, Inflation and Taxation

Unemployment rose partly because those in work proved unwilling to accept the diminishing share of the value of their output allocated to them as a reward for producing the nation's wealth. Egalitarian taxation to support generous social welfare depressed income differentials between white- and blue-collar workers, skilled and unskilled, employed and jobless. Workers responded by demanding higher money wages from their employers, to compensate for increasingly rapacious taxation. The result was cost-push (or more accurately tax-push) inflation (see Chart 3).

Somebody (probably writing for *The Economist*) brilliantly defined inflation as 'too much money chasing too few goods'. The description stuck and led to the corollary that limiting growth in money supply limits inflation. This, however, is the description of, and prescription for, demand-pull inflation. 'Too much money chasing too few goods' describes conditions in an overheated economy, one in which rapid growth and rapidly rising prices go hand in hand. But this manifestly does not fit the experience of the last two decades in which stagflation or slumpflation have been the norm – rapidly rising prices coupled with stagnant or falling output (see Chart 4). The 1970s inflation was

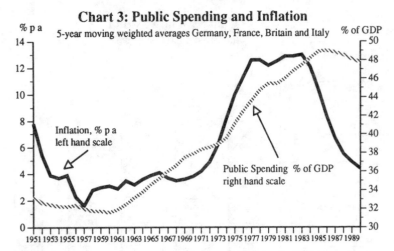

Chart 3: Public Spending and Inflation

5-year moving weighted averages Germany, France, Britain and Italy

Inflation, % p a
left hand scale

Public Spending % of GDP
right hand scale

cost-push, not demand-pull. It reflected too many claimants demanding too large a share on too small a real income. Instead of rising
unemployment curing inflation, rising inflation caused higher unemployment.

The prescription of the tight money solution to this different kind
of inflation produced perverse long-term results. (Controlling the
money supply may be a necessary condition for lowering inflation in
the short-term, it is not a sufficient condition in the long-term.)
Cost-push inflation, which reduced output and increased unemploy-

Chart 4: European Growth, Inflation and Unemployment

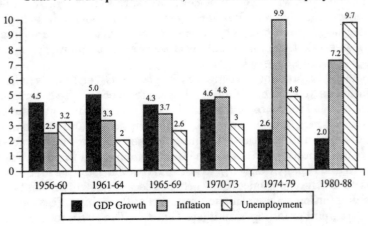

ment, was 'corrected' by demand-pull deflation, pushing output even lower and unemployment even higher. Inflation was contained during the 1980s, but in no way cured. Indeed it could not be cured, because it wasn't the problem. It was one solution to the structural problem presented by the financial crisis into which the social compact of the welfare state syndrome had plunged European economies. The exchange of the evil of still higher unemployment for less inflation has exacerbated that crisis. But at least it has also revealed its true nature, that of securing worthwhile jobs for all those available to take them.

Dimly governments have perceived this, but only at the expense of making matters still worse. A larger share of resources has been offered to the private sector through the fiscal ease which has alternated between bouts of monetary stringency. Instead of reducing the tax wedge by cutting back spending, they have 'cut it' by borrowing. Voters who could not stomach a decrease in the living standards of either the unproductive through social security cuts, or the productive through higher taxation, have been told that neither was necessary. Instead the burden has been transferred to future generations through the accumulation of massive public sector debts. This worked well when real interest rates were negative in the 1970s. But in the 1980s high real interest rates have driven another wedge between the productive private use of capital and the wasteful use of savings in financing public sector consumption.

The Threat from Low-Cost Producers

Europe's home-made employment crisis has been exacerbated by international developments. In a free-trade world, European producers must increasingly compete with newly industrialising nations, whose wage rates and social costs are a fraction of those they must pay. Where income differentials are exceeded by productivity differentials there's no problem. But the collapse in income inequality between skilled and unskilled, well educated and poorly educated European workers, means that Europe's semi-skilled, semi-educated workers in standard technology repetitive jobs earn more than can be justified by the level of their productivity. Competition from lower wage-cost economies cuts prices and reduces the value of their output below that which justified their continued employment.

So far, however, the post-war spread of industrialisation has been remarkably slow. Chart 5 compares shares in world industrial pro-

Chart 5: Relative Productivity and Shares in World Output and Population

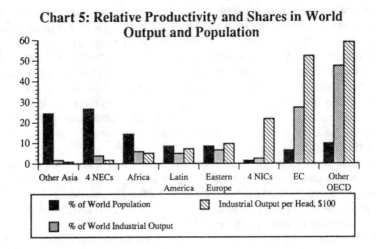

duction with shares in world population. The two ought to and will ultimately converge. With this convergence, incomes in developing countries will rise, while those for some workers in advanced countries will be dragged down to meet them. As yet the distribution of output versus population is grotesquely distorted in favour of America, Europe and Japan. This is largely because the majority of other countries adopted political ideologies and development strategies which inhibited rapid industrialisation.

Communist countries cut themselves off from the market economies and went their own way. Many post-colonial independent states adopted public ownership and control as the basis for industrialisation, hiding their home industries behind trade and exchange restrictions in the hope that they would grow and prosper by way of import substitution. Only a handful of countries, notably in Asia, adopted more liberal, export-oriented development strategies. These NICs – Newly Industrialised Countries – succeeded brilliantly. They have vastly out-performed the advanced OECD economies, substantially increasing their shares in world output and trade. The four Asian NICs, South Korea, Taiwan, Hong Kong and Singapore, accounted for 0.5% of world industrial production in 1965 and 1.5% of world exports. Today they account for five to six times as much.

Competition from NICs has caused job losses in Europe. Industry has migrated to where costs were lower. Multi-nationals have boarded the Orient Express. While painful for a limited section of European industry, this has been but a pin-prick to Europe's total economy. The NICs are mighty midgets. Their combined population is 1% of the world's and one-twentieth of the OECD's. But during the 1980s an ideological revolution swept through the world. Communism was discarded. Privatisation and de-regulation were embraced. Old unsuccessful development strategies were abandoned in favour of the liberal, export-oriented NIC strategy. The NICs are now being pursued by the NECs – Newly Exporting Countries – where the delayed take-off into rapid industrialisation has now begun.

The NECs represent an altogether larger threat. The combined population of those most likely to succeed – Indonesia, Malaysia, Thailand and China – is twice the OECD's. At present they account for only one-twentieth of world industrial production and exports, against over a half and three-quarters respectively held by the OECD. But double-digit annual rate GDP growth will rocket them into the big league before the twenty-first century is very old. (China was the world's thirty-eighth largest exporter a little over a decade ago. Since then its exports have risen six-fold, its share has doubled and it is now the world's thirteenth largest.) This ignores other counties such as Mexico, Brazil and India and countries in eastern Europe, following or set to follow a similar course.

The Need for a Change in Strategic Direction

Europe is already in crisis. It is structural not cyclical. It is a crisis of employment, not inflation. And it is set to get rapidly and disastrously worse. Having recreated pre-war conditions of high and rising unemployment, the leaders of Europe are now faced with those same social and political threats which tore Europe apart fifty years ago. This is a truth which ordinary people intuitively perceive, but it is one to which their myopic leaders are blind. No wonder governments everywhere are held in such low esteem. No wonder people are turning again for leadership to demagogues, such as France's M. le Pen (or America's Ross Perot) and to new parties, outside the established ones that have monopolised post-war power. The solution requires a return to fundamentals. Prosperity is Europe's true goal, not price stability. Maastricht makes the monumental mistake of supposing causation runs from latter to former. Stable prices do not lead to rapid growth and prosperity: it is the other way round.

The new vision for Europe must begin by abandoning Maastricht. (The collapsing ERM has already unnecessarily impoverished Europe's citizenry.) It must be based on a return to fundamentals. Some are simple to grasp. First, sovereignty, unlike virginity, is divisible. For each function of government there is an appropriate level at which it is best performed. Brussels, to give a trivial example, should not be responsible for emptying dustbins, nor should Broadstairs town council be responsible for local air traffic control. One task is to examine all functions of government to determine at which (lowest) level each can best be conducted.

Secondly, at every level of government there must be a democratic system of representation. The present undemocratic structure of European institutions means that it is unwise to allocate tasks to Brussels, even when they are genuinely pan-European. Dictats formulated by the Commission and imposed, following the secret deliberations amongst ministers, on member countries are to be rejected out of hand. A democratic system of European government accepted by referendum amongst all Europe's people is an essential pre-requisite to any hand-over of power to Brussels.

This is exactly how the American Constitution was established. We have the precedent for successful integration, so why don't we use it? Indeed to take another leaf out of this book, democracy is too precious to be left in the hands of politicians working with closed minds behind the closed doors of Inter-Governmental Conferences. An open European Constitutional Congress is required to hammer out proposals, made up of those considered by each nation to be their most gifted representatives.

Leaving this *cri de coeur* aside, let us see what would have happened to the proposed single currency if the first principle adumbrated above had been followed. There is an extensive body of theory concerning the optimum size of a single currency area. It posits that the benefits to trade across national frontiers from a single currency should outweigh the loss of flexibility in dealing with the differential impact of exogenous shocks or of differing rates of development. The more homogeneous a number of economies, the more similar their stages of development, the greater the area within which the benefits of a single currency will outweigh its disadvantages.

The European Community is, however, disparate rather than homogeneous. Britain and Holland are oil producers but other European countries, notably Germany, are energy importers. Sharp variations in the price of oil impoverish one part of Europe while enriching another. Exchange-rate changes lessen such shocks, but that is an example from the past. Consider the threat now posed by the NICs and the NECs. The social compact was carried to greater extremes in Germany, France and Northern Continental Europe than in Britain and Southern European countries. It was even extended on unification from West Germany to East Germany with disastrous results.

German and French producers suffer from greater actual and perceived social costs than British or Spanish, which was why Hoover recently closed its factory in Lyons and expanded its plant at Cambuslang in Scotland. These state-imposed payroll costs lead to market inflexibility. Measures which impede employers from making labour redundant, and impose harsh compensation payments on those allowed to do so, make every potential employer count the full consequences of establishing or expanding production facilities in those countries – whether or not they might find themselves facing closures. Where employers can fire employees with ease and minimum compensation, the burden of supporting their welfare falls on the state and is thus evenly spread amongst all producers. This increases the probability that new jobs will be created to replace old ones that are lost.

Table of Hoover's Payroll Costs

	Jacques	Jock
	£	£
Net weekly take-home pay	281	199
Deductions: Income Tax/National Insurance,		
Pension, holiday pay etc.	126	35
Gross Total Employer's cost	407	234
%age of Net to Gross	69%	85%
%age of Deductions to Net	45%	18%

Source: *Daily Mail* analysis

Where labour-market inflexibility drives major companies and industries into insolvency or foreign relocation, the solution governments are tempted to adopt is subsidisation. This inhibits the structural decline of old industries and, since the costs must be borne by industries not thus supported, it decreases the profitability of sound undertakings, thereby reducing the creation of wealth needed to finance the development of new and more advanced products. Onerous impositions on the employment of labour accelerate investment in labour-saving capital equipment at the expense of inhibiting job-creating capital investment in expanding production. It is no accident that, in the main, the application of modern computer technology has shrunk employment. Computers cost nothing to fire. Their use is not taxed.

Germany and France face a social-compact crisis on an altogether greater scale than Britain or Spain. This disparity is too great. In a single-currency area, with exchange rates frozen at levels reflecting the German Bundesbank's deflationary bias – i.e. with the Deutsche-mark grossly overvalued on a labour-cost basis and the French, if foolish enough, in the same boat – Germany and France will become Europe's depressed region. They will suffer job losses not merely to NECs and NICs, but also to Britain, Spain and Italy. Their social compact crisis would intensify.

The Maastricht 'solution' is irresponsible. It is to extend, through the Social Chapter, the area of labour inflexibility throughout the Community. Each member must suffer similar social costs if competition is to be fair. Social dumping must be proscribed. All of Europe will then become a disaster zone. Pressure for trade protection will become irresistible. Fortress Europe will be created. Eastern Europe will be shut outside its gates. We shall then have adopted precisely those illiberal trade policies which NICs and NECs have abandoned. Behind its barriers, an impoverished Europe will drift into deep stagflationary crisis. Democracy will be at risk. This approach is the exact opposite of the vision of the founding fathers of the post-war EEC.

The alternative is obvious. The European Community is too large and diverse to be an optimum currency area. If the French and the Germans cannot stomach the measures required to reduce the generosity of their social systems, the rigidity of their labour markets, the subsidisation of their declining industries, then they must go it alone. It would be appropriate for them to form a single currency area around the Deutschemark/French franc core, as a logical conclusion of the *franc fort* monetary policy. The D-franc could then depreciate against currencies of those left outside. Depreciation slows the process of job losses by spreading the pain of squeezed living standards throughout the economy, instead of leaving it to be concentrated upon the industrial, traded-goods sector. A two-speed Europe is a better way forward economically – perhaps not politically, but I am not addressing that aspect – because it would allow Germany and France to travel in the slow lane, instead of holding up the rest of the EC in its economic development.

Productivity versus Price Stability

Removing the threatened Maastricht impediment to the employment crisis will not provide a solution. It will merely prevent the situation from deteriorating so rapidly throughout the EC. Creating new jobs requires that costs be reduced or productivity raised. There may still be enough momentum in the Franco-German industrial engine to travel with the hand-brake of the social compact fully on, but the fringe economies are already too weak to contemplate such an absurdity. Lowering costs means reducing the relative living standards of those who do not produce, and the living standards of those the value of whose production does not justify a higher one.

The terms of the social compact may thus seem to be broken, which the pessimist may see as merely an alternative route to the same disastrous conclusion described above. Relative income decline can only be tolerable if accomplished by a rapid increase in living standards generally, so that absolutely no one need suffer. This can only be achieved by rapidly raising productivity. This is the challenge which governments face, not that of ensuring stable prices.

The challenge of the NICs, the NECs, eastern Europe and all other emerging nations must be seen as an opportunity rather than a threat. Rapidly expanding economies rarely generate excess savings. Their burgeoning exports are necessary to finance equally booming imports to sustain their rapid expansion. The coming quarter-century does not threaten the world with depression. It offers the prospect of the biggest boom history has ever seen, and a falling price boom to boot. There will be no general shortage of demand for European products, only for those products in which Europe is at a competitive disadvantage. The problem is to transfer resources as rapidly as possible from old to new industries, in order to meet buoyant world demand.

Paradoxically, the way to create employment is to destroy old uncompetitive industries as rapidly as possible. Europe's protective response to competition in agriculture, textiles, cars, iron and steel is mistaken and must be abandoned. It is probably cheaper in the long run to support the incomes of workers displaced during the interval before they are re-absorbed into other activities than to support their wasteful employment producing over-priced products. New jobs are generated by prosperous, not dying, industries. If we don't let east Europeans and others sell to us the things they can make more cheaply, we won't sell to them the things that we can make more cheaply. Consumers will benefit from lower prices. Our competitive industries will expand and prosper and employment will have a chance to recover. This means sharply reducing the Common Agricultural Policy, a wasteful and damaging way of failing to provide an adequate standard of living to a minority of ageing or part-time farmers, under which large and efficient producers reap excess profit from excess production. Support should be targeted on people, not on products. All other EC industrial subsidies, from coal-mining to semi-conductors, should go for the same reason.

The Dynamics of Employment and Trading

Displaced workers will initially fail to find employment. They are unlikely to possess the skills and education needed to work in the industries and services that boom because of this liberal trade policy. By this token booming industries will earn excess profit. Jobless growth may not boost incomes and consumption, but it will boost profits and tax revenues. The task is to employ these revenues wisely in upgrading the quality of the labour force. Training the unemployed is not normally a wise use of taxpayers' money and has been largely ineffective. They start at the bottom of a ladder of skills and education, while vacancies exist nearer the top. They cannot leapfrog these lower rungs, particularly at a time when others are increasingly being pushed off them.

Retraining is best focused on those in employment and capable of moving a step or two higher, leaving gaps below for others to fill. Europe's education system has not merely failed the unemployed, it has failed many in employment. Some have the wrong education and training, in arts rather than in sciences. Very many have never exploited their full potential in their youth. Very few can afford to take time off and start afresh. Provisions for those in employment to resume or complete their education and training would turn the employment ladder into an escalator, to the benefit of those at its bottom trying to get on it. A system of scholarship, offering preserved incomes during training periods, would be money well spent.

The abolition of all minimum wage requirements is equally necessary. There is no reason why all jobs must provide an income sufficient for a mature family man. Many are best done by students, teenagers, part-time workers and married women. Their employment does not deprive older male workers of full-time jobs. It adds to employment and incomes generally, boosting the prosperity of an economy for the benefit of all.

Harsh proposals to cut unemployment pay, to force people into taking the poorly paid jobs which would be on offer, are unacceptable, like fining the victims of a crime wave because there are so many of them. Hand-loom weavers in the last century were ground into poverty and desperation, but not on a scale to match that which would follow today from this approach. Better use of dole payments is preferable. An employment 'bounty' system could be constructed whereby employers are contracted to employ and train jobless workers in return for a significant contribution to their costs.

The Need for Fiscal Reform

Taxation is another field long overdue for reform. Horror is expressed at any proposal to tax wealth. Yet it is not obvious that workers and their employers should be taxed on incomes and profits generated by producing wealth, while the private enjoyment of the ownership of wealth is exempt. All taxes involve confiscation. Taxes on interest, dividends, capital gains and inheritance are indirect taxes on wealth used productively or handed to others. They could be scrapped.

A wealth tax could then be levied at a rate calculated to replicate that payable on income from the use of wealth. Where one might reasonably expect a real return of, say, 3% from capital invested in industry, and the basic tax on incomes was 25%, wealth in excess of a stipulated minimum might be taxed at a rate of 0.75%. It is not beyond the wit of man to devise a method of valuation. Taxing incomes presents equal problems. A wealth tax provides an incentive to entrepreneurs capable of obtaining above-average returns upon capital. The private enjoyment of wealth would be confined to those whose productive contribution to society gave them the income necessary to pay wealth tax.

The simplistic division of taxable categories into income and wealth (or capital) is to emphasise the importance of the incidence of taxation. If production is taxed then production suffers as the price of manufactures has to rise. The above table of Hoover's payroll costs makes this point in telling terms. Wealth, on the other hand, may be used either as a dynamic stimulant to production through direct capital investment or may be invested in non-dynamic assets, such as works of art or land values.

The difference, for example, between the way the German *Länder* raise revenue from local taxes and the way Britain's local authorities are mainly funded by central government support grants from payroll taxes has major implications, mainly of an adverse nature for Britain. For example, house prices and the level of ownership are both far higher in Britain, as is the consequent allocation of credit to this largely unproductive sector. A banking analyst at Nomura Securities calculated in 1992 that around 75% of total bank loans in Britain of £261.7 billion was secured on property, one way or another. When this £200 billion or so is added to the £800 billion lent out by other property-lending institutions, such as Building Societies on home mortgages loans, then there is clearly an imbalance which is injurious both to the lending institutions and to Britain's economy as a whole.

No wonder that Helmut Schlesinger, President of the Bundesbank, told the European Parliament in Strasbourg in November 1992 that before a common European currency could be considered, there was a prior need for greater convergence of national *fiscal* policies. The fiscal debate in Europe has only started on one tax, that of VAT, for which there are enormous variations in incidence, at widely varying rates, right across Europe.

The Need for Radical Debate

These proposals are illustrative rather than exhaustive. They may be extreme, novel or controversial. But the crisis facing Europe is grave. It will only be solved by those willing to embark on radical change. None of the above suggestions needs to be implemented at the European level. Even the complete abolition of the CAP would be possible, were the countries allowed to opt out from it. It is, after all, in restraint of trade and illiberal. Few of the proposals would receive, *ab initio*, pan-European support. There is no need for that.

The benefits of the single market can still be obtained by permitting, at national level, competition in discovering ways out of the employment crisis. The single market can best be exploited by allowing anybody to dig holes in the playing field if thereby they gain an advantage. Free competition between tax systems, trading systems, systems of labour regulations, etc., would encourage other European countries to harmonise on the best and most effective, or lose out.

The single market contains its own momentum for national reform. It does not need, nor is it helped by, regimentation by Brussels, which at German and French behest is far more likely to be in restraint of trade and competition. If they had a rocky coastline, while we had five deep harbours, they would probably want us to fill them in. The added beauty of a flexible, liberal and competitive approach to Europe's development is that it simplifies the expansion of the community. Expansion to other prosperous northern European countries is needed to share the burden of helping more backward members.

Germany is unable to shoulder this mostly alone. It may be said that this approach narrows the vision of a political, economic and monetary union embracing all of the EC and potential EC member countries to one of a mere free-trade area. Far from it, it is a different route to the same ultimate objective. Political, economic and monetary union is a matter of political will born of enthusiastic public support. Without it there is no European future. It is not an assault on the summit of Everest, to be reached by a phased climb to pre-ordained camps. The impoverishment of Europe, which Maastricht entails, will sap the political will long before the EMU summit is reached. Public support for Maastricht is at best luke-warm. Europe's deepening employment crisis will kill it stone cold. This is why Maastricht is doomed to certain failure.

No one suggested the phased introduction of the US constitution or of German unification. Like them, EMU is a bungy jump off the Forth bridge. An approach which gives the priority to prosperity will give people and their governments the confidence to make such a jump when the time is right. Europe's worst enemies are its over-zealous but misguided and supposed best-friends. They include, with a few brilliant exceptions, almost all its top politicians, whether leading governments or opposing them. They have allowed emotion to supplant reason. Facing the past, while marching backwards and blind into the future, they are leading us – without our consent – towards the destruction of all they hope to achieve. When they finally stumble over reality, it has to be hoped that somewhere the vision of Europe may still be alive.

10 June 1993   City of London

Monetary Policy in Europe 'after Maastricht'

Wilhelm Noelling

The condition precedent for monetary union in the EC is that Germany is prepared to allow the sacrifice of the Deutschemark – the strongest currency in the EMS – on the altar of European economic union. Germany is proud of the long history of the Deutschemark. Nevertheless, twice this century Germany has experienced the pain of hyper-inflation, so that its monetary policy today is governed by the need to control inflation above all other considerations. Consequently, any decision to subsume the Deutschemark in a new Euro-currency is a momentous issue for Germans, many of whom are deeply concerned about all-out monetary union and giving up the Deutschemark too quickly and unconditionally.

In the foreword to my latest book, Rudiger Dornbusch – Professor of Economics at Massachusetts Institute of Technology – comes straight to the point:

> 'EMU is gone, let's make the best of what is left. One Europe was not meant as a goal in itself, but rather as a means to afford peace and prosperity. The basic proposition got lost ... In the monetary area, convergence by conventional mechanisms has peaked and new answers are necessary.'

Must we lose sight of the idea of a Franco-German monetary union, including the Benelux countries, because of the foreign exchange turmoils of September 1992 and August 1993?

In retracing the history of the Deutschemark, I came across the Carolingian coinage reform around the end of the eighth century and recalled my proposal raised in January 1990 about the possibility of monetary union between Germany and France. Now that the attempts to rush through the Maastricht provisions have faltered with the collapse of the ERM on 2 August 1993, it is surprising that this alternative option had never, to my knowledge, been explored before the autumn of 1992. Given the common ground that was established in Maastricht, should it present fewer difficulties than appeared to be the case a year ago? On 21 September 1992 the former President of the Bundesbank, Otto Poehl, put forward a similar proposal on a visit to Washington, where he argued for 'the conclusion of an agreement that would be entered into only by those countries that are both willing and able to move towards integration'. Poehl clearly sees Germany and France as the core members of this exclusive club.

The political fascination of such a step could scarcely be overstated. If the two former arch-enemies at the heart of Europe could go back to the monetary legacy of Charlemagne, announce their firm commitment to that end and initiate the necessary measures in the very near future, something concrete would have been achieved – and something that is dependent solely on the will of the two governments concerned. There would be an end to the uncertainties that inevitably arise when concrete agreements between a multiplicity of parties have to be negotiated over a relatively long period of time. Economic and social policy, however, would have to be more closely co-ordinated, and in the medium term their political-institutional rulings would have to be adjusted at the supra-national level. This would clearly mean that the functions of the European Commission and the European Parliament would be affected, and the two national parliaments would need to be dovetailed – most certainly creating special problems.

France's fears – I reasoned – could swiftly be laid to rest and its reasonable insistence on having a full say in European monetary policy could be accommodated within a relatively short space of time. Germany's interests would need to be safeguarded, just as they needed to be safeguarded at Maastricht. There is no longer any danger of France exporting inflation: its firm commitment to a policy of stability has been convincingly demonstrated. France's representatives on a new joint central bank council would be no less conscious of the need for stability than their colleagues on the Central Bank Council of the Bundesbank. And clearly we can expect both countries to agree on the need for such a body to be independent.

The new governing body could be strengthened either on the basis of equal representation or by co-opting additional members to represent other countries as they achieve convergence. To enhance the attractions of the equal representation option it would be necessary not only to rotate the chairmanship every year but also to give the chairman a casting vote in the event of deadlock.

In my view the objections to a progressive and realistically attainable 'core monetary union' or two-speed Europe along these lines are more political than economic. A bilateral initiative to move Europe forward without involving all other ten members of the Community will probably be seen as a source of insuperable difficulties, and may well prompt fears that the cohesion of the EMS and the EC could be damaged.

But why should this be so? – I asked in my book.

A fixed Deutschemark-franc parity would replace the present anchor function of the Deutschemark. The other countries would align themselves around this, as they have previously done within the EMS. The Franco-German central bank model could be extended by the addition of representatives from The Netherlands and/or Denmark (whose central banks are to all intents and purposes independent), and they could be given a voice in determining common interest rates in Germany and France – and hence throughout Europe. If other countries wished to join this system of fixed exchange rates, they would be evaluated according to the criteria set down in the Maastricht Treaty. The whole process would resemble in principle the procedure for admission to the European Community, except that it would probably lead more quickly to a positive outcome provided the necessary pre-conditions had been met.

I proposed an alternative to a bilateral model as early as 1987. The proposal was prompted by the recognition of what was really a quite obvious fact – that the dominance of the Bundesbank in European monetary matters would probably prove unacceptable in the long term, regardless of whether its policies were, or were perceived to be, sound and conducive to the good of all. This was surely even more the case when the Bundesbank was obliged to clamp down long and hard on interest rates as a result of inconsistent and contradictory government policies – something which could not, of course, have been foreseen back in 1987.

The model proposed at the time seemed to me to be so simple that it appeared unrealistic – which is why I put forward the scheme only in very broad terms, omitting any reference to the institutional forms it might take. As far as I know, the proposal was not taken up or discussed further.

The structure of the proposed monetary union was indeed simple. A seat and a voice on a 'Europeanised' central bank council in Frankfurt would be given only to representatives of the central banks of those member countries who participate fully in the exchange rate system and are granted autonomy. Their number would be proportionate to the economic strength of the countries represented. Following a discussion of the economic and monetary situation in their respective countries, they would vote together at their regular meetings to determine interest rates in Germany, France, The Netherlands, etc. Naturally, they would vote on each country separately, because uniform interest rates in every country would not be required at this stage.

The enormous efforts that have subsequently been made to hammer out the status of an independent European Central Bank would thus have been superfluous, and national central banks that are not yet independent would have been forced to go down this road. Naturally, this applies in particular to France (as in the case of the bilateral model). In this way European monetary policy would have been effectively 'communalised'. However, the political objections raised in connection with Maastricht would probably still have applied – most notably the absence of political union and the persistence of national control over economic policy. At the same time, however, I do believe that the inherently irenic and stabilising tendencies of this model could have helped to build confidence and accustom Europeans to a greater sense of common purpose with respect to the achievement of full union.

Critics have maintained – even before the tumultuous events in the summer of 1993 – that the necessary preconditions for a bilateral approach as spelled out in my book could hardly be fulfilled in our lifetime. It has to be admitted frankly that the task of institutional reform and progress, i.e. to co-operate more closely, is more difficult now than it appeared to be even a year ago. However, this should not prevent us at all from thinking ahead.

Europe needs a positive vision to help stop the disintegration effect of the temporary collapse of the ERM. It was and still is my strong conviction that without a functioning ERM, more progressive ideas of monetary integration might be relegated to the status of a Glasperlenspiel. Therefore, the immediate task is to find out why the ERM went out of business for the time being. Here the much heralded free capital mobility comes into the picture. In my book I devoted a whole chapter to the role and inherent dangers of unchecked, massive speculative financial flows. We do have to give more attention to defining these fault-lines and seeking functional remedies.

5 August 1993

Hamburg

Economic versus Monetary Union

Sir Alan Walters

Britain Remains a Full Partner in Economic Union

Forebodings of catastrophe if Britain did not ratify Maastricht have been the stuff of official press briefings and the rationale of whips' threats. With the eleven marching forward to monetary and political union and Britain left out, we shall become 'detached' from Europe – that is the term used by the European Policy Forum (EPF) paper commissioned by the Corporation of the City of London.

Let us first be perfectly clear what Maastricht implies. First and foremost Maastricht is 'The Treaty of European Union'. It is primarily concerned, on the one hand, with the formation of a monetary union with one central bank and one currency and, on the other hand, with various moves to increase the power of Brussels in foreign affairs, defence, security and domestic policies. So if Britain does not ratify the treaty, it is literally opting out of a monetary and political union.

But Britain would not be opting out of the common market, the free movement of labour and capital and the barrier-free Europe implied in the Treaty of Rome and the Single European Act. In other words, Britain would continue to be part of the *economic union* of Europe; by saying thumbs-down to Maastricht, Britain would have opted out of only the monetary and political union, and would have freed up this option for the rest of Europe too.

Economic Union does not Require Monetary Union

But the Europhiles – notably in the shape of Messrs Delors and Bangemann and Sir Leon Brittan – continuously assert that an economic union can be completed only if there is monetary union, and by implication political union. The main argument put forward to support this proposition is that there are considerable costs in changing currencies and the market will be barrier-free only when there are no such costs intervening in inter-community transactions.

This is an absurd proposition. Such exchange costs are very small for perhaps 98% of transactions; it is only at the airport and at the actual retail level that one sees substantial spreads between selling and buying prices for differing currencies. One pays for that convenience, just as one pays for the use of the credit card to get a cash draft whatever the currency.

There is, of course, another reason which is not exposed. The monetary union is perhaps the only way in which countries will be prevented from asserting their rights to arrange their monetary affairs to suit their *domestic* circumstances rather than those of the country, Germany, with the dominant currency. The events of 16 September 1992 [and 2 August 1993] showed that, in the absence of a monetary union, the countries can engage in what is pejoratively called 'competitive devaluations'. They were, of course, nothing of the sort. They were an entirely rational reaction, alas far too long delayed, to the absurdity of imposing a massive monetary squeeze on an economy long in the depths of a slump.

We saw the *market* topple the idiotic policies that prevailed before 16 September 1992 [and 2 August 1993], but in a monetary union with one currency the markets would have no role. If there had been one European currency in operation there would have been no respite from the dominant German monetary squeeze. So monetary union will banish the market and impose the discipline of Brussels or Frankfurt. (Of course many sophisticated commentators regard such a surrender of market to bureaucrats as wholly desirable. And it is true that Central Bankers would have a much quieter life, but at the considerable expense of those in the dole queues.)*

Economic Union without Monetary Union

The idea that a complete economic union necessarily requires a monetary union has been widely accepted, however, by Euro-enthusiasts. This is an astonishing feat of public relations and press management by Brussels and its allies. Astonishing, because the most casual perusal of the facts so readily discredits the idea.

Consider for example the other great economic union in the world today – the union of the United States and Canada, shortly to be

[*Editor's note: On 18 May 1993 *The Wall Street Journal Europe* reported the words of Helmut Schlesinger, President of the Bundesbank, speaking in Los Angeles as follows: 'A single market can exist, and be beneficial, without inevitably requiring further moves towards integration in the monetary sphere.']

joined by Mexico. Canada and the United States have more trade than any two countries in the world. They have virtually free trade in the vast majority of goods and services and this is shortly to be made complete. There are no impediments of capital flows and few with respect to labour movements.

They have an economic union which, in terms of its performance, is far more complete than that of the European Community. The true test of an economic union is not in the number of directives it issues but rather in its *effects*. The acid test is whether prices for the same commodities, adjusted for local taxes, are broadly the same. In North America, the price of motor cars, net of local taxes, varies only with respect to transport costs from supplier to market. In the Community, however, the price in the dearest market is 80% more than the price in the cheapest market. And cars are only one example of the disparity of prices in Europe. The Community has a long way to go before its markets are really open.

So if the United States and Canada are in an economic union, one wonders why they have not found that their economic union is somehow incomplete and requires a monetary union to crown it? And what should be even more puzzling to Delors etc. is that the Canadians do not peg the Canadian dollar to the mighty greenback. True, during two brief periods since the end of Bretton Woods, the Canadian dollar had been pegged to the US dollar, but the peg had effects so dire that the Canadian government soon returned to a more or less free float. Furthermore, as far as I know, no one has seriously explored the possibility that NAFTA needs a pegged Canadian dollar or Mexican peso.

With tongues firmly in cheeks, one may enquire of the Europhiles whether these Americans and Canadians are stupid and fail to see the 'fundamental contradictions' in their policies which are so apparent to all Europhiles. But one can point to even closer examples of economic union without monetary union.

In our own islands an economic union has long existed between England and Scotland, since the accession of James VI of Scotland to the English throne. For most of these years, up to the Bank Act of 1844, Scotland had a banking and monetary system which was quite different from and independent of the English system administered by the Bank of England. But the point is that for about two hundred years (the exception was during the period of inconvertibility of the Napoleonic wars) an economic union worked perfectly well without a monetary union. The imposition of a monetary union after 1844 was no blessing to Scotland. Many scholars have argued that the Scottish monetary system of 'free banking' was far superior to the monopolistic Bank of England arrangements. (See 'Scottish Free Banking' in *The New Palgrave's Dictionary of Money and Finance*). But, willy-nilly, there was clearly no need for a monetary union to 'complete' the economic union of Scotland and England. Nor is Maastricht needed to 'complete' the economic union of the European Community.

What is needed is more open competition, reductions in trade barriers, more open capital markets etc., all of which do not require Maastricht. But it is clear that the Maastricht monetary union implies that there will necessarily be considerable transfers of power to Brussels in the form of a political union. Indeed the German government has made it clear that it regards progress of political union as an essential requirement of monetary union. The idea that, if Britain were not in this political union, we would be 'detached' from Europe has been much mooted as a major reason for ratifying Maastricht by the EPF paper for the Corporation of the City of London.

The EPF 'Detachment' Scare Tactics

The EPF authors have then gone on to calculate that, were such 'detachment' to occur, the south-east corner of England would lose as much as £10 billion a year in income, presumably to other Europeans in the Union. Furthermore Britain would also suffer, they say, from a reduced direct foreign investment (£10 billion again) which would add up to an annual loss of income of £6 billion. All this reminds me of Lord Justice Goddard's complaint: 'I am informed that figures cannot lie; but surely liars can figure.' Although these numbers are bandied about, there is no basis for them whatsoever even as ballpark figures or as orders of magnitude. In a literal sense the authors of the EPF paper do not know what they are talking about.

What they might consider is the immense loss of output (at least 7% of GNP) as well as reduced capital accumulation which we have endured since joining the ERM, *de facto* in 1987 and *de jure* in 1990. And the ERM is simply the trial canter before the monetary union stakes. Furthermore, although it is impossible to quantify the behaviour of foreign direct investment, we certainly know what motivates it – the prospective return on the assets. As we know, Britain outside the ERM but inside the Community has attracted more foreign direct investment than any other member during the 1980s, as can be seen in the many manufacturing implants in the United Kingdom financed by Japan and the United States.

Can anyone believe that if Britain continues to fulfil her commit-

ments under the Treaty of Rome and the Single European Act, she
will suffer because of the 'detachment' from the monetary and political union? The contrary proposition seems more plausible. Britain
will have all the advantages of being in an economic union, but none
of the disadvantages of being tied to the apron strings of a Franco-
German political and bureaucratic *dirigisme* with its monetary and
fiscal policies which are rarely suitable for Britain's domestic conditions. Rather attractive, I should think, for outsiders to contemplate.

The City of London

Behind much of the specious argument and fancy figuring of the EPF
report is the play on the underlying uncertainties of the financial and
commercial community (and to a lesser extent industrialists) of what
'detachment' will entail. Perhaps the biggest fear is that, if Britain is
not firmly in the monetary union, London will lose its status as the
great financial centre. It is even said that the financial community
will migrate, like drone bees following a queen, to gather around the
skirts of the European Central Bank or Institute – which looks likely
to settle in Frankfurt.

There are many confusions in this argument. First let us dispel the
notion that, if there is a European Central Bank, it will attract all
the money-men and women. As it happens, I live in Washington DC
where the Federal Reserve Board of the United States is located. Yet
Washington is no financial centre; indeed, compared with neighbouring Baltimore or Philadelphia, Boston, Chicago or New York, it is
pitifully small and underdeveloped. Of course most central banks are
located where there are substantial financial markets, but the belief
that central banks somehow create or retain a financial community
around them is far from proven.

On a more general plane, City dignitaries have argued that the
City will suffer severely if Britain is not firmly inside the Maastricht
bus. In their letter to *The Times* of 18 May 1993, the Lord Mayor and
the most eminent persons in the City asserted that if Britain ' ... were
to detach itself from developments in Europe, business which previously would have come to the City will be carried out in other
centres.' Put bluntly, on Maastricht, either sign up or suffer.

Yet we all know that the main reason for the pre-eminence of
London is that the authorities have ensured that there was light
regulation and little interference; so the City, more or less free of
political and bureaucratic interference, could get on with its business

of making money. This, together with its past reputation for integrity, had made the City a world financial centre. The City should now concentrate on preserving, or possibly re-establishing, its tarnished image and integrity rather than on Maastricht, if it values its future.

But if the assertion that staying out of the monetary and political union will damage the City is correct, this must be because a 'detached' British government will indulge more in restrictive regulation – and presumably the Franco-German Super-State will liberate Frankfurt etc. from its current red tape. This seems to lack credibility. Notwithstanding the various directives of capital liberalisation, the continental members of the Community are much more *dirigiste* than the United Kingdom, as France for example has recently shown with its policy of compartmentalising the short-term money market through its banking directives. Britain has much more to fear from a Euro-regulator, or possibly its own recent falls from grace, than from its own open and internationalist approach.

Finally many people, perhaps even a majority in the City, have succumbed to the oft-repeated assertion that London cannot conceivably retain its pre-eminence if it is not part of the vast hinterland of exchange rate stability epitomized in the monetary union. Such claims will not stand up to the most casual reflection. Counter-examples abound. Historically the great financial centres of the sixteenth century (Genoa) and seventeenth and eighteenth centuries (Amsterdam and London) through the eighteenth and much of the nineteenth century had no such monetary hinterland. In recent times, from the 1930s through Bretton Woods to our present float, there were only fitful periods of exchange rate stability and many restrictions on movements of currencies. Nevertheless, London's dominance grew dramatically in the 1970s and 1980s. The final counter-example is of course Hong Kong, on which perhaps no more need be said.

Conclusion

The City's great record of success was founded on light government, few regulatory restrictions and a well-earned reputation for integrity. All other arguments about monetary hinterlands, Euro-attachments, etc. are specious and discredited by the historical record. Can we not simply conclude that the continental record of stifling regulation, political interference and heavy-handed government, to say nothing of standards of integrity, should clearly put anyone who has the City's and Britain's interests at heart firmly against joining such a Union? The City had best look to its well-honed skills and to restoring its reputation for honest and straight dealing. That is the basis of its success.

17 April 1993   Washington DC

The City of London as Global Player

Rodney Leach

Not everything lends itself to boundaries. You do not ask if Einsteinian physics is European or American, or put tariffs on poetry and cancer research. The same is often true of business. Brands such as Coca Cola and Nescafé, and companies like Shell and Unilever, have transcended their national origins. Nowhere is this phenomenon more evident than in international finance, which nowadays is transmitted around the world's time zones by electronic mail, video screens, conference calls and fax machines, to the point where it is increasingly meaningless to say where a complex transaction has taken place.

Nevertheless, despite the erosion of the very concept of location in the more sophisticated reaches of finance, there remains a recognisable sense in which the City of London lies at the centre of the spider's web. It is a magnet of talent from the four corners of the earth, with more commuters than the entire population of Frankfurt. No other financial community even approaches the scope of its connections or the range of its activities – commodities, shipping, insurance, banking, gold, foreign exchange, investment management, securities dealing, as well as all manner of trading in futures and derivatives. It is supported by a professional army of lawyers, accountants, journalists and printers.

From time to time people ask whether such a problem or trend is a threat to the supremacy of the City. The current fashion is to ask whether Britain's reluctance to sign the full Treaty of Maastricht is such a threat – a question sometimes accompanied by an even more naive one, which is whether the City can retain its position if the EC's Central Bank is sited elsewhere than in London. Such questions betray a complete lack of understanding of the workings of this loose and disparate assemblage of market places. They should be replaced by two quite different questions – first, given that the EC has the good fortune to harbour the City of London within its confines, what can it do to increase the City's prosperity and help it draw further ahead of its rivals, New York and the Tokyo/Hong Kong/Singapore axis? And second, what factors, if any, could undermine the City's position?

To rephrase the questions in this way is to bring the City's relationship with the EC into clearer focus. Talk of signing up to Maastricht so as 'to protect London's position at the financial heart of Europe' can be seen to be as empty as the notion that failure by Germany to ratify the Treaty would jeopardise Stuttgart's position as a centre for the production of Mercedes. Far from appearing essential to the City's survival, the Continental hinterland starts to look irrelevant, while the EC's bureaucratic style of regulation and its indifference to labour costs risks strangling London's competitiveness. In a nutshell, Europe needs the City considerably more than the City needs Europe.

The City's position is not only independent of Europe; in many ways it is independent of Britain itself, for example in its widespread use of the dollar and in the predominance of foreign companies in its midst. Before sterling was freed from Exchange Control the Euro-currency markets, though they called London their home, found ways to operate as if on an offshore island, untouched by the regulatory framework, banking controls and demarcation lines of the UK's domestic markets. Today the Square Mile resembles a City State, like Renaissance Venice or modern Hong Kong, as much as a national capital's financial district. It thrives on its own particular attributes – the English language and the common law; a reputation, despite the inevitable scandals, for openness and probity; an international outlook inherited from one hundred and fifty years of maritime trade; a restless inventiveness, stimulated by financial boutiques, informal governance and executive mobility; the Bank of England's resistance to excessive statutory regulation; unique links with US and Asian markets. One thing that is striking about these characteristics is that they have precious little European flavour to them, sitting for the most part uneasily with the rigidities and the inwardness of the 'Brussels' mentality.

Official European thinking barely connects with the real business world – it tends to start with a visionary political preamble and descend promptly to the intellectual and ethical level of a horse-dealer. After months of haggling, London was given the Headquarters of the EBRD, in exchange for the appointment of President Mitterrand's friend and golf-playing partner, Jacques Attali, as its Chief. As is by now well known, Attali's first move was to hire a French chef and his next to spend a fortune changing the marble in the entrance hall and then another fortune on private jets. He went on to recruit the ex-nomenklatura to be his advisers. Somewhere along the line the original objective of lending money to emerging private enterprise in eastern Europe faded into relative insignificance, although Attali maintains there are many projects under negotiation.

The same sort of trivial squabbling is now going on over the location of the ECB. The Corporation of the City of London has invested far too much political capital in the quest to act as host to this unpopular, though as yet non-existent, organisation. As they lobby away, predicting woe if their campaign is unsuccessful, you have to wonder if they realise that when central banks intervene to support the Franc or the Peseta most of the dealing already occurs in London, the foreign exchange capital of the world, which trades more than six times the volume of Deutschemarks than does Frankfurt. Moreover if the Bundesbank has its way the ECB will never get off the ground – one example among many of the tacit mutual sympathy between the Bundesbank and the so-called Euro-sceptics.

In Westminster both front benches are united in arguing that Britain must 'establish its European credentials' to attract inward investment and win influence in the EC's counsels. At first blush, this appears absurd. After all, no one called the French marginalised when they so nearly rejected Maastricht, or questioned Germany's community spirit when Theo Waigel declared his readiness to opt out of the monetary union; still less has anyone suggested adverse knock-on effects for French or German industry. Yet Britain's political anxieties cannot just be dismissed out of hand, for these apparently irreconcilable responses to superficially similar symptoms of scepticism are in fact very revealing. They show that in current French and German political circles the Treaty is a prospectus for the agreed goal of a European Super-state, whose central doctrine of monetary union is both a by-product of that goal and a means to ratchet up the Federal pressure, to be postponed or accelerated according to circumstances.

British politicians, on the other hand, still comfort themselves with phantom opt-outs and the empty concept of subsidiarity, hoping against hope that the Federal dimension is so ambivalent that the Treaty can be signed now as a diplomatic gesture of goodwill, leaving the real debate till later. Referenda and opinion polls suggest that Continental and British voters have surprisingly similar reservations about bureaucratic Federalism: the great divide comes at the summit level.

Any attempt to link the ratification of Maastricht to prospects for investment from abroad is, however, based on ignorance of the way companies take capital expenditure decisions. The siting of a new plant or office is determined not by political atmospherics but by objective measures of competitiveness – wage costs, labour flexibility, communications, skill levels, transport, insurance and rental expenses, interest rates and so forth. One of the most active periods of inward investment in Britain's history was when Mrs. Thatcher was at the height of her opposition to the growing power of Brussels. Far from being put off by Britain's robust attitude to Europe, many overseas industrialists were positively attracted by it, despite the fact that their UK-built products were specifically destined for other EC markets. And what applies to intra-European industry applies much more to the tariff-free and global world of financial services.

The ultimate bogey, used successfully by Maastricht's proponents in Denmark and repeatedly aired in Britain, is that failure to ratify the Treaty might lead to expulsion from the Garden of Eden. In fact there is not even a mechanism to eject countries from the EC, nor is there any will to remove Europe's second biggest paymaster and its softest export market (see Appendix I). The EC is committed to widening itself to embrace Europe from the Atlantic to the Urals; it is also intent on developing eventually a common foreign affairs and defence policy. In that context, the idea of a Europe *with* Greece and *without* Britain is simply laughable. If the EC starts to lose its own strongest nations, that is the end of its geo-political ambitions. Where would be the moral authority or the deterrent credibility of a club which could not retain the loyalty of its foremost democracy and its leading military power?

Ever since I can remember the EC has promised a passport to prosperity. It has been a cruel deceit, for the region has become an economic black spot, with double-digit unemployment and the lowest rates of growth in the developed world. Elsewhere things are on the move. The US is forming a North American Free Trade Area without any of the EC's paraphernalia. Latin America and much of Africa have started a productive rebellion against their own forms of statism. But the outstanding feature of the business landscape remains the performance of Asia. Already as large as the EC or the US, the oriental economies will be twice the size of either within the next twenty-five years.

Europe is saddled with a lethal combination – super-power envy, rooted in nineteenth-century Great Power nostalgia; and the legacy of a post-war utopianism that has lost direction, resulting in universal welfare, bloated government deficits and high taxes. We have come to accept these as part of the furniture of a modern *advanced* state. By contrast, Asia is riding a wave of prosperity without cohe-

sion funds, social chapters or harmonisation, without central directives, collective international bargaining or exchange rate co-ordina-
tion. While a depressed Europe contemplates fiscal deflation in order
to meet Maastricht's convergence criteria, and counts the cost of
monetary deflation caused by the Bundesbank's domestic impera-
tives, Asia carries on blithely as if convergence and monetary union
were of no economic consequence in total refutation of the monolithic
economic doctrines which hypnotise Europe.

Watching these developments from afar, the EC's reaction is to
build barricades; not to question its own received wisdom, or to treat
Asia primarily as a potential customer, or to emulate its formulae for
success, but to punish it with tariffs and quotas. Whether Europe is
protecting its semi-conductor industry with tariffs, protecting its
communications monopolies, freezing out eastern Europe's goods,
pouring funds into the Mafia-ridden Mezzogiorno, cheating on the
Common Agricultural Policy or allowing national subsidies to industries from computers to energy, everywhere one finds the narrow
vested interests and the inexorable decline of Fortress Europe.

To stand against this tide is to find oneself confronted by all the
pressures that the machinery of European Governments can summon
up. They call their opponents 'Euro-phobes', implying that distaste
for the ideas of Delors or Bangemann means opposition to the Europe
of Degas and Beethoven; or that pride in the French countryside or
in British democracy is first cousin to insularity, not to say fascism.
They bribe the electorate with promises of subsidies or tax cuts and
frighten it with the spectre of still higher unemployment. They
suborn their opponents with promises of advancement or threaten
them with loss of contracts, loss of office, or ostracism from Ministerial favour. There have been concerted efforts to stifle debate and
deny freedom of speech. It has been an ugly year.

And who is behind this ugliness? The reputations of most of
Europe's political leaders are tarnished beyond redemption. It is
impossible to travel widely on the Continent without seeing how
people have grown disgusted with their governments and the
secretive bureaucracies which, collecting and dispensing over 50
per cent of each country's wealth, foster corruption and influence-
peddling.

Italians have reached the point where they have been driven to
political revolution. Until they see its outcome, they will continue for
a while to prefer foreign adminstration to their own degenerate
system. Spain, Greece and Portugal could be forgiven too, for favouring rule from Brussels. But British and Nordic businessmen, accus-

tomed to impartial law and honest administration, harbour justifi-
able reservations about the 'irreversible' transfer of more and more
legal authority to the politicised European Court of Justice and the
exchange of democratic accountability for deals negotiated by bureaucrats behind locked doors. Such rifts are ubiquitous in the EC –
between subsidisers and the subsidised, planners and marketeers,
compliers and dodgers, mercantilists and free traders. Hard enough
to resolve nationally, divisions of this nature are incapable of resolution across the whole of Europe, where they are reinforced by language barriers and by ancient lingering political, military or religious
animosities.

Every artificial political federation has resulted in bitter cultural
resentments, too often ending in civil war. At the civilised end of the
spectrum are the strains within Canada, Belgium and the United
Kingdom's Celtic fringe. At the barbarous extreme there are the
disintegrating remnants of what used to be Yugoslavia and the Soviet
Union. Nations, like human beings, need identity and space to be
themselves and to enable mutual respect and affection to flourish:
cram them together and they end up hating each other.

The battle for Europe's soul is just beginning in earnest. On one
side will be ranged Federalising bureaucrats and political mandarins
convinced of their own rectitude and careful not to be too well
informed about the Tammany Hall activities of many of their colleagues. They will regard democracy as tiresome and investigative
journalism as an assault on their honour and dignity. They will give
the European Parliament notional powers and treat it with the
elaborate contempt extended by Roman Emperors to the Senate.
Among their allies will be the poorer regions and big business interests, which benefit from hand-outs or need protection from more
efficient foreign competition.

Their foreign policy stance will have more than a hint of xenophobia, directed principally against the US and the East. They will speak
of a common army, but confronted by external crises they will be
indecisive, unable to evoke the loyalties which make soldiers willing
to risk their lives. Their economic vision will be interventionist
domestically, mercantilist abroad, their social vision that of the
welfare state. Their collective folk-legend will be the post-war reconciliation of France and Germany, fostered by Winston Churchill and
brought to fruition by Adenauer, Schuman and Monnet, leading to
the creation of the Franco-German alliance and independence alike
from Soviet and American domination.

On the other side will be those who see Europe in terms of its different artistic, cultural, literary and political heritages. Accepting the validity of the 1950s vision of a Europe in which France and Germany would never again be at war, they will see this as a danger overtaken by history. In their eyes Brussels will symbolise the degradation of the dreams of Europe's founders into a coercive bureaucratic nightmare. There will be British democrats, Danish fishermen, German bankers and French farmers, allied to small businessmen everywhere struggling in a morass of remote-control regulations. On the fringe will be crude nationalists whose own xenophobia, exacerbated by frustration over their powerlessness, will start nearer to home – with their European neighbours.

This other vision will be of a wide association of sovereign nations bound together by a single market, common ties of culture and shared environmental standards. Essentially free traders, they would nevertheless generally negotiate trade agreements as a bloc. Their economic vision will be of the enterprise culture, marked by de-regulation and competitive costs. They would consult and inform each other and would often work together in foreign policy; but their security would be based on NATO and there would be enough room to accommodate both neutrality and independent military action. Each would have its own currency, unless its particular trading patterns suggest a link, or even a merger, with a neighbouring currency. The transfer of further legal powers to the Community would be resisted. The Common Agricultural Policy would be a target for repeal, not a symbol of achievement. Democratic accountability would provide each country's outlet for self-expression and for determining economic policy. 'Brussels' would be the servant, not the master.

Hitherto centralism and bureaucracy have gained ground unopposed, through a mixture of deceit and singlemindedness. But now the repercussions of the Danish and French referenda, the rising awareness of the issues at stake in Britain and the prospective accession of eastern European nations which have had their fill of socialism; these elements together have the makings of a new set of forces which is capable of establishing a different and altogether more generous vision of Europe. It will not be a specifically British vision. But whether or not the Treaty of Maastricht eventually passes through Westminster it will be the one to which the majority of the British people, including myself, will subscribe.

21 May 1993   City of London

European Exchange Rate Economics

Howard Flight

While most of the opposition to Maastricht throughout Europe arises
from growing hostility towards the essentially undemocratic political
powers of Brussels, the Treaty itself is mostly about a phased path to
a common European currency. For the UK, moreover, where the
political divisions over Maastricht are amongst the deepest in
Europe, the UK government has explicitly reserved the right under
the Treaty not to participate in a common European currency. Unfortunately Maastricht has become a major political symbol or token of
'pro-European' commitment. As a result, no major European government has yet had the statesmanship to admit that the premises and
assumptions on which the draft Treaty was based have been effectively 'blown out of the water', consequent upon the economic problems of German re-unification. To do so is perceived as to invite attack
from the rest of Europe for being 'un-European' at a time in history
when everyone is frightened by what is happening in the Balkans, and
of rekindling the embers of nineteenth-century European nationalism.

It is arguably the government of Germany, in particular, which
should publicly admit what the Bundesbank has been revealing to all
by its actions – that a common European currency and more particularly common European interest rates are wholly impractical for the
foreseeable future, where the required fiscal and monetary policies
in a re-unified Germany are likely to differ very substantially from
those required by other EC countries.*

This is what the explosion of ERM parities of September 1992 [and
August 1993] was signalling. The Bundesbank had to chose between
continuing to follow interest rate policies which it believed (wrongly)
were correct for Germany and changing its interest rate policies to
accommodate interest levels required by the majority of other European economies. The Bundesbank was adamant that its first priority
was to look to its German interests. This did not mean that the ERM

[*Editor's note: in fact President Kohl made just such an admission on 9
August 1993.]

mechanism was inoperable. As Central Bank governors have recently pointed out, the ERM is a mechanism designed to provide relative European exchange rate stability but including the ability for member currencies to devalue or revalue, as required by their different economic circumstances. It is not a first stage towards a common European currency at a fixed exchange rate system.

The problem has been that since the early 1980s France sought to establish, by its own precedent policies, a phased route towards a common European currency, beginning with not changing ERM parities as required by economic circumstances and permitted under the Mechanism. Seeking to fix ERM parities was seen as a tool of monetary policy to achieve accelerated economic convergence amongst the states of Europe, thus in turn rendering a common European currency possible without excessive economic dislocation.

The policy, moreover, had substantial success. There was considerable convergence in the inflation levels of the states of the EC and partly as a result in EC members' interest rates. Without the impact of German re-unification, the process of accelerating European economic convergence by a fixed European Exchange Rate Mechanism might have succeeded in ushering in a common European currency. This seeming possibility generated the premises and assumptions on which the Treaty of Maastricht was conceptually based.

Unfortunately the recession started to bite seriously in Europe, beginning in the UK in 1990. This global phenomenon required interest rates to fall at a time when the inflationary impact of re-unification was seen by the Bundesbank as requiring German interest rates to rise, so the Maastricht game was up. Fixed exchange rates in Europe have had to be abandoned by all countries other than the core of Germany, the Benelux countries and France [on 16 September 1992, but on 2 August 1993 the game was up for the remaining core as well]. Now that France is facing similar problems to the UK, albeit a year or so later, if the Bundesbank still does not feel able to effect a substantial reduction in Deutschemark interest rates, France will be forced to abandon its fixed FFr/DM parity [which was what happened on 2 August 1993] in order to be able to implement the substantial cuts in French interest rates (4% or so) that her economy clearly needs.

Several eminent economists have argued that even without the particular problems of German re-unification, a common European currency was always either undesirable or premature. Here the crucial argument is that the inability to devalue by one economy suffering from the problem of relatively high inflation or other economic disadvantages could turn it into a permanently depressed

region. Arguably, in the USA this has been the particular fate of
Tennessee, if not most of 'the South' – at least until recently. The
main opposing argument is that until the 1931 abandonment of the
Gold Standard by the UK, Europe effectively had a common currency,
namely gold.

The Gold Standard dictated that real economies had to respond to
changes in their competitiveness, so that inflationary pressures in
any one economy were quickly checked by the Gold Standard monetary mechanism. Moreover, it may be argued that the maintenance
of the easy option of devaluation discourages businesses from fighting
against wage inflation, thus perpetuating an inflation/devaluation
cycle. Furthermore, foreign exchange transactions within Europe
represent an enormous and useless banking cost to businesses and
consumers alike. Mobility within Europe means that to change currency at non-existent borders has become an anachronism; no Lon-
doner would expect to have to change his currency when travelling
up to Edinburgh. Moreover, a common currency within Europe would
constitute an important stimulant to greater European economic
co-operation and a deterrent against any major lack of European
political co-operation – without broadly similar monetary and fiscal
policies a common currency would not work.

Before taking on board the full impact of German reunification
there was arguably a strong case in favour of striving for European
Monetary Union, although there were always those who objected in
principle and there was always the risk that different European
cultural and economic patterns would mean that not all EC states
could participate, e.g. Italy and Greece. German reunification has,
however, completely changed the position. The statesmen and economists of Europe were slow to realise this, despite the writing being
on the wall at the time the draft Treaty of Maastricht was signed in
December 1991. The economic strains of German reunification are
substantially greater and more difficult than were initially envisaged
and have put European monetary union to the practical test. It is now
clear that the priorities of German fiscal and monetary policies for at
least the next decade will be dictated by the course of reunification
and that these are quite likely to be considerably different from
appropriate fiscal and monetary policies for the rest of Europe.

The Bundesbank has made its position entirely clear. It is happy
to live with the ERM mechanism as a vehicle for relative exchange
rate stability in Europe, but permitting revaluations and devaluations (as the ERM mechanism allows) as economically appropriate.
It is not, however, interested in European Monetary Union or Euro-

pean-wide interest rate policies directed by a European Central Bank. As far as Maastricht is concerned, other EC states apparently prefer to overlook that it is the non-democratically accountable Bundesbank which wields ultimate monetary power in Germany, and not the elected government.

It is perhaps worthwhile focusing on why German reunification has made such a major difference to the situation. East Germany has added 15,700,000 citizens whose economy is virtually useless. As a result, and as East Germany is now part of greater Germany, there is the requirement to make massive subsidies to this population – now costing some DM200 billion per annum, or an annual DM12,000 for every citizen. The level of subsidisation may be somewhat higher than was absolutely necessary but was designed, successfully, to win votes at the last German election. A substantial degree of subsidisation is, however, still clearly unavoidable, or large numbers of people would simply move from east to west and citizens of one country have equal rights to social welfare entitlements. This massive subsidisation, ballooning Germany's government deficit, has inevitably caused inflationary pressures which the Bundesbank has felt obliged to seek to restrain by monetary policies, by raising and keeping relatively high interest rates.

Under a regime of fixed exchange rates, as the ERM had become in all but name, higher Deutschemark interest rates had to be at least matched in other currencies. Moreover, with the Deutschemark as the major European currency and enjoying a premium rating based on its historic strength, other European currencies required an interest rate premium if their parity was to be maintained. As recession bit hard in the UK it became an increasing economic nonsense to maintain very high real rates of interest. This is now happening in France too, where interest rates clearly need to fall by some 4% over the next year.

The impact of reunification in Germany is going to be prolonged, in part as a result of Bundesbank current policy. The East German economy would be regenerated more quickly if the West German economy were operating at full employment, as an incentive to German businesses to move East and to build modern plants in East Germany. A major recession in Germany, induced by Bundesbank policies designed to contain inflationary pressures, has resulted in many investment plans in East Germany being cancelled and is greatly delaying any material regeneration of the East German economy. In the meantime, subsidisation of living standards and trade union pressures for equal or nearly equal wages in East Ger-

many is making it a less attractive European location for new investment.

Across the border are Hungary, former Czechoslovakia and Poland
where wage costs are a fraction of those in East Germany and the
people are much hungrier for gainful employment. Meanwhile in
West Germany, having enjoyed a virtually unbroken rise in living
standards since WW2, people are unwilling to accept a cut in living
standards to accommodate the massive subsidies to the East. As
government tax policies, and more particularly the Bundesbank's
monetary policies, have sought to reduce demand in West Germany,
German trade unions have pushed to recover living standards with
wage increases and working practices which are now making West
Germany dangerously uncompetitive in its traditional industrial
areas.

Ironically, by the second half of this decade, we could well see a
reversal of recent intra-European monetary problems. By then the
Deutschemark is likely to be a weaker and less respected currency
after five or six years of unresolved German reunification economic
problems and relatively higher inflation. The German economy may
then desperately need a lower exchange rate and lower interest rates
at a time when four or five years of economic recovery in, for example,
the UK may require interest rates to move upwards.

In the meantime, and after the realignments of September 1992
[and August 1993], once the tug of war between interest rates in
France and Germany has been resolved this year, I would expect a
return to relative exchange rate stability in Europe – under market
forces – and some return of a pattern to interest rate and inflation
rate convergence. This should not, however, conceal the fact that the
economic imbalance caused by German reunification is likely to take
a minimum of a decade and possibly two decades to digest.

Put simply, German reunification has created too great a degree
of potential economic divergence within Europe as between Germany
and the other European economies for a common European currency
to be practically possible for many years. As a result the Treaty of
Maastricht is economically a dead letter, whether or not it is eventually signed by all EC member states. Unfortunately, the Conservative
government is badly placed to be able to tell the rest of Europe that
events have superseded the main aim of Maastricht – phased stages
towards European Monetary Union – as the UK anyway has an
opt-out under the Treaty. A reunified Germany, as both the major
European economy and the cause of the changed circumstances,
ought to be playing the role of European statesman and looking

afresh, with the other EC members, at the shape of a workable European economic environment. Germany however, appears to be as constrained as the UK, for fear of being thought a bad European in the context of twentieth-century European history.

It matters little, I believe, in the context of economic reality whether or not Maastricht is ratified. Just as with the 1688 British Act of Rights, if a piece of legislation is an impractical Dead Letter, even before its enactment, it will be consigned to the dustbin quickly in practice.

14 April 1993   London

Fatal Flaws at the Economic Heart of Europe

Stephen Hill

The problems of imposing a single currency, which is the main aim of the Treaty of Maastricht, on just two diverse economies is amply demonstrated by the current exercise in German reunification. West Germany is one of the strongest economies in Europe and East Germany is one of the weakest. Putting the Deutschemark on near-parity with the Ostmark turned the former eastern DDR into an economic wasteland, which now threatens to pull the former western BRD down with it for several years. In effect the near common currency conversion terms created an inflationary tendency within a deflationary whirlpool. It was a case of political *ECU*nomics over economics, justified no doubt because they are Germans in the east too and therefore rightful heirs to Teutonic equality.

How different it could have been if East Germany had kept its comparatively worthless Ostmark. Then the east would have enjoyed a strong competitive currency advantage that would have attracted inward investment and led to the gradual revival of its near-bankrupt economy. The west had better learn the lesson quickly, as east Europe has another hundred million inhabitants living with economies equally debilitated by communism. The Germans will eventually achieve an economic reunification, but it would be unwise to attempt to repeat the exercise following this blueprint – it's a long, long way to the Urals from the Oder River.

The idea of a common market with a common currency covering twelve or possibly fifteen or so different economies by 1999 – as currently envisaged by certain unelected European Commissioners – is the stuff of economic nonsense. It would be the most certain way known to man of causing a depression. This is the great danger posed by unelected *fonctionnaires* dabbling in matters of which they appear to have little knowledge or foresight, and without being accountable to an electoral review.

This is neither a sweeping nor an unwarranted claim. In 1992 we witnessed at first hand the British economy turned into 'an economic desert' in the words of the chairman of BTR plc, one of Britain's most successful manufacturing companies. The worldwide recession was generally to blame, but specifically it was Britain's membership of the ERM that nearly caused final economic asphyxiation. Now the same is happening in France and for precisely the same reason.

Britain's economic policy consisted solely of membership of the ERM from October 1990 to 16 September 1992. The only aim was to bring inflation down from an unsustainable 11%, by maintaining the pound sterling within either side of 6% of 2.95 Deutschemarks. Because of the high costs of German reunification, however, their Deutschemark was losing its non-inflationary characteristics at exactly the moment Britain was attempting to hitch its currency to the Deutschemark's seeming virtue. The result was that German interest rates rose, so Britain's had to rise too to maintain the ERM parity-band. This monetary axis squeezed both economies, but whereas Britain's inflation had fallen to 4% and was still falling, her Base Rate had still to be maintained at 10%, thus yielding a 6% real interest rate.

The British economy could not stand this massive deflationary squeeze. The foreign exchange markets came to Britain's rescue and forced sterling into a free float. Once again the deliberate policy of forcing two currencies to converge against a background of two different economic structures was proven to be an impossibility. On 2 August 1993 exactly the same forces led to the effectively free float of the French franc.

The notion that Britain's inflation came down as a result of its brief membership of the ERM is a complete fallacy too. In 1980 Margaret Thatcher was faced with inflation of over 20%, but by 1983 it was back down to 4%. At no point in the 1980s was sterling ever even in the ERM. When sterling inflation hit 4%, the ERM currencies were still experiencing inflation of 8%, according to H.M. Treasury's *Red Book* for 1992-93. Yet it is H.M. Treasury that now claims that Britain's current low inflation was achieved through ERM membership. Get away! Inflation came down in 1990-92 for exactly the same reason that it did in 1980-83: high real interest rates, regardless of ERM membership. In fact, inflation got out of control in 1987-90 when Nigel Lawson, the Chancellor of the Exchequer, was tracking the Deutschemark at a rate of DM 3.00 to the pound in the run-up to ERM membership.

The truth is that exchange rate movements are the effect of many causal components. When they are fixed artificially, as in the ERM or the Gold standard, they have a counter-effect on these underlying components, such as demand, output, employment, credit and interest rates, which is usually negative on at least one side of the exchange between two trading currencies, if not both. The beauty of exchange rates is that they adjust in the market place so as *not* to interfere with the causal components in the economy. When exchange rates are fixed it has the same effect as putting a spanner in the works.

For example, West Germany's decision to put East Germany's Ostmark on a partial parity with the Deutschemark has seized up the eastern economy by removing its competitiveness. At the same time the resultant German high interest rates have forced France's economy to the west into a massive deflationary squeeze, as France refuses to realise that its *franc fort* policy is a losing strategy. The way out of this economic cul-de-sac is simply to let the exchange rates float to their market rates and ease the gridlock affecting the causal components in the underlying economies. This is exactly what the markets did anyway in September 1992 and August 1993. The bureaucrats then blame the markets as being manipulated by speculators, which is sublime nonsense. The so-called speculators are various economic entities, from pension funds to industrial companies, who know more about the economic reality of markets and the effects of bad policy than the bureaucrats themselves who framed the unworkable policies in the first place.

There is another and bigger risk that would be created by a new single currency across Europe. Every major nation in the EC is taking on vast national debts in the early 1990s recession to support their bloated social security programmes. A single currency would bundle these respective national debts into a single debt behind a single currency – with no democratic accountability, and therefore focus, on managing and repaying that debt. We have only to look across the Atlantic to America and see the slumpflationary effects of its massive federal debt, which is holding back recovery and causing President Clinton to seek US $500 billion expenditure cuts, while the lowest interest rates for over two decades fail to prevent recovery slipping and sliding, and possibly stalling.

The effective collapse of the ERM on 2 August 1993 is viewed as a national tragedy in France; as a matter-of-fact proof of the law of economic gravity in Germany; of passing importance to the Bundesbank; and as an object of mirth and much rejoicing in the UK. So what exactly was the ERM, what was it meant to achieve and does it matter if it suddenly emits scalding hot blasts of escaping currency, before finally exploding in a whirl of flying shards of coinage from equally shattered realms?

The seed of the ERM was conceived some three centuries ago in the minds of French mercantilists such as Colbert. As they surveyed the vast fields of France, it was clear that her largely agrarian population could be 'held to ransom' by imports of relatively cheaper foodstuffs and that her export values could suffer with relatively lower produce prices. The argument for protectionism seemed compelling and stable produce prices within a tariff barrier became a key French objective. This approach inevitably led to the perceived need to maintain stable exchange rates, for there seemed no point in achieving a stable price if fluctuations in exchange rates eroded produce prices and either let in cheap imports or devalued exports. This twin approach to agriculture – of stable prices and fixed exchange rates – was the cause of the French propensity towards protectionism and mercantilism, first manifested in this century by France's adherence to the Gold Standard. It manifests in the late twentieth century as the twin French policies of the CAP and the ERM.

After the Second World War, this central French idea was reinforced in two ways. First, the re-emergence of German industry and the relative weakness of French manufacturing industry in the 1950s and 1960s meant that Germany was France's major trading partner and main export market for her biggest industry and employer, namely agriculture. Second, Jean Monnet conceived the EEC as a mechanism for the future peace, by harnessing German economic power into a monetary and eventually a political union, in which stable produce prices and fixed exchange rates would lead to a single currency, the D-franc. This single currency would be managed by a joint Franco-German central bank, so that France would have a considerable measure of control over monetary policy in Germany, and her main industry would be heavily subsidised, so that the French economy would keep pace with the German juggernaut.

French policy in the 1960s was driven by the need to establish the CAP in the core of the new Europe, which was why De Gaulle kept the British out. The British would have wanted a real common market with no subsidies, however, as their cheaper food imports came mainly from the Commonwealth. This would have been directly contrary to the French objective. The CAP was established with German compliance as West Germany was out to make amends for the two world wars and did not consider itself so much a nation as a federation on the eastern edge of the EEC. When the British were

allowed into this uncommon market in 1973, the Franco-German core
was already one step ahead devising the second leg of the strategy,
the EMS, which was referred to at that time as the 'snake', in which
the franc would closely follow wherever the Deutschemark led. The
EMS was formalised in 1979, but the policy started much earlier in
the decade.

The French socialists' key monetary policy in the 1980s was to
achieve a stable parity between the franc and the Deutschemark,
which was achieved with considerable deflationary pain by means of
high real interest rates, to the point where French inflation did
converge with German inflation, just as envisaged by the monetary
convergence criteria of the Treaty of Maastricht. Unfortunately, this
treaty was a direct product of 1950s thinking and failed to accommodate the major fault-line that unexpectedly appeared in 1989 when
the Berlin Wall came down. The French economists had forgotten the
first rule of European history: the winds of change blow through the
Brandenburg Gates.

The collapse of the Iron Curtain had the immediate effect of
re-uniting Germany. It was a sovereign nation state once again, and
began to walk, talk and think like a nation state for the first time
since 1945. The monetary terms set by Chancellor Kohl for the
reunification with East Germany, however, led to an explosion in
Deutschemark M3 in the early 1990s, causing a 10% surge in monetary growth in 1993 alone. The speed of the German legerdemain in
granting parity for the Ostmark with the Deutschemark for the first
4,000 Ostmarks and two-to-one thereafter worked like smoke in the
French *franc fort* eye.

The pain for France is immense, particularly as Balladur has the
socialist President Mitterrand for the next two years and cannot
easily drop the *franc fort* policy. Thus the politicians' pain is translated into economic grief for the French people. An elaborate policy
pursued at great expense for forty years has only succeeded in
snatching failure from the jaws of success. Just as French inflation
at 2% is running at under half of Germany's 4.5% in 1993, the
Deutschemark leaves the franc floundering in its wake as the foreign
exchange markets perceive that, whereas Germany will eventually
succeed in reunification despite high interest rates, France's existing
economy can no longer withstand high real interest rates of over 6%.
If one wished to add insult to injury, one would have to question the
assumption of the efficacy of a single currency as an agent of an
enduring peace in the first instance. The *slotje* came a cropper in the
peace stakes in former Yugoslavia, just like the dollar in nineteenth-

century America and sterling in seventeenth-century Britain. The agent for peace between countries is *free trade*, not a common currency.

This fundamental fact brings the discussion round full circle to the Anglo-French free trade agreement of 1860. (Did the socialists ban history these past twelve years in France?) Gladstone found himself in 1859 in a most unusual position for a British Chancellor of the Exchequer: he presided over a £2 million budget surplus caused by the remission of the Long Annuities. In the interests of European peace, Gladstone determined that this windfall would be allocated to reducing customs duties on French imports.

Cobden was appointed envoy and met the Emperor Louis Napoleon in Paris in the autumn. The Emperor was impressed by the success of Britain's free-trade policies and he saw that France's protectionist 'ironmasters' were holding the wider economy back by promoting their sectional interests. His finance minister, however, was a 'furious protectionist' and rallied the ironmasters, but between January and September 1860 the treaty was negotiated in detail and then signed in November.

Cobden was present throughout the negotiations and observed that 'The ironmasters are the landed interest of France. They constituted the Praetorian guards of monopoly. Bankers, courtiers, authors, bishops and priests are to be found in the ranks of the ironmasters. The French witnesses of course all tell the old story of alarm and ruin ... if their protection is withdrawn'.

The only thing that has changed 133 years later is that the ironmasters are now the farmers. The bankers are now assisted by the EC bureaucrats. The farmers' subsidies are now to alleviate 'social problems', regardless of the economic problems they cause to other sectors of the French and world economy. Worst of all, French defence of the CAP subsidies threatens a trade war with America; if the GATT talks remain stalled by French intransigence on what is perceived as this paramount issue, the Americans will probably further reduce or even withdraw their military presence and thus remove the basis for Europe's security.

The massive subsidies of the CAP are the fatal flaw at the economic heart of the EC. They undermine the common market, impede economic growth and threaten Europe's stability. The CAP should be phased out – sooner rather than later. Even for France it remains an industry of declining employment, whereas France has developed world-class industries in other leading sectors, from telecommunications to nuclear energy, defence and in general manufacturing from automobiles to aerospace. France should look back to the example of Emperor Louis Napoleon and move decisively to free trade, abandoning the flawed socialist programme of the ERM and the CAP.

Everyone is agreed on one issue concerning Europe: that the evolution of a peaceful and united Europe depends on economic prosperity. If the violent first half of the twentieth century taught us anything, it was this fundamental reality. So the need in post-war Europe was for reconciliation and for a means of exchanging 'blessings instead of curses'. The essential strategy was meant to be the creation of a common market as the central plank of a revitalised and cohesive continent, for history has shown us time and again that free trade and peaceful prosperity go hand-in-hand, just as protectionism in all its forms inevitably leads towards economic deprivation and eventually to war.

The economic malaise caused by the First World War was not addressed as the essential post-war issue, however, and the League of Nations failed to achieve American endorsement. The Fordney-McCumber tariffs imposed by America on mainly European imports in the early 1920s were a direct cause of the Great Depression. (Historians generally refer to the 'infamous Smoot-Hawley protectionist tariffs' of the 1930s as the cause, but it was these earlier tariff barriers that started the whole destructive process.) Then the Great Depression led to the Great Inflation in Germany in the early 1930s. The lack of any coherent economic action created the vacuum that allowed the Nazis to seize control of the most powerful country on the Continent. Hitler's economic recovery was led by the revival of the armaments industry. The pocket-battleships, U-boats, fighters, bombers, dive-bombers, tanks and self-propelled artillery required steel and engines and drove new technologies and, above all, generated full employment. The inevitable outcome was the Second World War.

The lesson of this murderous cycle, however, was not lost on the allies the second time around. The Marshall Plan for the economic recovery of the Continent was funded directly by America – and indirectly by Britain as she repaid her war debt to America. The concept of a customs union as a free trade area throughout western Europe, from the Atlantic to the Iron Curtain, was established by the Treaty of Rome in 1957, as economic reconstruction became increasingly evident. For forty-five years the Continent of Europe – the western part of it as least – enjoyed the longest period of peace in the millennium, along with the greatest prosperity.

The eastern half of Europe, however, enjoyed neither peace nor prosperity. For forty-five years, while the west recovered and then prospered, the east was held in subjection by the heavy centralist hand of the former USSR. A workers' revolt in East Germany was crushed in 1953 with a still unknown number of fatalities; in 1956 Hungary was invaded; in 1968 Czechoslovakia's democracy movement was stamped out; and in the former USSR dissidents were regularly imprisoned without trial. The communist regimes were military-command economies in which the secret state police and part members prospered, while the mass of the people struggled endlessly and queued forever for life's necessities – when they were available.

Whilst the economies of eastern Europe were on the point of collapse in 1990, those of western Europe had just reached their post-war peak. More extraordinarily, just as the centralised economies of the east imploded, the twelve EC members in the west were determined to move towards more centralisation, in the form of monetary union, monetary policy determined by unelected central bankers, standard social security impositions on employers and extension of the Common Agricultural Policy of unproductive and costly subsidies.

Western Europe was living in the past. While it was seeking to produce a federal socialist structure directed from the centre, its not-so-distant cousin in the east, namely a federal communist structure managed by the military-command centre, was collapsing. The west was seeking convergence or 'ever closer union': more power was being moved to the centre, with more corruption set to follow in its path; the centre was moving to deny democracy, with more decisions behind more closed doors; regional governments were being deliberately weakened. A parallel tendency to protectionism was being fostered in the west, just as it was failing to give effective economic aid and assistance to the east. In the east, the military has been molly-coddled; in the west, inefficient farmers and other industries are being cosseted. An inability to repay or even service debt emerged first in the east, but now threatens to spread to the west.

The grim reality is that west Europe could implode in the future in much the same way as the east, under the weight of the most costly social security and payroll tax structure in the world, compounded by a severe deflationary monetary policy at a time of world recession. In short, two of the main concepts of the Treaty of Maastricht are bringing west Europe to her knees in a massive sea of national debt, while at the same time consigning the east to virtual economic exclusion. Meanwhile, the price of gold soars, along with unemployment.

The leaders of west Europe have lost sight of political and economic reality. The political reality is that the Iron Curtain no longer exists. The economic reality is that the EC is no common market in the true sense. It is an outmoded, post-Second World War, west European defensive structure that has outlived its useful life in its present form. With its growing tendency towards subsidies, minimum social security standards and centralised directives, it is no longer economically viable in today's environment of fierce global competition. The Treaty of Maastricht not only does not deal with the real problems facing Europe, but it actually exacerbates them and excludes real debate by setting the wrong agenda.

It is time to resurrect the forgotten agenda of Maastricht and return to the essential strategy: the need to create a common market where manufacturers, labour and capital can move freely to maximise their market potential. Whilst there has been apparent progress in the more obvious and visible aspects of a barrier-free Europe, such as the removal of customs duties, border checks and lengthy delays caused by paperwork, the fact remains that the EC is riddled with latent protectionism in all its many forms and guises.

Customs duties on imported goods are the most obvious protectionist device. There are, alas, many others: price support mechanisms, production subsidies, non-production subsidies, employment subsidies, export subsidies, criteria on technical and safety regulations, outright bans, 'voluntary' restraints, price fixing, checks on capital movement and even subsidised interest rates.

This list of anti-common market mechanisms bears comparison with current practice within the EC: the CAP subsidies for farmers cost a massive £88 billion in 1992, according to the OECD; farmers are even paid subsidies not to farm, under the 'set-aside' programme, so that prices are maintained; semi-conductor manufacturers are heavily subsidised both by the EC and by the nation-states; so are coal-mining, atomic power, railways, high definition TV and many other sectors in general manufacturing; import quotas are placed on a whole range of goods, from bananas to pigs; production quotas are placed on another range of items, from rape-seed oil to motor-cars made by Japanese European implants; technical restrictions run through many key industries, such as telecommunications; the British fishing fleet is allowed to go to sea for only two days a week; cartels exist across a whole range of industries, from cement production to airline tickets; capital movements on the Continent are severely restricted, for example by the distinct lack of data on ownership and financial statements widely available in the UK public domain; and in Germany the KFW (Credit Institute for Reconstruction) even provides industry with subsidised low-interest loans.

Far from being a common market, the EC is an elaborate system of economic bluffs and baffles, which enables the centre to trade off one subsidy against another's production quota, one nation's open procurement policy in one sector for protection in a different sector, and one trade alignment for another regional development grant, guarantee or loan. It is a structure that every bureaucrat dreams of, for all these trade negotiation instruments are currency to their power and their own self-advancement. As power gravitates to the centre, so does corruption inevitably follow.

A common market worthy of the name is a quite different structure, based on the economics of common sense. One person's subsidy is another person's cost, either in taxation, debt or the price paid for goods. One person's subsidised job is another person's unemployment. It cannot ever be otherwise. So the £88 billion annual cost of the CAP translates into an annual cost for a British four-person family of £1,020, which sum cannot therefore be spent on other goods and services. So consumer demand for products of industries other than agriculture is reduced by this amount – less any portion that would have gone to savings or investment. This structure contributes to the fall-off in demand and investment that is so evident in the world recession of 1991-93. In this way does the redundant, but subsidised, farmer's job destroy the possibility of an alternative job emerging in a healthy industry elsewhere.

It is precisely the same with all other types of subsidy. Government procurement programmes, for example, that are biased towards national suppliers invariably increase the cost of the resultant service, which is usually a less effective service anyway. The denationalisation of British Telecom has broken its monopoly of the single biggest service market in the UK and led to a whole range of cheaper and more efficient services from a wide range of suppliers. The resultant efficiency and productivity gains help make the rest of the UK industry more competitive too. In effect, the UK telecommunications sector has become a common market and not a closed market, which is the exact opposite of the EC's approach to agriculture, the largest industrial employer in Europe and on every continent.

The challenge in the 1990s is to establish a free trade common market in the EC; to extend this common market to the Urals; then to promote free movement of capital across the world. Any impediment to this new global order in the making will only sow the seeds of protectionism and future discord.

12 August 1993   London

A Japanese View of European Unity

Dr. Toru Nakakita

What are the major factors that will steer the world economy in the future? Europe will no doubt be one major influence, as it attempts to break free of the traditional framework of autonomous nations and move into as yet uncharted territory. It is a daunting task for a Japanese author observing this transition from within the traditional structure correctly to assess the significance of European integration.

How has Japan viewed European integration thus far? The understanding of the average Japanese citizen is that EC integration in 1992 would also mean the eventual addition of Austria, Sweden, and Norway, typical European states, to the membership of the EC. As a result national boundaries would be redrawn and the traditional view of Europe held by the Japanese and that of a unified EC would overlap. On the economic side, expansion of the marketplace and the benefits of a larger-scale economy would open up new possibilities for business development.

At the same time, conflicts within the region would be reduced while the economic dynamism of Europe as a whole would be augmented. The scale of financial and capital dealings especially would expand rapidly, increasing the degree of integration. On the other hand, however, there would be a greater tendency for the EC to transform into a bloc and raise trade barriers against countries outside the region, such as the US and Japan. For that reason, members of the business community, the mass media and academics continue to sound the alarm against a Fortress Europe and to bolster their warnings with numerous comparisons of GNP, trade, and population figures between the EC, Japan, and the US.

Even if these aspects are very important, though, they are not the whole issue. The crux of the problem is that EC integration will attempt to do away with states hitherto autonomous and replace them with a supra-national institution. The Maastricht treaty assumes that financial and currency systems will be integrated, and a uniform currency, the ECU, will be introduced at the latest by the turn of this century. This is an ambitious design, aimed at eventually establishing greater trust among the citizens of Europe towards economic activities. A unified currency, however, will only find acceptance by these citizens through naturally-occurring processes, not through any exchange of treaties between governments.

In the areas of finance and currency, the focus of debate will likely shift to the issue of how many representatives each country may send to occupy posts in the European Central Bank. After economic liberalisation has been achieved through political decision-making, attention will return to political affairs. In other words, the debate will come full circle, with the emphasis once again falling on politics.

If and when complete economic integration is achieved, the financial policies of individual EC member countries will naturally disappear, essentially to be incorporated into a regional policy. Can these individual states overcome the regional ego? Can a unified monetary policy work across so many different economies? If disputes over assistance funding arise during the design of unemployment policies, however, EC integration could lose all meaning.

Euro-federalists, trying to break up the European mould of traditional national autonomy, are now experiencing a variety of birthpangs in trying to form a supra-national institution. The transition is such a difficult one that it can be likened to a transplant operation to replace a weak heart with an artificial one. It is hence surprising that the national representatives involved in negotiations to overcome this framework of individual states have been taking such direct approaches to resolving the issue. Has the idea of a European Super-State matured so much?

What can be inferred from a comparison between Japan and the whole of East Asia? The Asian countries that broke free of colonial rule in the post-war period had as their ultimate objective the achievement of independence and autonomy. Other than this, however, there is little common ground in language, ethnic composition, history and culture among the countries of East Asia. Until recently, the region was thus plagued with such chronic problems as Communist insurgency, refugees from Vietnam and border disputes, all of which greatly hinder regional development; indeed, increased contact with different cultures and ethnic groups among the poorer nations has become a potential cause of international conflict.

From the mid-1980s, nevertheless, the export-driven economic development of East Asia has proved successful and continues to show dynamism and promise. East Asia in this context refers to the intermediate-developed countries of South Korea, Taiwan, Singapore, Hong Kong, the ASEAN countries of Thailand, Malaysia, Indonesia and the Philippines, and the coastal provinces of China.

This region is shut into a rigid framework of national autonomy, which protects authoritarian governments and pursues no higher goal than the maintenance of political stability. Progress is being made, however, through liberalisation in accepting foreign capital, and increasing interdependence means greater opportunities for growth and, through that, greater political stability. This marks a major revolution in thinking. Once the economy reaches the take-off stage, living standards will begin to improve and mutual exchange will increase; this cycle will deepen the friendly relations between the countries of the region and will propel the Pacific rim towards economic integration. Unlike the EC, the resultant entity would be a de facto economic sphere founded on a network of corporations working through private initiative. In this manner, the economics and politics of East Asia will gradually mesh, leading to a reduction in the distinctiveness of the autonomous states.

Compared to Europe, the economic development of East Asia is still at an early stage and is really no more than the prelude to the tremendous development to come in the twenty-first century. It is very possible that by the beginning of the next century the Asian NICs will join Japan alongside the other economically advanced nations. In 1965, Japan's GNP per capita was only one-fourth that of the US, but in 1985, only twenty years later, Japan had pulled level. This process of catching up with the US is being echoed in the intermediate-developed nations of Asia and in ASEAN, and has now reached the coastal provinces of China. Given the dynamism of East Asia, it can be expected that very early in the twenty-first century, say around 2005, the presently intermediate-developed countries of Asia will achieve parity with Japan, while several of the ASEAN countries will surpass the present levels of South Korea and Taiwan.

What conditions must be met for this to come about? Economically, much depends on whether or not East Asia can expand and develop a horizontal division of labour, and above all on whether or not Japan will continue to expand its import of manufactured goods. Hence, it is vital that East Asia itself increases its supply capabilities. This period offers Japan a good chance to break away from the one-set production pattern that has drawn so much disapproval from overseas and to deflect criticism about its closed markets.

The inter-penetration of the economies of East Asia will progress considerably. For example, at least one or two major manufacturers from South Korea and Taiwan will probably have entered the Japanese markets for passenger cars and home appliances etc., and will be able to compete on an equal footing. Towards this end, it is very important that Japan carries on with technology transfer to the other countries of East Asia and that it supports marketing efforts made by those countries in the Japanese market. It is extremely important that the countries of East Asia proceed more actively along the road to market liberalisation and deregulation. Such efforts will help check the protectionism that appears on the increase in certain western countries and will be of considerable help in strengthening the GATT system of world trade.

Will the basic driving force for the twenty-first century come from the EC and Europe west of the Urals? Or will it stem from the diversity and dynamism of Asia-Oceania? Or might it arise from a successfully reconstructed American economy? In any case, due consideration must be given to internal structural changes in, and the economic maturity of, the US, Europe and Japan, which will be the focus of economic development.

The Asia-Pacific region will be one of the focal points of future world growth, and continued rapid expansion may allow some countries in the region to attain national incomes on a par with those of European countries. Trade and investment activities are liberalised, and progress in liberalising these areas will likely increase the economic benefits enjoyed by the countries doing so. Because these countries are young, it does not seem for the time being that the increased burdens of social security programmes will be a cause for worry.

There will be fewer constraints on trade with and inward investment in the NICs and ASEAN; Japan's economic strategy towards them will provide useful experience on how the EC should approach the former Comecon countries to the east, to the advantage of all. To compound Europe's competitive problems, it seems that America is likely to maintain its technical and productivity advantages.

Japan's manufacturing and banking industries, amidst the calls for a fundamental globalisation of economic activities, will continue to have strong incentives to branch out further into Europe. Certainly, the break-up of the ERM on 16 September 1992 [and on 2 August 1993] means that a serious reconstruction of the prospects for a unified EC currency is due. But Japan will continue to invest in Britain, where its open capital markets and atmosphere of free trade are attractive, whether a two-speed Europe evolves or not.

Japan, like the UK, is separated by the sea from its continental neighbours, permitting it to take a more objective position regarding moves towards regionalism as well as to provide a certain direction to the world trading structure. There is little doubt that the affinity between the UK and Japan will provide support both to the future integration of the EC and to the development of the Asia-Pacific region.

21 June 1993   Tokyo

For 'Russia' read 'Borassic Park'

Franco Racca

The dinosaur of the Russian economy has a political backbone of clay and lives in a polluted habitat. Its continued existence is truly 'a riddle wrapped in a mystery inside an enigma'. If this nearly extinct species disintegrates, however, the threat to Europe is incalculable. To begin to imagine the scale of this threat, take a map of Russia and Europe, turn it upside down and look at the capitals of Europe from the viewpoint of Moscow – how can Europeans talk now of a common market that excludes east Europe and White Russia?

The west must provide urgent help for the communist dinosaur to come in from the cold. When President Gorbachev came to the G7 summit in London in June 1990, he asked for US $10 billion in loans. He was refused and rightly so, for the money would have gone to bank accounts in Switzerland and elsewhere and would never have been repaid. A different approach is required, but first the problems must be analysed.

The only part of this dinosaur that really gallops is inflation. Monthly inflation in 1992 was in double figures every month. First, the government and central bank continue to sanction ever more credits for loss-making state enterprises and just keep on printing money. Then consumer prices keep on rising every month – 25% in December 1992 alone. The official budget deficit in 1992 was only 4% of GDP, but total credits issued by the central bank to the state sector alone totalled 40% of GDP. While the impetus for economic reform falters and political will is sapped, the IMF argues that it cannot lend because of the Russian government's profligacy rather than any excessive caution on its own part. The World Bank's real concern is about the capability and will of the Russians to implement reform and deliver a consistent economic programme.

Second, the privatisation programme appears to have been successful – over 50,000 SMEs had been privatised by January 1993 – but the reality is a far grimmer picture. Most of the privatised companies have retained the same management structures, methods and personnel as under the Soviet regime. There has been little or no new investment, restructuring or formulation of strategy. Most companies are majority-owned by management, employees and the enabling bureaucrats, who were able to secure their controlling positions in the best companies as they had prior access to the limited financial data available. These owners defend the *status quo* on employment levels and welfare, rather than adapting to a market-oriented economy.

Third, the military-command Soviet economy has either to find new export markets for arms, or convert to civilian products, or simply shrink with the declining military budget. Of these options, conversion requires new investment and management which is simply not available. So there is no quick-fix miracle cure even for the pride of Russian industry, which is a world leader in aerospace, ships, submarines and metallurgy. In addition, regional governments are hesitant to divide their monolithic defence concerns into separate economic units. This top-level indecision has prevented clear plans on what to convert to what, what to leave alone and how to convert from this to that. Whole factories are thus left in limbo, hoping for more subsidies and orders and surviving by selling off bits and pieces. The Aviastar aerospace complex at Ul'yanovsk, for example, makes the largest aeroplanes in the world, along with flat-pack furniture and barbecues. The plain fact is that there is nothing much to attract investors, other than the possibility of quicker returns from service industries.

Some of the medium-technology firms have succeeded in establishing joint-ventures with western firms by offering well proven know-how or 'dual-use' products for military or civilian applications, ranging from helicopters to electronics and sporting guns. These are the exceptions, however, because most products are well below world standards and many firms that have started the conversion process are finding that their products are not good enough for export markets. This is a double blow, as hard currency export earnings are needed to sustain investment in the conversion process. Moreover, production volumes were the only objective under communism, so research and development, marketing, distribution, quality control and after-sales service all suffered. Seventy years of communism have ensured that companies are not market- or consumer-driven.

Finally, the military-command economy had no use for costing and accounting, so companies are not profit and cost conscious. At Aviastar, for example, which is also the world's largest aircraft manufacturing complex, the workers still rivet and hammer aircraft wings rather than employing aluminum-stretch technology. The company keeps no cost records, so it cannot measure efficiency.

Turning any company's culture around is a difficult task, as people the world over are naturally more comfortable doing what they are good at or at least used to doing. So there is a trend in Russia to invest in developing existing technology instead of analysing potential markets for new products.

The fourth major problem facing the CIS is the antipathy towards Moscow from the former USSR republics. (The dinosaur has a message here for M.Jacques Delors: for 'Moscow' read 'Brussels'). To take an extreme example, consider the port of Nakhodka with its 225,000 inhabitants on the Pacific, some 8,000 kilometres and seven time-zones to the east of Moscow. The port, following the introduction of the market economy, is now trading with other regional centres such as Shanghai, Tokyo and Seoul and attracting inward investment, including from China. Nakhodka's aim is to have the whole area declared Russia's first free economic zone. The dinosaur in Moscow, however, reacts by banning the import of right-hand-drive cars from Japan.

Such absurdities are now causing Vladivostok, the territorial capital, to consider declaring the Maritime Territory a republic. At the heart of the tug-of-war are two simple issues – first, who receives and spends the taxes and, secondly, democratic accountability. Nakhodka has privatised the port facilities in the initial free economic zone and they handle 25% of Russian exports, so the bureaucrats now have to sit up and listen. The plain fact is that Moscow is too remote and it seems inevitable that its sphere of influence will soon terminate at the Urals.

The Russian dinosaur is a question-mark waiting for answers. Money is not the answer, but the dinosaur needs help in formulating the right questions and establishing priorities. It is in the west's interests to help too. There are environmental threats from the failing nuclear power-stations, and another Chernobyl cannot be ruled out. There is a military threat as Russian armaments, missiles, enriched plutonium and scientists seek new markets. There is the economic threat of inability to repay debt. There is the political threat of anarchy should the reform movement fail. Alarmingly, all four threats could crystallise at once.

The IMF and EBRD may find some projects that are economically viable on their banking criteria, but most projects cannot yield hard currency. So the preferred approach must involve barter and most projects must find western joint-ventures and managers. Rather than western governments and agencies lending money, they should underwrite private sector joint-ventures and set the industrial priorities, by sector and region. In effect, the west must realise that the common market goes all the way to the Urals as an essential fact; it is just that barter replaces currency in Russia as the principal medium of exchange.

Russia has many commodities and skills. She is rich in natural minerals which the west needs in abundance: oil, diamonds, gold, titanium and rare metals. Russia needs food, especially wheat, and manufacturing machinery. Russia has world-class skills too: in aerospace, ships and metallurgy. Russia needs management, and effective and visible systems of distribution that modern micro-chip technology can provide at realistic prices.

As in the west, political stability can only be achieved if a certain measure of economic progress is maintained. Russia can only achieve this with western help. The largest export order ever won – the Al-Yamamah project in Saudi Arabia managed by British Aerospace plc and worth £20 billion – was in part a barter deal. Saudi supplies 500,000 barrels of oil a day and some cash, while BAe supplies Tornados, Hawks, ground facilities and training, as well as minefield clearers from Vosper Thorneycroft. The model is in place, but the agencies and priorities need to be put in place for Russia – rapidly.

As well as moving to safeguard its own security, there could be other bonuses for western Europe. The manpower involved could make a considerable dent in unemployment; there will be new markets; there will be double-sourcing for key commodities such as oil; there will be cheaper prices for consumers. Failure by the west to exploit the opportunity with the suppressed citizens of Russia for mutual advantage could easily mean that the ugly prospect of the Borassic Park in the east becomes the Jurassic Park of the west, as the result of avoidable catastrophe. That could come to a television-screen near you in the discomfort of your own home, if the west lacks the will and runs out of time.

10 July 1993   St. Petersburg

Prescription for the New Europe

Sir Donald Maitland

The nine o'clock news: Martin Bell of the BBC crouches at the roadside, behind him the ruins of a village in central Bosnia. A British patrol of the UN Protection Force has found the remains of a family burnt alive in the cellar of their home. Bell tells us: 'This is happening today, in our Continent – Europe.' He has seen too much of this already and wants us to share his anger. And we do.

Meanwhile at Westminster, the more the debate on Maastricht continues, the greater the confusion over the future shape of Europe. Crowds demonstrate outside the house in Solingen whose long-standing Turkish residents have been incinerated in a racist attack. The German Chancellor deplores hooliganism; immigration policies are revised. The result of the Danish referendum prompts a leading Belgian to urge immediate progress towards the next stage of integration. Italian politics remain in turmoil. Opinion polls show a decline in popular support for the Community. The European Commission revises downwards its forecasts of economic growth. Divergence is more evident than convergence. Two strong advocates of European union break ranks in trade negotiations with the United States – France over farm products, Germany over telecommunications equipment. Another currency is forced out of the Exchange Rate Mechanism. Unemployment in the former German Democratic Republic and France reaches new heights. Farming and fishing lobbies flex their muscles. And so on; and on and on.

The conclusions a disinterested observer might draw from what is happening today in Europe would be disagreeable. First, proposals for the closer integration of the Community initiated by the European Commission and adopted by the Council of Ministers over the past several years have run far ahead of public opinion. In those member states, especially the largest, where the sense of history, tradition and national identity is strongest, the trend towards centralisation – which many British politicians erroneously equate with federalism – has become increasingly unpalatable. This fact seems not yet to be fully recognised in Brussels.

Secondly, member states' efforts to develop a common foreign policy failed the first real test. The end of the Cold War and dismantling of the Berlin Wall seem to have taken foreign ministries in the Community by surprise. The consequences of the removal of the regimes which had suppressed individual and national expression for forty years were foreseeable, but not foreseen. Likewise, the threat to the integrity of Yugoslavia was evident the day Tito died. The catalogue of political and diplomatic errors since fighting broke out in former Yugoslavia has led not only to widespread destruction, human misery on a massive scale and the betrayal of the people of Bosnia, but also to severe damage to the standing of western Europe.

Thirdly, economic prospects for the Community make the timetable for economic and monetary union even more unrealistic than when the Maastricht Treaty was signed.

Fourthly, western Europe has difficulty in coming to terms with the advent of new faiths and cultures.*

Finally, it is not easy today to identify any political figure able to lead it. Those who have been in power for many years have run out of ideas, and scandals and the relentless scrutiny to which they are subjected by the media have diminished respect for politicians in general.

We who live in Europe are not disinterested. So we have to turn our dismay at what has been happening into constructive criticism.

If the European Community is to regain momentum and the goodwill of its citizens it should return to first principles. The vision of the 'founding fathers' deserves to be honoured. 'Ever-closer union' is not an involuntary erosion of sovereignty, real or notional, but the most ingenious formula yet devised for ordering relations between peoples. We should take pride in the evolutionary character of the European enterprise, animated by the continuous dialectic between the Commission, representing the Community interest, and the Council of Ministers, representing the interests of member states. We should bear in mind, however, that the original signatories of the Treaty of Rome assumed that economic integration would constitute a sufficiently robust base for the union. Of the conference at Messina in June 1955 Paul-Henri Spaak said: 'We set out to built a new Europe and ended up arguing over the tariff on bananas.' Jean Monnet on the other hand had set a different aim: 'The real change we are after

[*Editor's note: these 'new faiths and cultures' might actually become the agent for the revitalisation of western spiritual life.]

is not the free flow of goods. It is change in the relationship between people.'

In the 1950s reconciliation and reconstruction were prime objectives. These were to be achieved by the establishment of a large European common market which would lock together the economies of western Europe. These aims were set in the context of progressive integration by consent of those European nations who shared the same ideals. Of course, when the Treaty of Rome came into force in 1958, this ambition extended only to Europe west of the Iron Curtain.

What causes distress today is that the Maastricht debate has been conducted in terms which obscured many of the factors which will influence the future of our Continent. Demographic, societal, economic and political changes on the scale we now perceive were not imagined in the 1950s. Population growth, especially in developing countries, has reached unprecedented levels. The population of Africa, which today roughly equals that of its northern neighbour, Europe, is expected to have grown to three times that of Europe within twenty-five years. By the end of the first quarter of the next century three billion will have been added to the world population – an increase of 60%. Population growth has been accompanied by large-scale migrations – Asians from the sub-continent and east Africa into the United Kingdom, Arabs from the Maghreb into France, Turks and east Europeans into Germany. European society is now multi-cultural and multi-faith.

The marriage of telecommunications and computer technologies has facilitated the creation of countless electronic networks. Trade and the increasing coherence of economic and monetary policies in recent years have stimulated interdependence. But, thanks to revolutionary advances in methods of handling information, interdependence is yielding place to interconnection. Economic activity is being globalised. Cross-border mergers and acquisitions, world-wide procurement, international joint-ventures, the establishment of common standards, collaborative research and development programmes – all these are becoming commonplace.

These developments offer opportunities and pose threats. Electronic networks are a means to an end. They can strengthen the fabric of international understanding. On the other hand, because they disregard frontiers, networks can diminish the capacity of nation states to confront challenges to their economic interest and, in so doing, they can undermine traditional ideas of sovereignty. Moreover, networks can encourage a market-led international division of labour. International conglomerates are able to locate their production facilities in low-cost areas of the world with important consequences for patterns of employment. Already the total annual sales of the 350 biggest multi-national corporations are equivalent to one-third of the gross national products of the entire industrial world and far exceed sales of developing countries. Clearly, serious issues affecting the relationship between commerce and governments and the role of international regulation need to be addressed.

Power has been diffused in other ways. Living standards have risen, the aspirations of the working class have become more ambitious, ownership of property and other assets has spread, individual citizens and groups have been exhorted to assume more control over their affairs. These social changes and the decentralisation of decision-making have altered attitudes to authority.

Changes in the economic field have been even more dramatic. The countries of the Pacific basin are now major economic players. Brazil, China and India have made spectacular progress. Recession in the United States and western Europe suggests no return in the foreseeable future to the high rates of growth achieved in the 1980s. Long-term unemployment and ageing populations place an extra strain on public finances.

In the 1950s no one foresaw the sudden collapse of communism. The removal of the tyranny in the Kremlin brought to an end not only the immediate threat to world peace but also the suppression in central and eastern Europe of basic freedoms and the sense of national, cultural and religious identity.

These are among the considerations which should shape the future of Europe. The Inter-Governmental Conference to review foreign policy and defence in 1996 will provide European leaders with an opportunity to re-launch the Community and to correct the error made by their predecessors at Messina. Events have shown that the view taken then that the creation of a common market would provide a sufficient base for a union of European states was mistaken. Without close alignment of foreign policy, underpinned by joint action in the defence field, progress towards ever closer union will continue to falter.

The immediate task, however, is to end the bloodshed and to promote a viable settlement in former Yugoslavia. The lessons of this shameful episode need to be taken to heart. In future Community governments should devote as much effort to eliminating the causes as to mitigating the effects of such calamities. The decision in 1991 to recognise the separate states was a blunder. In the summer of that year, when the Community offered its good offices to help the peoples of Yugoslavia settle their differences peacefully, it should have been made clear that any attempt to resolve these problems by force was unacceptable in the Europe of the 1990s and that, unless fighting stopped at once, a total embargo would be placed on the whole territory. What was happening in the Balkans was a more obvious threat to peace than anarchy in Somalia and the need for humanitarian aid in the wake of ethnic cleansing just as pressing. It was therefore open to European governments to call on the Security Council to make the embargo universal and to authorise the use of all other means to end the fighting. Air strikes at that early stage could have sent a clear message to potential ethnic cleansers elsewhere in Europe.

The Balkan tragedy underlines the urgency of enlarging the Community to include all those states which qualify politically and are willing and able to accept the disciplines of membership. Negotiations to admit Sweden, Finland, Austria and Norway should be concluded without delay. As a reward for their democratic progress and an encouragement to their neighbours, the four central European states – the Czech Republic, Slovakia, Hungary and Poland – should as soon as possible be accorded a special status, superior to association but short of full membership; this would entail enhanced access to the Single Market for their products – a small price to pay. Between the present and 1996 a programme for the association and eventual accession of other states in eastern Europe should be drawn up.

In anticipation of the 1996 conference, the Western European Union should plan for the gradual integration of parts of national defence forces into a combined European defence force. To support this, military procurement should be more rigorously co-ordinated, drawing on the best skills of the European defence industries. The United Kingdom and France should find a means for effectively pooling their nuclear forces and holding their deterrent forces in trust for western Europe.

The end of the cold war enabled the UN Security Council at last to act as originally envisaged in the United Nations Charter. By the same token, despots in developing countries have been deprived of the means of playing Moscow off against Washington. Nonetheless, unacceptable situations have arisen in parts of Africa and South East Asia. The effect of the international community's response to these has been the gradual erosion of Article 2(7) of the Charter, which precludes intervention in the internal affairs of a member state. European governments should encourage this process by supporting more effective intervention to stop bloodshed, end the abuse of human rights, eradicate the production of drugs and support for international terrorism. The efforts of the Secretary-General to establish more effective means of co-ordinating humanitarian and military operations authorised by the Security Council deserve wholehearted European support. The combined European Defence Force could contain rapid reaction elements which could be placed at the disposal of the United Nations for such operations. British and French forces already have a splendid record in this role.

In preparation for enlargement and a more effective international role, the Community should set its own house in order. The Maastricht Treaty has added to its existing burdens. Emphasis now needs to be placed on a critical review of the structure of the Community, the respective roles of its institutions and its methods of work. Application of the principle of subsidiarity should include study of existing Community functions in order to distinguish those for which responsibility could be restored to national administrations.

Much could be gained by reducing the size of the Commission. Fewer people will mean less activity; only the essential should survive. As the Community expands, not even one Commissioner for each member state will be practicable. The number of directorates could be correspondingly reduced – by amalgamation, by delegating operational functions to national administrations or executive agencies, or by shedding them absolutely. While its right of initiative should be retained, the Commission's proposals should be more closely and systematically scrutinised by the European Council, the European Parliament and representatives of national parliaments. Strict observance of Community law should be verified by a multinational corps of monitors.

In the field of domestic policy, alongside measures to stimulate growth and promote employment, the liberalisation of telecommunications throughout the Community should be accelerated and assistance provided for investment in this sector in central and eastern Europe, in order to stimulate the growth of continent-wide electronic networks.

By themselves a shift in direction and internal reforms on these lines, even if carried out effectively, would do little more than arrest the decline in the Community's international prestige and make its institutions marginally more acceptable to public opinion. Community leaders should recognise the urgent need to articulate its purpose

and ambitions in more imaginative terms. For forty years foreign and
defence policies were dominated by the need to contain the Soviet
threat. John le Carré has recently reminded us that the end of the
Cold War meant we could no longer put our humanity on hold in order
to defend humanity. 'We no longer need to clip the wings of our
humanity', he said. 'It's time we flew again.'

It is indeed. In 1977 the then President of the Commission, now
Lord Jenkins, proposed that the Community should concentrate on
those 'functions which will, beyond reasonable doubt, deliver significantly better results because they are performed at Community level',
while leaving to member states 'those functions which they can do
equally well or better on their own.' It is a pity, to put it no higher,
that fourteen years had to pass before the principle of subsidiarity
was enshrined in Community law. It is also a pity that the Treaty of
Maastricht did not specify in more detail how this principle is to be
applied. Nonetheless, subsidiarity offers not only to the citizens of the
present Community, but also to our European neighbours to the east,
the twin benefits of a secure place in what Mikhail Gorbachev called
the 'European House' and the right to take those decisions which
affect them most intimately at the lowest effective level and in the
most appropriate form.

Through the horizontal division of sovereignty into layers of power
which subsidiarity entails – and this is one of the more apt definitions
of federalism – the Community could demonstrate a degree of respect
for the sensibilities and aspirations of minorities. In so doing, the
Community would take another precious step towards accepting the
realities and enjoying the benefits of our multi-faith, multi-cultural
society. This in turn would encourage Europeans to recognise that,
despite recession, high unemployment and the social tensions these
create, we cannot shed our responsibilities towards the rest of the
world.

The younger generation, to whom WW2 is grainy newsreels in
black and white, cannot be expected to understand what motivated
Jean Monnet and Robert Schuman. Skinheads apart, the young are
concerned above all about people – people not only in Europe but
people everywhere – and they deserve a contemporary statement of
mission. They want to be told the moral values which will guide the
construction of the enlarged Europe and inspire its policies towards
the rest of the world. They want to know what balance will be struck
between rights and obligations whether at Community, state, corpo-
rate or individual level. When our political leaders have the wisdom
and courage to compose a statement of mission worthy of the more

noble aspects of Europe's heritage and consistent with Europe's potential, perhaps Martin Bell will be on hand to tell us: 'This at last is happening in our Continent – Europe.'

24 June 1993   Bath

Is it Time for a Common Defence?

Col. Frederick Bonnart

The need for a United Europe and the Maastricht treaty has been widely discussed in the recent past. At this stage, the Treaty on European Union, to give it its proper title, will come into force on the first day of the month in which it is ratified by the Federal Republic of Germany, where a decision by the German Constitutional Court is still outstanding. This day could well be 1 November 1993.

Although this act will set the seal on a detailed process of unification, it is common knowledge that many of the objectives are unattainable in the time-frame envisaged and that the whole process is suffering from general disenchantment in all the member countries. This is partly caused by the adverse economic situation and the widespread feeling that it has been brought about by the rigidity of the system. But there is also awareness that the process is driven by enthusiastic politicians and senior officials who are themselves tied into it and who are trying to force it through by institutional measures regardless of popular feeling. This applies also to the defence dimension in which hopes and aspirations are taken for facts, resulting in actions which fly in the face of reality.

The British government, however, has pledged itself, together with the other eleven signatories, to establish a European Union. One of the primary objectives of this Union is the assertion of its separate identity by the implementation of a common foreign and security policy, 'including the eventual framing of a common defence policy, which might in time lead to a common defence'.

This cautious wording must be the background to any examination of the development of a European defence identity. Without, however, assuming that it is necessary or even desirable, I intend to deal with this subject by looking briefly at the history and concepts of European defence, and then its new significance in the light of developments after the end of the Cold War. I will look at a European defence structure as envisaged and cover some of the main difficulties and possibilities. Finally, I will make a careful assumption about its likely development and give my view about the best way forward.

Definition of Europe

An initial definition of Europe is essential since, in the first place, Europe is a geographical expression – and not a very clearly delineated one at that – rather than a political one. It has become the latter only very recently and, although the Union has a formal external frontier, Europe is far bigger than that, so that its boundaries remain to be determined.

The formal geographic definition of 'from the Atlantic to the Urals' begs a number of questions which need not affect the argument too much, but it is worth remembering that for some nations it includes islands off Africa or in mid-Atlantic as well as parts of the North African coast, and that Turkey extends into the Near East and hence into Asia.

As for the political definition, there is the Europe of NATO, formally defined in the Washington Treaty; that of the European Community contained in the frontiers of the twelve signatories of the Rome Treaty; then when the members of the European Free Trade Area (EFTA) are added; and, finally, the Europe which includes Turkey, with the dimensions already mentioned, the former Warsaw Pact countries, including the new European democracies of the former Soviet Union, in particular Russia, stretching well beyond the Urals to the Pacific coast.

For the purposes of this chapter, unless specifically stated, Europe will mean the area covered by the treaty and the twelve nations that have signed it. Before going into the subject, however, a look at different attempts at a common European defence in the past, necessarily in a more loosely defined geographical area and with various partners, will be important.

Origins of Common Defence

Since, for much of Europe, the nation state only arose after the French Revolution, any previous military alliances are irrelevant. It is perhaps worth remembering that these were generally either religious or dynastic in nature and often only lasted for the length of one campaign.

To see the build-up to the present concept we need go back no further than the First World War, in which two groups of European countries fought each other, one side being joined by the United States half-way through. Again, the term 'European' and 'Europe' is flexible in this respect. In the war, Britain, France and Italy on the one side, and Germany on the other, had overseas possessions, some of which provided considerable numbers of forces. Also, the war was not only fought on the Western Front in France and Belgium – although that is where the main battles with their enormous losses took place and where it was finally won – but also in the Near and Middle East, in Africa and in Asia, as well as on the seas between these areas and between Europe and North America.

This geographic spread also applied to the Second World War in which the line-up of countries was somewhat different. Moreover, Japan and China then joined in on opposite sides, which gave it an even bigger dimension and extended it far into Asia and onto the Pacific. Although, like the First World War, this was a war of nations, universal ideological motivations played an important part and showed the trend to transnational fundamental objectives.

However, in each of them, Germany was considered the main culprit in Europe and, as it was undoubtedly its most populous nation, was looked on again at the end of the Second World War as the main potential danger for the other west Europeans. Shortly thereafter, the continued expansion of Soviet power led to their early recognition of the need to pool their defences and to continue firmly to link America to Europe. The result was the emergence of various concepts of European defence, leading to the North Atlantic Alliance which brought in the United States and Canada. Later attempts were made to establish a common European pillar within the Alliance, which will be discussed in more detail.

Winston Churchill had promised continued close ties to France after its defeat in 1940, even suggesting a common nation. Britain made good on this in the Dunkirk Treaty of 1948. However, in 1946, Churchill had given his warning about an Iron Curtain descending onto Europe and, with Stalin's rejection of Marshall Aid and his establishment of the Cominform in 1948, the break with the wartime ally was complete. The Communist *coup d'état* in Czechoslovakia and the Soviet blockade of Berlin led respectively to the establishment of the Brussels Treaty in March 1948 and, via the Vandenberg Resolution, to that of the North Atlantic Treaty Organization (NATO) in April 1949. These laid the foundations of a completely new form of military co-operation between nations in peacetime.

The experience of the two great wars had shown the need for considerably closer alignment of allied military forces as well as that of a common command. Before either of them broke out, each group of countries had held military staff talks, exchanged officers for training and later established liaison arrangements. In the First, it took a number of costly misunderstandings and jealousies to arrive at unity of command. In the Second, a common War Council was created at the beginning but it gave its instructions, arrived at by consensus after discussions, to its constituent nations which passed them on to its commanders. Liaison was instituted from the start but it took defeats and emergencies to begin to make it effective.

Detailed common command arrangements began with the American intervention in North Africa and continued thence into Italy. They were considerably further advanced for the final phase, the invasion of Europe. The lessons were learnt the hard way but, fortunately and exceptionally, seemed to have been remembered thereafter.

The Sovereign Nation

Needing to show unity to obtain the American commitment, the Europeans gave teeth to the Brussels Treaty by setting up a Western Union Defence Organization in September 1948. Field Marshal Montgomery was nominated Commander-in-Chief with his headquarters at Fontainebleau, and land, air, and naval commanders from different nations were appointed, but its independence did not last long.

When NATO came into being in April 1949, the Western Union happily agreed to transfer its military responsibilities. General Eisenhower accepted them when he was appointed Supreme Allied Commander Europe (SACEUR) and set up Supreme Headquarters Allied Powers Europe (SHAPE) in April 1951, incorporating the Western Union's commanders and facilities. These were not entirely negligible as the Union had created an infrastructure programme in which they shared costs for airfields and communications.

NATO and SHAPE then set out to organise a common military network of headquarters and infrastructures which would enable allied forces to co-operate immediately and effectively in a crisis or war. The first step, highly unspectacular but most essential, was to ensure that all spoke the same military language. English and French were agreed as the standard languages, but even more important were the early attempts to obtain common procedures. These had to run from the most mundane, such as a common phonetic alphabet – hotly discussed, as each nation had good reasons to prefer its own, – to highly sophisticated scrambling techniques for aircraft which were much easier as during the war most allied aviators had trained in the United States or Britain.

Out of this there arose in the end an organisation unequalled in the history of peacetime armed forces: the allied integrated military structure. On land, in the air, at sea, national commanders and units were able to enter combat at a moment's notice and find their place in plans worked out by allied staffs and exercised over the years. At the height of NATO power, only a few years ago, 20 army divisions, supported by tremendous air potential, stood ready across central Europe where the main Soviet surprise effort was expected, with 60 more on call within a very short time. Aircraft and ships were earmarked ready to transport reinforcements across the Atlantic for some of whom heavy weapons, transport and stores would be rolling out of European depots in the meantime. Detailed arrangements for tactical nuclear support were backed by the vast power of the strategic nuclear force.

At the same time, attempts at European military integration continued apace. Driven partly by the evident need to bring in Germany, France proposed as early as 1950 a European Army, integrated at divisional level, with a common uniform, unified command structure, as well as common arms procurement and production. This was superseded in 1951 by a proposal for a European Defence Community, consisting of France, Italy and the Benelux countries, as well as Germany. Britain, alas, kept out and was given observer status.

A more remarkable but less well-known institutional proposal for a European Political Community, based on the then nascent European Coal and Steel Community, was made at that time to control the defence forces. This gave a Council of Ministers with an associated Executive Committee wider powers than those envisaged in European Union today. However, although signed by the governments of all parties, the project failed to run as, without British support, it was passed over by the French Assembly in August 1952.

It was the Paris Agreements, in October 1954, which finally crossed the threshold. The Brussels Treaty powers were joined by Germany and Italy in the Western European Union (WEU). This enabled the new Federal Republic of Germany to set up armed forces while providing means of keeping its armaments under control. At the same time, Germany was able to join NATO (Italy had been a founding member). But, like the Western Union, the WEU refrained from duplicating the NATO command structure and deliberately passed all military planning and execution to SACEUR.

Gradually, as Germany became more accepted and, indeed, needed NATO membership, the arms restrictions agreed in the Paris Protocols were lifted, until only the nuclear prohibition remained (and still remains). The WEU's Agency for the Control of Armaments virtually became redundant, the Council met periodically but decided nothing of note and the parliamentary assembly was active in voice but not in influence or power. Having seemingly achieved its purpose, the organization then went to sleep. The reactivation only came in 1984, under French impetus, with the sharpening of European self-consciousness.

Of other notable attempts to promote a European pillar in NATO, one was the proposal in 1962 for a Multilateral Nuclear Force (MLF), where all member nations were to participate in operations with nuclear forces assigned by the United States and Britain. Nothing came of it but it was replaced in due course by the Nuclear Planning Group, in which most (and later all) Europeans except France participated. This still exists and involves the Europeans in nuclear targeting of the assigned elements, as well as a large number of measures concerning control, safety and storage. France, however, continued to look at its nuclear force as a strictly national element, designed and operated exclusively for the defence of France.

Another step was the creation of EUROGROUP in 1968 to co-ordinate European defence ministers' opinions in NATO. Again France did not take part as it does not take its place in the Defence Planning Committee (DPC) meetings of NATO's defence ministers. The Europeans' meetings always preceded the regular six-monthly DPC in which they could co-ordinate positions and discuss the Group's practical dimension. This consisted of a number of sub-groups on different military aspects (training, communications, logistics, etc.). However, far and away its most important task and achievement was its propagation in the United States of Europe's contribution to the Alliance. At their last meeting in May, the European ministers passed a number of their functions to the WEU and the Group is likely to be absorbed in it by the end of this year.

Perhaps the final effort worth mentioning is the Independent European Programme Group. It came into being in 1976 at the initiative of EUROGROUP, so as to enable France to participate in NATO's very serious search for rationalising arms procurement and production. In a large number of meetings it produced much paper but little else over the years. However, under much ministerial pressure, nations at least agreed to ensure that national information about future procurement requirements would be passed rapidly to all the other members so as to enable their industries to bid for contracts. The Group has recently been incorporated in the revitalised WEU.

As is now clear from this lengthy review of post-war efforts towards a common European defence, only one, that of NATO, has until recently been of any significance. Although perhaps long-winded, it was essential to run through it to show that, indeed, some pressure had always been exerted for a separate and cohesive European element, but that the necessary basic assumption for it was never there. This assumption is the abandonment of national sovereignty which is implicit in subordinating military forces to an extra-national command.

The Break with the Past

It is important to stress here that, in spite of its evident capability, NATO is not a supra-national organisation. Every step is negotiated individually with nations, and agreement to participate depends ultimately on the government and parliament of each individual member nation. Until the recent force reorganisation, national delegations and support units existed at every command level, excepting only the small wholly integrated organisations of the brigade-size Allied Command Europe Mobile Force (AMF) and the wholly international Air Early Warning Force which supplies the AWACS aircraft, some of which are now operating in the Balkans.

In NATO's new force structure, the truly multinational level has been raised to that of army corps which has considerably increased international integration. Also, common procedures and the routine of rapid consultation worked out and practised over 40 years have resulted in large measures of agreement enabling rapid decisions to be made. The reaction speed is further increased by a certain degree of automaticity in placing national elements under international command.

This last point has always been contested by France since De Gaulle's decision to withdraw from the integrated military structure and illustrates the difficulties of overcoming national prerogatives. However, even France was tied into most of the automatic defence arrangements by bilateral treaties, so that the Alliance was ready to cope with a massive surprise attack, which had been considered a real threat since the build-up of effective nuclear forces by the Soviet Union in the early 1950s.

The disappearance of the Soviet threat has meant a fundamental reappraisal of security needs and consequent action to conform with it. Clearly, a surprise massed armoured thrust into central Germany – or any other anywhere else – is now wholly impossible. Equally, the game of nuclear threat and counter-threat is utterly incredible.

Yet, except for the removal of medium- and short-range nuclear weapons – on which agreements were obtained while we were still in the confrontation mode – the main nuclear arsenals remain in place and are maintained and modernised, regardless of their present uselessness as a means of security or power projection. With the break-up of the Soviet Union, the Ukraine has emerged as the third biggest nuclear power, China is known to be improving its potential and several other countries are either believed to possess or be on the verge of creating their own. Others which do not, like Germany and Japan for instance, must have cast-iron assurance of protection.

Nuclear proliferation is therefore an acute danger to stability which requires a capability to respond or, better still, to prevent it. Recent declarations of good intentions, including that of the Group of Seven in July, may result in agreement to abandon testing for a period but, unless and until the danger is wholly eliminated, a reliable nuclear capability must remain in reliable hands. This, for Europe at present, means the continuation of the American nuclear umbrella and the British and French national arsenals.

In order to cash in on the peace dividend, the allied nations have rapidly shed considerable elements of conventional forces. NATO has evolved a new strategy to meet the new situation and a new force structure has been devised accordingly. Although NATO's primary function remains unchanged as that of the common defence of the territory of its members, the new dangers of widespread instability, caused by the break-up of highly centralised totalitarian systems accompanied by economic disruption, require a more sophisticated approach.

Allied armed forces are therefore being redesigned to support United Nations decisions about possible intervention to deal with trouble spots. At the same time, the political element is deeply involved in assisting the new democracies in establishing democratic and legal frameworks to reshape their own military establishments, as well as in the conversion of the defence industries to civil use.

NATO's new force structure consists of rapid reaction, main defence and augmentation forces. The rapid reaction forces are divided into two elements, immediate and main reaction forces of the three armed services which are available at very short and short notice, respectively. Some of these forces and headquarters are in previous locations, mostly in Germany, but a large number of troops have now returned to their home territories. Main defence forces are the national forces which remain on call under existing plans, while augmentation forces are mainly reserves at different stages of readiness.

Of the first category, naval on-call forces were recently deployed in the Adriatic, AWACS aircraft in Italy and Hungary, and an *ad hoc* allied military headquarters in Bosnia to deal with the Yugoslav crisis. An allied air force element was assembled under Commander-in-Chief Southern Europe (CINCSOUTH) in Naples to enforce the no-fly-zone decision of the Security Council. At the time of writing this force has been augmented to enable it to carry out air attacks to support the Geneva peace negotiations and lift the blockade of Sarajevo.

The European Element

The desire for a cohesive European element has, as we have seen, existed since the beginning. It has also been encouraged by the American partner as the concept of a two-pillar alliance, of which one is European dating back to President Kennedy. The Americans thought of it mainly as a means to ensure that Europe takes on a greater share of the burden, while some Europeans, led by France, saw it as a way to greater power in the Alliance. This resulted in considerable differences of opinion which found expression in the run-up to the Maastricht Treaty.

In good time a solution was found and in the declaration appended to the treaty its members agreed to develop the WEU as the defence component of the European Union and as a means to strengthen the European pillar of the Atlantic Alliance. The relationship is to be characterised by transparency and complementarity. In other words, the two organisations are to keep each other fully informed of their respective plans and actions which should neither contradict nor duplicate those of the other. WEU was given the dual role of the elaboration and implementation of the decisions and actions of the Union which have defence implications.

To this end it has moved its Secretariat from London to Brussels where it is in easy contact with the European Communities and NATO. It has established a permanent council and a military planning cell, both of which are functioning. These bodies are able to prepare the regular ministerial meetings (foreign and defence minsters) and begin to work on contingency plans. Some of the permanent representatives and senior military officers have a so-called 'double-hat' function, in that they represent their countries on both organisations, which improves the exchange of information.

Like NATO, the WEU's military forces remain under national command (and, mostly, have a prior NATO assignment), but unlike NATO, it owns no multinational units (such as NATO's AWACS, satellite and other communications networks, or integrated headquarters), nor has it any stand-by forces (like Allied Command Europe Mobile Forces, or SACLANT's naval on-call forces).

WEU prides itself on its execution of three main operations: minesweeping during the Iraq-Iran War to protect international shipping in the Gulf in 1987, a similar naval undertaking in the Gulf War, and the recent naval exercise in the Yugoslav conflict where WEU was responsible in the embargo monitoring and later blockade for a sector of the Adriatic.

None of this was either necessary or particularly difficult. Naval forces consist primarily of ships which are self-contained compact force units. With common communications, procedures and a little practice, any naval ships can work together with others. The nations concerned agreed to send them into these operations under the WEU flag for political reasons. They could work together since, as they were all also NATO members and had co-operated for years on allied exercises, they were fully familiar with the common operational practices. With goodwill – and it was there in plenty – they were able together to work out coverage in areas and time and they achieved a splendid success.

In the Adriatic, however, the existence of a WEU command separate from a NATO command was clearly an anachronism. It also offended against the complementarity principle and rapidly became an obstacle to a rational military command chain. It has fortunately now been eliminated and the forces in the Adriatic function under a single NATO command.

One of the biggest events where the wish became the father of the thought and thus became a contributory element to the Yugoslav mayhem was the assumption at the beginning of the crisis that Europe was capable of dealing with it. This began under the Luxembourg presidency when, buoyant with the success of the Maastricht negotiations, Europe virtually told the United States to stand off as the Community intended to resolve it. A little later, under the Dutch presidency, the then Dutch foreign minister Hans van den Broek, actively supported by his French colleague Roland Dumas, virtually intended to throw the European forces into the breach, only to find that, first, he did not have the support of all his colleagues and, second, there were precious few forces to throw.

Another element that can properly be called purely European has appeared. This is the European Corps, formed at Strasbourg by France and Germany. It was also a bone of contention between NATO and Europe which has now been amicably resolved by the agreement that its primary role would be that of the common defence under Article 5 of the Washington Treaty for which it would come under command of SACEUR. This was essential as the German combat formations belonging to it would necessarily have come out of NATO-assigned forces and none of the other European countries would have joined without that pre-condition.

As a consequence, Belgium has now joined, Spain will do so soon and others have declared an interest. The command element is functioning and some exercises have taken place. Having learnt the lessons of earlier fiascos with the experiences of the Franco-German brigade, these are now kept within manageable dimensions. A good deal of harmonisation will have to occur but the will and enthusiasm seem to be present, so that difficulties will not be insuperable. One overall advantage is that French armed forces will be able to catch up on NATO procedures, tactical doctrines and equipment and thus co-operate more closely with all their allies, whether in the Eurocorps or outside it.

An All-European Defence?

If the WEU were to replace NATO it would have to start taking on all common activities, facilities and responsibilities. Many of these, such as reconnaissance, surveillance satellites, reinforcement transport (heavy air and sealift), tactical helicopter lift, are either wholly or mainly American-owned or supplied. A large proportion of infrastructure funding is also provided by the United States. The Europeans would have to find resources for these activities and they are unlikely to be available in the foreseeable future.

Even more weighty is the nuclear problem. All nuclear forces remain under strict control of the nations that own them. We have seen that the United States and Britain put a certain proportion at the disposal of NATO for planning purposes, but the ultimate release would come from the owner-nation. France has kept out of this and keeps its nuclear force exclusively for national defence, and even Britain has put the reserve of supreme national requirement on its allocation.

Initially, there were some in France who believed that a deal could be struck with Germany whereby the latter would provide the bulk of the conventional forces while France would be responsible for the nuclear element – but this is now considered naive. France has been negotiating with Britain about the joint development of a nuclear-capable medium-range air-to-ground missile, but even if the project takes off in these nuclear-adverse and tight-budget days it is unlikely to lead to common control of separately owned weapons. An arrangement for joint targeting could theoretically also be made under the WEU aegis, which could eventually turn into a European nuclear planning group. The means at its disposal would, however, be significantly smaller than those now available to NATO and would not be a due counter-weight to those of Russia, the Ukraine or the United States.

Conventional forces would be scarce, as the Europeans have been reducing at a more rapid rate than the United States. The exceptions are Greece and Turkey which still spend a sizeable proportion of their GDP on defence, but they have different reasons. The headquarters structure could be maintained, provided sufficient infrastructure funds were made available, but many of the units to be slotted into the formations would be cadre elements only. The present tendency to replace the unpopular national military service by regular volunteer forces not only makes soldiers expensive, and therefore reduces their numbers, but it eliminates the possibilities of trained reserves. If these are not available in a crisis, then cadre units could not be filled.

Similarly, defence industry problems would be aggravated by the exclusion of the United States from a common alliance. Admittedly, a good deal of European equipment has been bought in the United States in the past, partly because American industry was organised more quickly and more rationally and because it invested a considerably larger proportion in research and development. Europe is beginning to realise this but has to compete with a number of difficulties, such as state ownership of the armaments industry in some countries, more difficult work practices and labour relations, and heavy subsidies to maintain employment.

Even if these were overcome, the contraction of defence procurement has meant very sudden reductions in demand and many such industries are in difficulties. If they want to survive they will have to modernise, specialise and join forces with each other to create bigger and fewer units. Some of this is already under way but change is slow and adaptation difficult. This problem would, however, apply in any case, whether Europe relies on NATO or only on itself for its defence.

The Way Ahead

The question then arises whether NATO is now redundant and should be replaced by the WEU for the defence of Europe. As far as the allies are concerned, the answer was given at NATO's Rome Summit in November 1991 when President Bush put the question baldly to his European allies: 'Do you want the United States to remain in Europe?' and received a resounding 'Yes!' as answer from all present, including President Mitterrand of France.

Also, it is to NATO that non-members look for ultimate military security. It is for them the one international military body capable of exercising military power. This applies to the east central Europeans who view with troubled minds the events further to the east. It applies also to Russia and the Ukraine, in spite of the resentment in some of their more nationalistic circles. It applies, finally, to much of the world population which looks on the Alliance as a force for democracy and hopes that it will remain there, in the background, in case their fragile democracies run into difficulties.

Yet the purpose of NATO has always been the defence of Europe. When it came into being, the American involvement was essential, as Europe, alone and consisting of nation states debilitated by a long and costly war, was quite unable to stand up to the mighty Soviet threat. With the threat gone, and with the increasing cohesion of Europe's nation states and their solid wealth, Europe should in theory indeed be in a position to defend itself – but to assume that it can would be a monumental error.

The reason for America's involvement in the late 1940s was not only its concern for Europe, to which its population was tied by culture, roots and common values. It was the sense that Europe's security was essentially also that of America and that only a complete commitment in peacetime would be able to prevent another world war. This sense has necessarily become attenuated with the disappearance of the previously very tangible Soviet threat. It would thus not take too much effort by Europe to make America abandon its peacetime commitment.

But Europe is far from being a single nation. It is quite unable at this stage, and for the foreseeable future, to abandon its structure of different nations with their different traditions, cultures and languages. It can only, therefore, establish a defensive system on the lines of NATO, where each nation has an equal voice in decisions and these have to be unanimous to be carried.

If Europe decides to do so alone, it would alone have to provide adequate forces for its own defence, bear alone all the costs involved, and carry on alone the formerly common technological effort in equipment development. It would lose the reduced but still powerful American force elements permanently stationed in Europe, the automatic reinforcement commitment, several basic military capabilities and, above all, the nuclear umbrella.

The potential for all this is present in Europe – but the will certainly is not. For the will implies real sacrifices in well-being in order to build up the inadequate military capabilities, increase national armed forces, and move to a degree of cohesion which the populations of its nations are quite unwilling to give.

There is a way ahead, but it is a different route. Europe can be made increasingly secure as it continues on its slow but steady road towards greater cohesion only by persevering in the methods it has begun to adopt. It must build up gradually European elements closely linked to NATO, preferably within the Alliance where it can attempt to make a reality of the tenuous concept of the European pillar. It should continue to experiment with integrated European military elements so as to spread accepted NATO procedures, tactical concepts and organisations. It should take on as much as it can of the common burden of infrastructure costs and participate as much as possible in common technological research.

Such action will enable the Europeans to accept greater responsibility inside the Alliance. When the force relationship makes it evident, the position of SACEUR would become European, but power must continue to be spread evenly to ensure a continued American commitment. For, as far ahead as can be seen at this moment, it is on the North Atlantic Alliance with its transatlantic link that the security of Europe will rest.

In the distant future and gradually, as the nations grow together, Europe may well evolve its own armed forces. But by that time, one hopes, their numbers may not have to be very great, and their tasks will be mostly in the service of humanity under the United Nations, leaving that of Europe's own defence as a most unlikely eventuality for which they would be the final guarantee of safety.

10 August 1993   Bruxelles

Beyond Politics

Dr. Jean Klein

When talking about a united Europe, one must first look at what it means to be united. The underlying reality of all human beings is one consciousness, manifested in very similar ways. Whether we are black, white, yellow, red or British, German, Belgian, French, we all have the same body structure, same liver, same breathing systems, and these are affected similarly by the same fears, anger, hate, jealousy, sexual urges, anxieties and so on. The body can be treated universally, the psyche and soul can be healed in universal ways. Humanity is profoundly one. We are in any case united. We only need to be aware of it. Without feeling this oneness we can never come to a united Europe.

There are two aspects to the unity I mean here: actual oneness and multiplicity in oneness. The most important is the recognition that our very homeground, our origin, is one. It is not a composed oneness, but actually *is* oneness. It is called by many names – consciousness, stillness, our original nature. It is present when all aspects of individuality are absent. When there is no more object, it is there as presence – presence in the absence of anything.

We are, however, educated to take the absence of objects as an absence of awareness. This is a profound error. We have identified with the world of referents and only know ourselves in relation to objects. We know only the qualified I, as in 'I am English, I am French, I am a lawyer, a man, a woman,' etc. But our original nature which we have in common with all is when the I stands without any qualification. This unqualified I is presence, consciousness. It is our homeground out of which all phenomenal existence arises and into which it returns.

Before we can be united, or even truly related, we must accept intellectually, even before we have the living experience of it, that our homeground is one. This is the only *a priori* conviction that can ever work in solving conflict in our world society. It is the only workable structure, because it is the only truth. Out of this truth comes authority. Truth is the only sovereign. Truth is ethical, functional and aesthetic. It is the fundamental knowing that consciousness without objects is our original nature and that to take ourselves for individual personas is the sole cause of conflict and suffering.

Every undertaking of a human nature must have, as its background, that which binds everyone together, which all have in common, which gives support to the phenomenal world, namely consciousness. The expression of this deep conviction is love, openness, humility, and the seeing of facts as they are, not the seeing of the products of wishful thinking and illusion based on the misconception of the existence of a personal entity. True thinking comes from non-thinking, from silence, from stillness, from this background. Thinking that comes from thinking is obviously based on memory, on past conditioning. And all thinking that is creative must be fresh, new and free from preconceptions. It is not thinking that can change society but rather a looking away from thinking.

On the level of objects and ideas, there can be no solution to any situation. We turn in the vicious circle of the divided mind, caught up in endless choosing and arbitrary decision-making, arbitrary because the premise is arbitrary – that there is a chooser, someone to decide. There can be no authority based on arbitrariness. When we take ourselves for individuals we take ourselves for a fraction. No situation can be clearly seen from the fractional point of view. No facts can be clearly put on the table when clouded by the idea of the person. In the absence of a personal entity the situation unfolds in all its possibilities and the facts are presented. The person can never bring a solution. It is the situation itself that brings its own solution, the right solution. It may not be pleasant for the ego, but it will be ethical, functional and aesthetic. The truth is never personal. Right thinking, right acting and right feeling are not personal. This impersonal vision is the ground of all harmony.

An harmonious society must be built on the inner state of every human being. This inner state is not an appropriation of moral, spiritual and functional rules, but the building of an inner foundation grounded in knowledge and love.

In observing the seed of truth, unity will inevitably evolve, not as something constructed by the mind in an arbitrary fashion, as in a written treaty, but as an organic happening. A united Europe is an inevitability. In 1928 students in Berlin, myself included, were shouting in the streets for pan-European unity. Our deepest desire is to be united. If it is not today, it will be tomorrow, because it belongs to the survival of the human race to unite, to unite in love. So, before embarking on uniting Europe the perspective must be clear.

The perspective of a united Europe cannot become clear in an evening! It is a kind of living together, living with the question, the inevitable question. When the perspective is clear, all practical issues will be resolved. Economic and political unification cannot take precedence over, but is a result of, a clear perspective based on the oneness of humanity.

The second aspect of unity is multiplicity in oneness. It is clear that when we realise, in the absence of the notion of an individual, that the original homeground of all phenomenal existence is consciousness and that we are all essentially one, the cause of conflict disappears. The great majority of conflicts are caused by psychological survival, the attempt to protect one's ego or national ego in its many forms and extensions. In the absence of the person as chooser, judge, comparer, there is a welcoming of life and all that life brings.

This welcoming and openness is love. It is only in love that the infinite diversity of life's expressiveness can co-exist harmoniously. Love cannot be adopted or attained. It is what we fundamentally are. Each person and nation must come to the understanding of this underlying principle called love. It is an experience without an experiencer. When the experiencer is absent there is no more conflict. Differences are faced purely functionally without psychological involvement. Differences are respected. When one nation faces another nation with historial, not psychological, memory, it appeals to its greatness, its richness of culture, language and tradition.

The power of a United Europe lies in maintaining the different traditions, cultures, languages, myths of each country. It is the dynamism of a country that keeps it alive, virile and powerful; otherwise it calcifies and loses all vitality and interest. In any case, true culture belongs to no one and to all. It is the same humanity in many aspects. Whether expressed in religion, art or language, it is all from the same origin. Orchestras, paintings etc. have long been cross-cultural. There needs to be a coming together of the great minds and hearts in the arts, sciences, law and philosophy to expose the seeds of culture in each country.

To be identified with cultural traditions is the beginning of unification. It is in learning about and respecting the great thinkers and artists of one's own country that one can learn to admire the cultures of other nations. Basing unity on economics is doomed to failure because it emphasises the object rather than its origin. In a society based on acquisition, on greed and consumerism, a species of competition is born which has nothing to do with creative production and beauty. But when we live intelligently, without anticipation and end-gaining, the roots of our society will change. The object will no longer take priority, but emphasis will be given to the ground from which it comes.

A new Renaissance is only possible when art and science is an offering to the Ultimate. Without a feeling of the Ultimate, it is not possible to create a cultured and happy society. And no society can be happy when it is culturally stagnant, when it has nothing to offer, nothing to be proud of, nothing to be admired. In adoration, however, there is togetherness. In listening to music there is togetherness. In seeing painting or dance, there is togetherness. In the act of admiring we are one without admirer or admired.

By the Ultimate I do not mean a personal or conceptual God. Although this was a beautiful pretext for creativity and offering in the Renaissance, today's 'God' language is purely conceptual, a nuisance which prevents new knowledge and new discovery. God can only be discovered, never attained. The European God is a sleepy person – responsible for two great wars in this century. Today, we must find what is beyond objects, and to find it we have to look where thinking cannot take place. Each one of us must find our true nature, not based on contrived morality and beliefs. It is this true nature which is the only sovereign. Sovereignty based on self-image, religious, political or any other, is completely hypothetical – an illusion. It will inevitably bring conflict. No nation in the world today can live in isolation. Real sovereignty is not based on competition and self-image but on knowledge and love. It is the sovereignty not over others but of oneself. There is only spiritual sovereignty. Temporal authority flows from this knowledge, from this alone.

What is called for is an exchange between people of competence, with knowledge and experience in all aspects of culture. We need a kind of Academy of people who are rooted in this spiritual authority, who are educated and cultured and who see facts as they are, free of interpretation and wishful thinking. The united Europe currently under discussion is a purely intellectual construct that has no basis in real knowing, no basis in reality. Goethe said to Linné: *'Da hast du die Teile in der Hand, fehlt leider das geistige Band'* (You have details in your hand but unfortunately no spiritual binding). The present rule of bureaucracy, where the so-called leaders are devoid of culture, authoritarian without authority and acting from the personal point of view, can never bring harmony. One cannot construct unity on the phenomenal level. There is no mental or phenomenal way out of the situation we are in. Only unity based on the non-phenomenal principle is consistent. There is only one sovereign authority, but it is not authoritarian. Loving and giving to our surroundings must be beyond the personal, as it was in the Renaissance. An Academy approaching things through knowledge, beauty, kindness and love is the only way to a united Europe. For Beauty has its own authority.

Education will then come out of love. One learns because one loves it. Then we will be able to give, to share, what we have loved and learned and which is the inheritance of all humankind. Ultimately, when we have acted on the principle that binds us together as human beings, there will be no nations, but the culture and traditions will remain in all their richness. When our wrong thinking, a thinking that is based on acquisition, is righted, we will live in offering and openness. The new Renaissance will be based on what is actual, on real knowing, not on the accumulation of fundamentally unrelated facts. When we no longer take ourselves for an image inevitably arguing with other images, there will be no more talk of blending the practical with the spiritual because the spiritual is the only practical way. Nothing else works.

12 August 1993   Santa Barbara

Conclusions

When Europeans look towards America they sigh wistfully at the federal perfection of the New World. When the *Mayflower* landed at Cape Cod in 1620 the settlers had the great advantage of a blank sheet of paper, or as Sir Richard Body puts it, 'happy is the Continent with no history'.

The population of immigrants slowly built up on the eastern seaboard over the next hundred and fifty years until the Declaration of Independence in 1776, when the population had grown to nearly four million. The thirteen revolutionary states had then fought their way to independence at the Treaty of Paris in 1783.

The first pioneers to head west were the hunters and fur-trappers, followed by the stage-coaches bringing the settlers intent on farming and mining, followed in turn by the railroads with merchants and bankers. As the New Frontier expanded ever westwards, so did the English language, a derivation mainly of English common law and an essentially Calvinistic brand of Protestantism, with Quaker and Methodist influences also prevalent.

Meanwhile George Washington and his Secretary of the Treasury, Alexander Hamilton, had prepared a Federal franchise package comprising the Constitution, certain Federal legislation and the dollar. At the Convention of Philadelphia in 1787 the founding fathers set the precise parameters of sovereignty between the Federal and State governments, so that their respective duties and powers were divided and clearly delineated at the outset of the new Union. They succeeded in creating a central government strong enough to maintain order, pay its debts, promote economic development and protect American interests abroad, while at the same time satisfying the popular sentiment in favour of the States' rights for local self-determination.(If only the EC Commissioners had had the good sense to agree such a division at the outset, instead of relying on the vague notion of subsidiarity.)

As the new territories to the west became ready for statehood they exchanged their unpaid debts and the inevitable overdue interest for the new Federal franchise and currency. On independence, Alexander Hamilton had the sense to back the revolutionary deadbeat dollar with gold, and so the bankers in London, Paris and Frankfurt were only too ready to exchange monetary paper of questionable value for a currency with such solid backing. In this uncontrived manner did a common market, currency, law, language, culture and constitution spread across this vast continent. No wonder that Gladstone described the Union as 'the most wonderful work ever struck off at a given time by the brain and purpose of man'.

Nations, however, live in a body spiritual as well as a temporal body politic. Whereas America contrived a perfect federal system of self-governing states, her philosophical foundation was rooted in somewhat stonier ground. Article I of the Virginia Declaration of Rights of 1776 set the grand aim of 'pursuing and obtaining happiness and safety'. One has only to read Jean Klein's contribution on the supreme philosophy to appreciate that happiness cannot be pursued: however elusive the apperception may be, happiness is one's own very nature. And as for the idea of 'obtaining' happiness, an act of *becoming* cannot possibly exist in relation to that *which Is*. So these two false concepts led to a society where happiness exists, not as the realisation of an inner harmony, but objectified as a materialist advance; and where safety exists, not as the realisation of an harmonious society, but as a result of the right to carry a gun.

Likewise, it is clear from the discussions on sovereignty in the contributions of Leslie Blake and John Laughland that the Anglo-Saxon notion is essentially Platonic, whereas the continental notion as described by Dr. Manfred Brunner is essentially Aristotelian. In philosophic terms, Platonic sovereignty derives from the transcedent Form, Idea or *eidos* of Sovereignty Itself. As the Idea Itself is beyond time and space, so the nature of the participation of the many transient forms in the One Form is an ineffable relationship. Aristotelians, on the other hand, only accept that the Form or reality is in the immanent forms of this world. Their 'basic principle' of sovereignty does not change. Their second concept of 'potentiality' requires an ever greater perfection towards the pure Form in this world. For as Aristotle put it: 'Where there is a better there must be a best'. (Aristotle's name is a compound of *aristos* meaning 'best' and *telos* meaning 'goal' or 'end'.)

This philosophical antithesis has important implications in the realm of practical politics. The Anglo-Saxon concept of sovereignty, being Platonic, has no written constitution, for the crown and the law derive their authority in a mystical way from a transcendent spiritual source. The law is therefore above the King and freedom derives from obedience to the law, as Leslie Blake describes. The continental concept of sovereignty is Aristotelian, so the consitution must be written down and sovereignty resides in the people, who are the 'basic principle' realising their 'potentiality' through republican ideals such as equality, fraternity and liberty – but not necessarily much Anglo-Saxon flexibility.

The trouble comes when a new European Super-State requires a new constitution. The Germans only accept a new constitution that Aristotle would approve of as having the same 'immanent form'; in fact an exact replication where the 'basic principle' as actually defined in the 'Basic Law'. The terms of the Treaty of Maastricht would then transfer this Aristotelian constitution to Platonic Britain, thereby replacing 700 years of hard-won, continuously evolving, finely balanced, unwritten, constitutional evolution that has withstood the test of time, with a written rival that is not yet half-a-century old.

More importantly, it is a subtle threat to the very substance of the British nation – the nation that has continually championed freedom, free trade and self-government. Britain's constitutional monarchy and parliamentary democracy lose their spiritual and mystical authority and are forced to evolve their 'potentiality' along republican lines. M. Jacques Delors as Head of *European* State effectively replaces H.M. Queen Elizabeth II of Britain too. Fighting for Queen and Country is a natural bounden duty in time of war, but dying for Delors? It is ironic that Britain's national sovereignty may hopefully be protected by Dr. Manfred Brunner's action in the Constitutional Court at Karlsrühe.

Almost as dangerous, the essential commercial character of the British people as spirited free traders on a global basis is now to be redirected into realising 'the potentiality' of the new European bureaucratic, protectionist Super-State. The choice for Britain, as Lady Thatcher, Godfrey Barker and Bill Cash explain, is whether to join this unaccustomed and possibly uncertain path, or to maintain Britain's historic stance and freedom of action and nudge Continental Europe towards real liberalism.

A Minister of today's government saw the danger fifteen years ago:

'The greatest danger to the vision of effective European co-operation is the over-ambition of proponents of what amounts to a truly integrated European state. The disastrous doctrine that stealthy alignment of all sorts of regulations, major and minor, in the individual nations will somehow breed a common 'European consciousness' – seen as the epiphenomenon of standardised styles of administration – has already done enough to damage popular trust in the benevolence of the existing European Community ...'

The publication was *The Binding of Leviathan* and the author was the Rt. Hon. William Waldegrave, the Minister for John Major's *Citizen's Charter*, no less.

This clash of wills and temperaments is set to spark serious riots in the streets before long. It only needs Brussels to alter the pint measure or outlaw daily milk deliveries in their search for *total harmonisation* and all Hell will break loose. The scenes of cobble-throwing youths rioting on the streets of Copenhagen after the second Danish referendum on Maastricht is a warning to the European Commissioners of just how near the surface lies the ugliness of discontent. For the plain fact is that the more the centralist Super-State seeks to extend its competence, the more resurgent will nationalism become. The example of the disintegration of the former USSR is before our very eyes.

Nor can the electorate derive comfort from the manner and style of the Maastricht debate, where disinformation and deceit replaced open debate based on honestly proven facts. Lord Harris tells us about the ill manners in the Lord's debate, Rodney Leach calls it 'an ugly year', while John Laughland has to remind politicians that 'honesty is the best policy'.

Take the Conservative Party's *allied* membership of the European People's Party as an example of Euro-doublespeak. Chris Patten, as Chairman, wrote on behalf of John Major to Wilfried Martens, President of the EPP, seeking membership, and citing full support for a social dimension to the social market. Whereas John Major had said at the Conservative Party 1992 conference words that amounted to 'Federalism over my dead body,' the EPP's *Basic Programme* states (Article 213): 'the European Parliament [will be given] direct responsibility vis-à-vis the taxpayer'; 'that the review of the Maastricht Treaty ... will lead towards greater communitarization and restore the unitary nature of the draft treaty' (Article 218); and 'the Qualified Majority Vote has to apply to ... taxation, freedom of movement of persons etc.' (Article 224), and so on. When challenged on the contradictions inherent in this alliance, Douglas Hurd said that the alliance, with its 32 British, two Danish and 129 EPP MEPs, 'is designed to consolidate the centre-right within the European Parliament, where there is a Left-wing majority', but in the same breath he said, 'no policy programme agreed by the EPP is binding on the Conservative Party or its candidates'. I ask you! Where does that leave a Conservative MEP in the June 1994 Euro-elections?

Hence the wisdom of the approach suggested by Dr. Manfred Brunner and Philippe Séguin, of tapping the collective strength of Europe's nation-states through the principles of *mutual recognition* and *democratic self-determination*. Germany retains her sovereignty, as do Britain, France and the others. A Federal Europe of autonomous states, based on a common market underpinned by military commitments, evolves its truly federal functions by carefully delegated authorities, step by step, in accordance with the *best interests* doctrine expounded by Sir Richard Body.

When you pass through the Ventimiglia border-check heading east, there is no doubt that you are leaving France and entering Italy and that the two countries are separate nations. They speak differently and act differently. Within a hundred yards the sights, sounds and smells all change. So does the food they eat, the beer they drink, the flags that fly, the songs they sing and everything else. So what? *Vive la difference!* It is precisely these differences that make international travel so pleasant and refreshing – nowhere more so than in the mountains, fertile plains and historic cities of western Europe.

The first distinguishing characteristic of every nation is its language. Nothing so clearly delineates the peoples of the world as the wonder of their different tongues. The grammar of each language also profoundly affects the formulation of thought. The ancient Romans could not aspire to the philosophical conceptions of the ancient Greeks with their wonderfully flexible language, any more than the Greeks could give precision to laws with the same exactitude as in the marvellously logical structure of the Latin language. Whereas eighteenth-century America had one language, twentieth-century Europe has over two score. The EC is destined always to have more indigenous languages than actual nation member states. The only language that could possibly become the common language of Europe is English, which is on the way to becoming the first world language of every continent.

The effects of language, however, do not just play on the surface of the human psyche or human affairs. Language is powerful and has its political implications too. The French, for example, are determined to make foreigners speak their language in France, and who can blame them? The trouble comes in far-away Canada, where the French-speaking Quebecquois population even dreamed in 1991 of breaking away from the English-speaking provinces and breaking up the confederation. The linguistic difference threatened the constitution of this vast country with such a relatively small population, which to an outsider's casual gaze appears to be so at peace with itself.

Nearer the heart of Europe, Switzerland embraces three main languages and this confederation has uneasy moments too, with the latent border drawn on the demarcation of language. Nevertheless, the *Confederation Helvetique* holds together, since it has a single economy, the unifying presence of the Alps as a protective shield and a fine balance between the three 'nations'. The former Czechoslova-kia, however, had no such unifying geographical feature and she split on linguistic lines on 31 December 1992, at the very moment that the twelve different tongues of the EC had decided to take a step in the opposite direction.

There was no such unifying movement in former Yugoslavia either, alas, where Serbo-Croat is the main language. Tito held the union together for more than thirty years through force of personality and the long arm of the law, to the point where economic growth appeared to be a self-sustaining agent of unity, but the country fell into civil war in 1992 along racial lines. And did the USSR really collapse in 1989 as a result of economic failure, or was it the absurd notion that diverse peoples with more than 130 different alphabets could be held together in a centralised union? This 'union' fell apart when the military-command economy no longer had the wherewithal to enforce it against the people's will and between so many different tongues.

The second distinguishing feature of a nation is its law, used here in its wider sense of customs upholding the life of a nation. The British constitution goes back to Magna Carta established in 1215, and its system of statute and common law has evolved over almost eight centuries, as so amply described by Godfrey Barker. France and West Germany on the other hand, the most powerful continental countries, depend mainly on Napoleonic law and have had several different constitutions since the French Revolution and the German customs union of 1806. When language and law differ, there is a gulf in meaning and understanding.

The precision of the English language, and the general respect for the rule of law in Britain, make the British negotiate agreements to a point of exactness which often exasperates the counter-parties. Once they have signed an agreement, however, they can generally be relied upon to keep to it. (There are, unfortunately, exceptions that prove the rule.) The French, on the other hand, love to use the richness and fluency of their language to set out grandiose views of distant aims. Having set the parameters for *La Grande Vision*, the French are usually prepared to sign something that approximates to the overall objective and then deviate to do whatever seems to be in their best interests.

The third defining characteristic of a nation is its religion, used here in its widest sense to include art and culture and spiritual life.

It is hard to say more on this subject than is set out by Jean Klein, other than to emphasise his view that unity can only begin in the cultural realm.

The conclusion must surely be that the EC comprises twelve separate and distinct nations, each with its own language, law and degree of religious zeal, not to mention history, geography, alliances, cultural pursuits, industries, sports and pastimes. Yet it is also true that these distinct families inhabit a common region which contains the greatest cultural, artistic and natural phenomena of the western world. And regrettably, it is a region that has descended into bitter feuds and wars that twice this century have embroiled the rest of the world as well and threatened the end of civilisation. The challenge to Europe must be to evolve its unity in many spheres and spread its treasures on a mutual basis, while respecting national institutions and sovereignties, as so comprehensively described by Lady Thatcher.

The contributors to this book on Europe set out with one common perception — that the centralised bureaucracy envisaged by the Treaty of Maastricht is not the answer to Europe's evolution. Indeed, as a socialist attempt at centralisation it is both seeking to deny democracy and heading inevitably towards protectionism and corruption, as it seeks to expand an unsustainable social security system and a single currency across the whole Continent. The Treaty of Maastricht is not just not the answer to Europe's problems, it also threatens to become the cause of its future ills as it sets the wrong agenda for debate. Nevertheless, the contributors — working independently of each other and at diverse times and in different places — have produced a unified vision of the concept of a 'United Europe'. Remarkably, this anti-Maastricht, pro-Europe collection is epitomised by none other than John Major, speaking in the House of Commons debate on Maastricht on 22 July 1993:

'The European Community will continue to develop, whatever else may happen. But we need to influence the way of that development and to see that it moves in a way that is congenial to the British interest.

'I want a wider European Community. I regard the present Community as but a fragment of Europe. That is why I wish to see the European Free Trade Association countries join, and a little later, our old friends in central and eastern Europe. The wider that we can spread the European Community, with a free market concept not only in economic terms but in military and security terms, the more we shall be able to hand a glorious bonus to the next generation that we should not throw away.

'So I want that wider Community – a free-market Community, a Europe with the minimum necessary centralisation, a Europe that exercises more powers through the elected Governments of its member states and fewer powers through unelected Commissioners, a Europe in which national governments exercise undiluted control over genuine domestic policy matters from national elections to our education system, from health care to religion. That is the sort of Community that has been our agenda for a long time, and we are beginning to make progress in encouraging others to support the development of that sort of Community.

'We seek a Community that emphasises co-operation between governments, not imposition from the centre. We seek a Community where member states freely decide the agenda and the outcome. We see a Community which limits common rules and the jurisdiction of the Court of Justice to matters such as free trade and free competition, where they are genuinely necessary for any level playing field to be established. That is the Community that we seek to develop and shape ...

'I do not want to see either a centralist or a federalist Europe. I mean federalist in the sense in which we refer to it, not in the sense in which other countries refer to it. They mean something different by it. Yet when I say that to some Hon. Members, including some of my Hon. Friends, they are apt to say to me, "What about this country or that? There are federalist countries in the Community." That is true. There are. That is why we need influence and allies in Europe to build the sort of European Community we want.'

Source: *Hansard* 1992, Cols. 523-524

If Her Majesty's Government wanted to see a family of democracies across Europe, why are they determined to ratify – without consulting the people – the Treaty of Maastricht? This is a federalising treaty, designed by socialists with the intention of creating a centralised bureaucracy, with a uniform monetary policy across completely disparate economies, to be determined by unelected central bankers. The treaty imposes an expensive welfare system through the Social Chapter, which will cause unemployment and thus pave the way for protectionism. (This and other opt-outs negotiated by John Major will be overturned as soon as the Conservatives inevitably lose power, as Godfrey Barker points out.) The treaty sets conditions that will positively exclude eastern Europe and divide rather than unite the Continent, creating at the same time the economic dislocation which Brian Reading, Rodney Leach and Sir Alan Walters clearly warn us about. It has already led to the conditions whereby Germany and

France may proceed to a core union in the way described by Wilhelm Noelling. One cannot blame these Continentals for favouring this approach, but far-sighted observers like Bill Cash positively disfavour such a development for the Continent as a whole.

The government's response is – 'Precisely! That's why John Major negotiated the opt-outs from EMU and the Social Chapter, and insisted on the inclusion of subsidiarity.' The trouble is, that having negotiated these precious terms, the government is then in no position to kill the treaty. Even those who support the treaty freely admit its inadequacies – even Delors and Bangemann. In effect, the British Government has ratified a treaty that sets out to achieve the very opposite of its declared aims. The Commons Select Committee on Foreign Affairs, whose chairman is the Conservative David Howell, observed recently that as soon as Maastricht is ratified, the government should immediately work out its plan for the sort of Europe Britain is seeking.

In the ordinary world of everyday folk, some of us would have preferred that the government had done that *before* they signed this irrevocable treaty or had taken the timely opportunity not to ratify when the ERM collapsed. And yet Bill Cash provided the government *before* the Maastricht negotiations – attached as an *addendum* to his contribution – with a comprehensive rationale and brief. The government, however, allowed itself to be ratcheted back a notch, opting out of Stage 3 of EMU rather than simply vetoing it, and accepting Stage 2 rather than opting out of it. If the government had taken the Bill Cash approach, it would now appear prescient and statesmanlike and really would have influenced events 'at the heart of Europe'. Instead, the government has set the scene for the eventual absorption of sterling into EMU, as Godfrey Baker warns, with the consequential loss of national sovereignty over UK monetary policy.

Incredibly, the disastrous Treaty of Maastricht has been portrayed as a symbol of European unity. The Eurocandle is flickering and a failure to ratify Maastricht has been promoted as a psychological disaster, despite the fact that it is possible that Germany will eventually reject anyway. Germany's blunder with its own reunification was to put economic and monetary union before its own political union. Maastricht is seeking to create the same blunder on a megascale right across western Europe, but Germany is hardly likely to let the unforced error happen again, surely? So the British government sits on its precious opt-outs, lets it become clear for all others to see that Maastricht is a nonsense, while at the same time ratifying it as a symbol of unity.

This may be clever diplomacy but does not constitute sound long-term foreign, or rather domestic, policy. Having ratified this treaty, the British government will have endorsed the inevitable and harmful consequences. In a frank interview with *The Wall Street Journal Europe* on 4 May 1993, Martin Bangemann, the sometimes charming and at all times voluble German *bête noire* EC Commissioner, spelled out exactly what ratification of Maastricht would lead to. His view of 'ever closer union' is for 'an integrated political system', based on a federal structure of sharing power. He does not foresee just a loose association of independent states or 'family of democracies' as envisaged and preferred by John Major. 'Sorry!' boomed the bulky Bangemann. 'I know that some British prefer that [loose association], but they will have to accept that there are other Europeans ... who have their own political ideas.'

Some British indeed! It is not hard to see the origins of a mighty quarrel brewing under Maastricht. Far from being a symbol of European unity, it will become an explosive and destructive device in the hands of the federalist Euro-tinkerers. Sensing that this interpretation would be put on his patronising remarks, Bangemann quickly affirmed: 'I'm not aiming at a centralised Super-State'. Oh, no? All he wants is a federal structure modelled on the Federal Republic of Germany, where the centre 'is controlled and even managed by the member state.' But on a European scale, the Palace of Westminster will become one of twelve regional offices, housing some managers trying to control 'Head Office' in competition with eleven other regional offices. Head Office will rule supreme, naturally, on the classic management stance of divide and rule.

This is what Maastricht is really about in political terms. The fact that it also contains the economic blueprint worthy of an inverted Micawber glorying in continuing recession does not bother Bangemann. 'We have always been able to use a weak instrument in a better way than normally the instrument would allow us', he says. Perhaps he was speaking with the Single European Act of 1986 in mind. This act was meant to be about establishing a common market, but because it replaced the national veto by majority voting in certain areas, it unleashed a torrent of directives and regulations which had everything to do with federalisation of agriculture and trade. Maastricht will do exactly the same with monetary policy, justice and defence.

Bangemann now intends to use majority voting to move the EC forward towards his vision of a Federal Europe, no doubt supported by the European Court of Justice at every step and case in the way described by Martin Howe. Member states that do not wish to bow to the majority 'would have to leave' the community, he said firmly. It is easy to see how Maastricht will simply transfer power from elected representatives to unelected Commissioners, supported by so-called judges, turning democracy into legalised bureaucracy at the stroke of a pen. The possibilities had not escaped Bangemann's attention either, but the prospect caused him no problems whatsoever. 'Commissioners are not *fonctionnaires*', he said tartly. 'They are *political* figures. They have their own political ideas. If not, it would be a shame, by the way. If a Commissioner would just function like an official, you could throw them out.'

Quite. In other words, what Bangemann was actually saying was this: 'Once Maastricht has transferred political and economic powers from freely elected representatives, who can be voted out of office by the people they are elected to serve, to unelected Commissioners and central bankers like myself, we shall have dictatorial powers freely to impose on the people whatever we think is best for them, as they cannot even vote us out of office.' To underpin this monstrous arrangement, the Treaty of Maastricht proclaims itself to be irrevocable. It will soon be time for the constitutional lawyers to brush up on the principle of *res pactae sunt,* loosely translated as 'fings ain't wot they used to be'.

Bangemann is, unfortunately, not a mere official. He is a consummate politician too. Anyone who thinks he is a fool is the bigger fool. You have only to compare the above comments with, for example, the recent patronising remarks made by Lord Wakeham to see why Maastricht will split Europe. Lord Wakeham maintained, as he concluded his recent speech for the government commending the treaty to their Lordships, that the current agenda in Europe was not about a federal union, it was about job creation and economic growth. Would that it were! That is the trouble with this treaty, it addresses none of the issues that really confront Europe, but is capable of interpretation in any way the federalists may, or may not, want. This is because the treaty only achieves one purpose – only ever had one purpose – to transfer sovereign national power to the unelected Commissioners, bankers and judges of the new Super-State.

Britain's foreign secretary, Douglas Hurd, has complained on a number of occasions that those who opposed Maastricht had not proposed any viable alternative. The Maastricht vision of Europe fosters bureaucracy, restricts democracy, is protectionist, excludes eastern Europe, is deflationary, destroys jobs, fosters subsidies, hinders competition, is silent on details of military commitment, formulates no foreign policy objectives but gives away self-determination in this vital sphere, promotes largely meaningless citizenship, encourages immigration, spurs corruption and dilutes sovereignty. It augments Brussels, but it is a myopic vision that never sprang from any metaphysical rallying-point. Maastricht is the Trojan Horse of the bureaucrat spirited under cover of darkness into the heart of Europe. It is the deadly agent of the thirteenth nation.

The alternative vision from this symposium unites Europe from the Atlantic to the Urals as an agreed association of democracies. It creates the biggest common market the world has ever seen, in accordance with that part of the original vision of the founding fathers. It promotes healthy competition in trade and enjoys the economic advantages – denied to America – of regional currencies and effective foreign exchange markets. It ensures the safety of the region by a common system of commitment to military deployments. It diminishes Brussels.

It is, on the other hand, a United Europe in which the human spirit can evolve. It emphasises national sovereignty and allows for a process of self-determined, natural integration wherever this is feasible and desired. It is also the British Government's stated aspiration. If only they would listen to the Europeans in this debate who have the people of Europe behind them! Then there could be a realisation that Europe can work and realise the collective strengths of her sovereign nation-states to which her peoples relate naturally. There might then develop a prosperous and peaceful Europe fit for self-governing nations, living harmoniously in a continent fit for renaissance.

S.R.H.

15 August 1993   Andover

Appendices

Appendix I
UK's Trade with the EC
1983-1992

	Exports	*Imports*	*£ billions* *Balance of* *Payments**
1983	28.0	31.0	-2.9
1984	33.1	36.6	-3.6
1985	38.0	40.7	-2.7
1986	34.8	43.8	-9.0
1987	39.0	48.7	-9.8
1988	40.8	54.6	-13.8
1989	47.1	62.6	-15.5
1990	54.2	64.2	-10.0
1991	58.7	59.2	-0.5
1992	60.9	63.5	-2.6

**Balance of Payments Cumulative Deficit –
10 Y/E 1992:**   £70.4*bn*

Source: Developments in the European Community CM 2168, London: HMSO

* cross-totals not additive due to rounding

Appendix II
Population

	Millions
Western Europe:	
The EC members	
Germany	78
Italy	57
Great Britain	57
France	56
Other states	93
	341
The EFTA members	26
Switzerland	7
Sub-total: west Europe	374
Eastern Europe:	
Former Yugoslavia	24
Former Comecon *etc.*	99
Sub-total: east Europe	123
'White Russia':	
Russia (incl. Siberia)	149
Ukraine	52
Moldova	4
Belarus	10
Baltic states	8
Sub-total: 'White Russia'	223
TOTAL	720

Sources: *The Times Concise Atlas of the World 1990,* and *National Geographic Magazine 1993* – for former USSR entities.